STUDIES IN GLOBAL EQUITY

PORTRAIT OF A GIVING COMMUNITY:
PHILANTHROPY BY THE
PAKISTANI-AMERICAN DIASPORA

STUDIES IN GLOBAL EQUITY

PORTRAIT OF A GIVING COMMUNITY:
PHILANTHROPY BY THE
PAKISTANI-AMERICAN DIASPORA

ADIL NAJAM

PUBLISHED BY
GLOBAL EQUITY INITIATIVE
ASIA CENTER
HARVARD UNIVERSITY

RESEARCH COMMISSIONED BY
PAKISTAN CENTRE FOR PHILANTHROPY

DISTRIBUTED BY HARVARD UNIVERSITY PRESS
CAMBRIDGE, MASSACHUSETTS, AND LONDON, ENGLAND 2006

Library of Congress Cataloging-in-Publication Data

A copy of the Cataloging-in-Publication (CIP) Data is available from the
Library of Congress.

ISBN 0-674-02366-8

Cover Design by Jill Feron/Feron Design.

Main cover photograph by Dan Koik (back of a 'Pakistani Painted Truck'
displayed at the Smithsonian Institution Folk Arts Fair, 2005).

Cover border photograph by Zahid Ali Khan (traditional Pakistani ceramic
tiles).

Design of interior text and illustrations by Matthew McCaffree.

For

Musa, Amineh and Eesa

and the new generation of Pakistani-Americans

Contents

List of Figures

List of Tables

A Note of Thanks

This initiative has been a long, sometimes tiring, but always fulfilling exercise. Like so many labors of love, it grew into more than what had originally been planned and took far more time than I had anticipated. I must begin, therefore, with an apology to all those who have been so patient with me as I struggled to complete this report. I hope that I have not lost all their confidence and that the results of this long process will meet their expectations. Intellectually, this has been an exciting journey of exploration. One that has allowed me to study a topic that was not only intellectually challenging but which is important and timely for a community that I am myself a part of.

This book is the result of a multi-year project on 'Philanthropy by Pakistanis in America' that was conducted for the Pakistan Centre for Philanthropy (PCP). I am grateful to PCP for giving me the opportunity to conduct this research, and to the Aga Khan Foundation-USA (AKF-USA), which coordinated the project through a grant from the Rockefeller Foundation. I am indebted to Shahnaz Wazir Ali, the PCP Chief Executive, for her many insight that shaped the results and her patience with me. Members of the PCP Board, especially Dr. Shams Kassim Lakha, Syad Babar Ali and Mahomed J. Jaffer, were supportive and the advice from the PCP Board and its Research Committee helped shape the final structure of the report. PCP staff—including Zubair Bhatti, Ali Raza, Ahsan Rana, Eazaz Dar, Tasneem Saeed, Bushra Asif and Sarah Pervez Afzal—were helpful in many ways and at many critical junctures of the project. Comment from two external reviewers—Dr. Aliya Khan of the Quaid-i-Azam University (Islamabad) and Paula D. Johnson of The Philanthropic Initiative (Boston)—were useful in refining the final draft. I am also thankful to Victoria Waimey of AKF-USA whose gentle prodding made the completion of this project possible.

The team that worked with me on this research—many in a volunteer capacity—was an absolute inspiration and a testimony to the dedication of Pakistanis in America to contribute to the wellbeing of Pakistan. Dr. Salal Humair, in particular, was a pillar of dedication and was extremely generous with his intellectual input, time and support. He conducted more than a third of the focus groups and Chapter #6 of this report is based on his original analysis and draft. However, his imprint on this report is both wider and deeper than just this and his advice and analytical insight has influenced every aspect of this report. Dr. Bilal Zuberi also made critical intellectual contributions to the project at various stages, including in the original conceptualization, in conducting a number of focus groups, and in the final analysis.

Other members of the team that helped in the research in various ways included Khurram Khan Afridi, Sabahat Ashraf, Durriya Farooqui, Ali Hasan, Momina Suleman Malik, Bilal Musharraf, Maha Qazi, Tariq Qureshi, Lama Rimawi, and Sumbula Safavi. In Pakistan, Khalid Ali, Shoaib Zahidi and Muhammad Zafar ul Malik at epoor.org played a key role in developing the internet version of the survey form for data entry and analysis. Hasan Usmani and Dr. Musadik Malik were key intellectual sounding boards and advisors throughout the project. Important ideas about research design also came from Dr. Saad Ayub and Dr. Khalid Saeed. The project also received useful advice from Shahid Ahmad Khan and Shahid M. Qureshi, particularly in terms of hosts and locations for various focus groups. The Deputy Chief of Mission at the Pakistan Embassy in Washington DC, Mohammad Sadiq, provided invaluable assistance and advice in a variety of ways, most especially with regards to providing the most current demographic data on Pakistanis in America.

A report based on the work presented here was earlier published in Pakistan by the Pakistan Centre for Philanthropy. I am very grateful to the Global Equity Initiative (GEI) at Harvard University, and particularly to Barbara Merz who leads the Philanthropy Program at GEI, for suggesting that the original report should be converted into a book. She and her team, especially Iris Tuomenoksa and Erin Judge, were instrumental in guiding me through the process of turning this into a book and through its publication. Matthew McCaffree and Khadija Amjad, respectively, designed and copy-edited the final book version. Both are at the Fletcher School of Law and Diplomacy, Tufts University, and have left deep imprints on the final product. Seema Patel, also at the Fletcher School, provided a fresh eye and useful insights in her reading of drafts at earlier stages of its completion.

Resources made available to me as a Faculty Fellow at the University College of Citizenship and Public Service at Tufts University were instrumental in my ability to update the text of the book and include discussion of the response by Pakistani-Americans to the devastating 2005 earthquake in Pakistan.

Above all, I am grateful to all those Pakistani-Americans who so generously gave us their time, knowledge and wisdom by attending our focus groups and filling out our survey forms. My special gratitude goes out to all those who helped arrange our various meetings, who introduced us to potential hosts, who spoke out on our behalf when other's doubted our intent, and without whom we could not have completed the 54 focus groups or collected the 461 survey forms that we did. There are, of course, too many people to thank here and I will nearly certainly embarrass myself by forgetting to mention some; to those, I apologize in advance.

The following were all amongst those who were particularly helpful in this regards (not including those already mentioned): Aftab Ahmed, Dr. Nuzhat Ahmad, Riaz Ahmed, Ali Asghar, Aziz Ahsan, Ahmed Ali, Chaudhry Usman Ali, Dr. Saud Anwar, Imran Baqai, Rubina Byramji, Dr. Barkat Charania, Andaleeb Dawood, Prof. Ahmed Durrani, Akhtar M. Faruqui, Khadija Haqqi, Fariha Haque, Khurram Hasan, RazaHasan, Dr. Arjumand Hashmi, Musa Jaffar, Abdullah Jafri, Arshad Javed, Zaheer Khawaja, Arif Kazmi, Adnan Khan, Dr. Ejaz Khan, Jamshed Yar Khan, Seeme Hasan Khan, Dr. Shahnaz Khan, Dr. Wasiullah Khan, Zainab Khan, Kamran Kizilbash, Khalid Mahmood, Bano Makhdoom, Muzammil Malik, Suleman S. Malik, Dr. Sohail Masood, Huma Najam, Dr. Maqbool Qureshi, Prof. Malik K. Rahman, Mohammad Razvi, Dr. Ahmed Saeed, Malik Sarwar, Najmi Sarwar, Khurram Shahzad, Mudassir Sheikha, Shakeeb Syed, Saad Tabani, Syed Umar, and Shahzad Warraich.

This work has benefited from the wisdom, enthusiasm, ideas and generosity of time of many; too many to mention. To all of them, I am deeply indebted. Even though I hold the intellectual responsibility for what follows and any mistakes within it, the ideas you see reflected in this report are the accumulated ideas of a community. It is to this community that I owe my greatest debt of gratitude.

-- Adil Najam
Boxborough, Massachusetts, 2006

Overview

This book seeks to understand the giving habits and impulses of Pakistanis in the United States. The focus is not only on what Pakistani-Americans 'return' to their country of origin, but also on their non-Pakistan-related giving practices. The study covers a broad range of giving practices, including giving to institutions as well as individuals and including giving in cash, in kind, and in time. The analysis is based on a set of 54 focus group discussions conducted around the United States, mostly in 2004, an analysis of 461 completed survey questionnaires, interviews with community leaders, philanthropists, and representative Pakistani-Americans, and a review of the relevant literature. In this overview we will only provide a summarized snapshot of some of the key findings. We invite the reader to peruse the entire book for a nuanced and detailed discussion of these and related issues.

Chapter #1 reviews the context, constraints and criteria that define the parameters of the research. This chapter includes a discussion on why diaspora giving by Pakistanis in America is a particularly important topic for Pakistan and for Pakistani-Americans today. The chapter also includes a discussion of the methodological constraints that had to be overcome in conducting this research. The bulk of this chapter is devoted to an exposition of the demographic and other characteristics of the 54 focus groups and 461 survey questionnaires analyzed for this research.

Chapter #2 focuses on the history, demography and institutional geography of Pakistanis in America and is based on original research, and adds new information to our understanding of each of these. This chapter provides a new and original analysis of the history of the Pakistani diaspora in the USA, particularly focusing on the growth of the Pakistani-American community over the last half century. The chapter identifies five distinct historical phases, starting with the pre-Pakistan phase and ending with the post-9/11 phase. It presents a synthesis of available official information to provide a systematic demographic snapshot of the Pakistani population in the United States. The chapter concludes, quite conservatively, that there are at least 500,000 Pakistanis in America; that the majority of them live along the East coast of the

USA; New York City has by far the largest number of Pakistani-Americans, while Houston, Washington DC, Chicago and Los Angeles also have very large concentrations of Pakistanis; and that comparatively smaller but sizeable populations of Pakistanis can now be found in just about every major metropolitan city in the USA.

Importantly, the chapter concludes that while the Pakistani diaspora in America is both young and new (relatively recent arrivals), two groups within this diaspora are of particular importance: (i) a first generation of Pakistani-Americans now retiring in the United States and (ii) a second-generation of younger Pakistani-Americans who were born and/or raised in the United States and are now entering adulthood.

The chapter also provides a detailed introduction to the very wide array of Pakistani institutions that operate in the United States. This points towards an active and involved community that invests large chunks of its time and resources in trying to retain its essential 'Pakistani' identity. This spirit of community activism and giving for Pakistan's development was particularly evident during the aftermath of the 2005 earthquake in Pakistan, which literally turned just about every Pakistani institution in USA into a philanthropic organization. The chapter identifies five key categories of Pakistani institutions in America that particularly relevant to the giving practices of this community. These include: (a) cultural identity and civic organizations, (b) professional and business associations; (c) religious institutions; (d) information and advocacy platforms; and (e) charitable and development initiatives.

While the rest of the book reports on research (and estimates) completed before the 2005 earthquake in Pakistan, this chapter has been updated to highlight the various ways in which Pakistani organizations so generously responded to this horrific tragedy.

Chapter #3 presents the findings about the estimated total giving by Pakistanis in America. It is estimated that the total giving by the Pakistani diaspora in the United States is approximately $250 million per year in cash and in kind, and about 43.5 million hours per year of volunteered time. The dollar cost of the volunteered time is approximately $750 million, which would imply that the total giving by Pakistanis in America is to the tune of $1 billion per year. More importantly, the time volunteered by Pakistanis in America is the equivalent of 25,000 full-time employees and is a central component of the institutional infrastructure of the Pakistani-American community.

About 40 percent of the monetary and in-kind giving is directed towards Pakistani causes in Pakistan, another 20 percent towards Pakistani causes within the U.S., and the remaining 40 percent towards causes unrelated to Pakistan.

Our survey respondents report that about half of their monetary and in-kind giving is motivated by faith-based obligations to be charitable (but not necessarily directed towards religious organizations) while the remaining half is motivated by specific issues that they hold dear (such as poverty reduction, education, health, community development, civil liberties, etc.). Our survey findings suggest that, much like the rest of America, faith is a major motivator for giving by Pakistanis in America. However, much of this giving is directed in the form of individual support for the poor and needy, especially based on kinship networks, rather than as direct giving to faith-based organizations. Our survey findings suggest that Pakistanis in America are as or more generous in their giving habits when compared with either their compatriots in Pakistan or their neighbors in the United States. This is important because the community seems to believe the opposite to be true.

Chapter #4 focuses on the trends and tendencies in the giving practices of Pakistanis in America. Not surprisingly, the chapter concludes that total giving tends to rise with increasing income and with increasing education (the two are possibly correlated). However, lower-income households tend to volunteer more of their time. The level of giving in our survey sample tended to increase up to the 40-50 years range and then declined; however, the amount of time volunteered increased steadily with age.

Households that were more involved in Pakistani organizations tended to give more and volunteer more, as did households with Pakistani-Americans who have lived in the U.S. longer. A clear finding of this research is that while Pakistan and Pakistani causes remain a major focus of giving by Pakistanis in America, a significant proportion of giving by Pakistanis in America is also directed to causes unrelated to Pakistan. One interesting finding is that the overall giving rises with length of time spent in the USA but proportionally more of the increase is directed towards causes not related to Pakistan.

Social issues—including education and health, poverty reduction and help-ing the needy—are by far the most important issues for Pakistanis in America, and particularly so for Pakistani causes in Pakistan. In terms of Pakistani causes in the USA, community development (of the Pakistani-American com-munity) and civil and human rights were the highest ranked causes in our sur-vey. In terms of causes unrelated to Pakistan, religion and civil and human rights were the two highest ranked-causes. Our research suggests an overall inclination amongst Pakistanis in America to give directly to individuals in need and an apparent distrust of formalized institutions whether they be non-governmental organizations, educational institutions or religious organizations. However, our respondents were much less likely to focus on giving to individuals when giving to causes outside of Pakistan.

Another key finding of this chapter is that Pakistani causes—whether in Pakistan or in the United States—simply do not ask the Pakistani diaspora for contributions as often as causes unrelated to Pakistan. For example, as many as 81 percent of our survey respondents reported receiving three or more requests per month from causes unrelated to Pakistan; by contrast, only 4 percent and 10 percent, respectively, report that they are courted at the same frequency by Pakistani causes in Pakistan or the USA. The final, and important, finding of this chapter is that the giving patterns of the majority of Pakistanis in America have remained unchanged since the tragic events of September 11, 2001. Indeed, slightly more Pakistani-Americans have increased their giving since 9/11 than have decreased their giving; and the greatest increase in this period has been in causes unrelated to Pakistan.

Chapter #5 moves the focus of the report towards the giving attitudes and preferences of Pakistanis in America. Our analysis suggests that the single most important giving impulse is the desire to directly help individuals in need. Faith and a sense of community are also strong motivators of giving for Pakistanis in America, but there is an obvious lack of enthusiasm for giving to educational institutions, except for a handful of prestigious institutions that have cultivated a strong sense of identity amongst their alumni.

In terms of fundraising, nothing is as effective in raising funds as personal testimonials and appeals by friends and family. Interestingly, the means of fundraising that are most commonly used—including cultural events, formal fundraisers, and celebrity endorsements—seem to solicit only lukewarm approval from our survey respondents. Equally interesting is the fact that many of the methods that are most popular for fundraising by U.S. organizations—websites, membership dues, mass mailings, media advertising, phone requests and pledges, and email solicitation—also receive little enthusiasm from Pakistanis in America.

This chapter also finds that organizations working in a region that people 'belong to' seem to get only marginal advantage; that the view is mixed on the importance of getting a tax deduction but an organization having officially registered status in the U.S. does give people a greater sense of comfort; that celebrity endorsement and marketing material seem to hold little importance but the reputation of an organization is a key factor, even though its size is not.

A key message from this chapter confirms the well-known adage that 'people do not give to causes, people give to people'. More importantly, people tend to give most to the people they trust and for the most part Pakistanis in America do not trust institutions in Pakistan. In particular, we find that the Pakistani diaspora in America does not have much trust in nongovernmental organizations (NGOs) in Pakistan and a very large proportion of our respondents consider them to be inefficient, ineffective, unethical and inattentive to the most pressing issues. This perception is clearly an important impediment to institutional giving in Pakistan and needs to be addressed before more significant resources can flow from the Pakistani diaspora to civil society organizations in Pakistan.

In terms of the future giving potential, an overwhelming majority of our respondents believe that both their own, and the Pakistani community's giving to Pakistan-related causes can increase significantly, but only if certain conditions are met: (a) *if* they had more trust that their contributions would be put to good use, (b) *if* it becomes easier to give to Pakistan-related causes, and (c) *if* they had more and better information about causes in Pakistan.

Key priorities for our respondents, therefore, include easier mechanisms for transfer of funds to organizations in Pakistan, independently verified information about and certification of organizations in Pakistan, organizations' acquisition of officially registered status in the U.S., and better monitoring of how contributions are utilized.

Chapter #6 analyzes the group discussions in the focus groups and uses this as a means of deciphering community perceptions about giving and volunteering. The chapter concludes that the Pakistani diaspora is a dynamic and philanthropically active community but has within it significant pockets of disengaged subsets, including younger populations. The community has a very low self-image in terms of how its own philanthropic activities compare with philanthropy by other peer groups in America (even though our survey results indicate otherwise). The focus group analysis suggests that the institutional hurdles in Pakistan remain a greater impediment to giving to causes in Pakistan than the post-9/11 policy environment in the United States. Indeed, a key impact of the events following 9/11 seems to have been the emergence of a very strong perception amongst Pakistani-Americans that they need to become much more active in US-based philanthropy, even if that means cutting back on Pakistan-based philanthropy.

Chapter #7 concludes the report by drawing out key trends and larger lessons that emerge from this research, with a focus on themes that are of greatest intellectual and practical value to our key audiences: the Pakistani diaspora in America, the Pakistan Center for Philanthropy (PCP), Pakistan-related philanthropic organizations that wish to engage the Pakistani diaspora, and the scholarly and policy communities.

The chapter highlights a set of seven key overarching lessons that emerge from this research:

Lesson #1:
Pakistani-Americans are a generous, giving and active community.

Lesson #2:
There is a strong preference for giving directly to individuals in need.

Lesson #3:
People are motivated by faith, but mostly give to social issues.

Lesson #4:
The philanthropy of Pakistani-Americans is not limited to Pakistan.

Lesson #5:
9/11 made the Pakistani diaspora more vigilant, but not less giving.

Lesson #6:
There is significant potential for more giving by Pakistanis in America, including more giving to Pakistan.

Lesson #7:
There are serious hurdles that make it difficult to give more to Pakistan, including a chronic lack of trust in the civic sector in Pakistan, practical difficulties in giving to causes in Pakistan, and a lack of credible information about philanthropic organizations in Pakistan.

The chapter then suggests some practical measures that can be adopted to alleviate the challenges identified. Suggested measures that could build greater confidence in the civic sector include: creating a trustworthy independent agency for certification, developing guidelines for standard financial and management reporting and for standard impact reporting, investing in a culture of regular audits and transparent reporting of financial and management performance, and better measurement and communication of achievements and results. Measures identified for the facilitation of easier giving to causes in Pakistan include: preparation of user-friendly inventories of new US laws and regulations about international philanthropic transactions, facilitation of 'pooled funding drives' for sets of smaller NGOs and organizations, supporting educational institutions in Pakistan to harness diaspora funding, development of reliable and transparent options for international money transfer, the acquisition of registered nonprofit status in the US by more Pakistan-based organizations, and support from the Government of Pakistan in seeking more clarity on changes in US laws about monetary transfers to Pakistan.

In terms of improving the outreach on impacts and achievements of the civic sector in Pakistan, some of the identified measures include: creating a web-based clearinghouse of information on relevant organizations in Pakistan, facilitating visits to the USA by team delegations of NGO and philanthropic sector leaders, establishing channels of better and more frequent communication to existing and potential donors, targeting visits by representatives around key diaspora events in the US, seeking non-monetary contributions including knowledge-giving and volunteering by Pakistanis in America, and partnering with Pakistani organizations in America.

CHAPTER #1

Context, constraints and criteria

The purpose of this book is to better understand the giving habits and impulses of the Pakistani diaspora in the United States of America. Possibly the first study of its kind, this research also begins to shed light on how Pakistani-Americans balance the pulls of their multiple identities. The research adopts a broad and inclusive definition of philanthropy that includes all giving and volunteering (in cash, in kind and in time), to and by institutions as well as individuals. Although giving and volunteering is our primary lens of enquiry, the research also helps to better understand how this diaspora has navigated the various dimensions of its immigrant identity. It is different from most studies of 'diaspora philanthropy' because it does not restrict itself only to what Pakistani-Americans 'return' to their country of origin. There is an equal interest in the non-Pakistan-related giving practices of Pakistani-Americans.[1]

Like much of the research in this genre, we are particularly interested in the role that the Pakistani diaspora can play in the social and economic development of Pakistan. However, the focus of this enquiry is more exploratory than evaluative. A determination of exactly what (if any) impact the Pakistani diaspora and its philanthropy has had on Pakistan and its development is beyond the scope of this book and is left to future researchers; and particularly to researchers based in Pakistan. We focus, instead, on a more basic set of questions: What is the broad size and scope of philanthropic giving by Pakistani-Americans? Why do they give? What are the types of causes that they feel motivated to give to? What are their concerns about giving to causes in Pakistan? What can be done to encourage more giving by them to causes related to the social and economic development of Pakistan?

In the following chapters we will explore these and related questions in detail. The goal of this first chapter is to set the context for the rest of the book by outlining, our research methodology, how we gathered data in the absence of any baselines and in the face of great community unease and apprehension about such data collection, and, importantly, to lay out the limitations of our approach and to identify for the reader which part of the findings are the most robust and which are only indicative. Being the first study of its type, the key challenge and goal has been to set a benchmark—in terms of information as well as methodology—one future scholars will hopefully build upon and re-fine. We begin in the first section, however, by setting out the context within which this research was conducted.

Setting the context

This research was borne at the confluence of four related trends.

First, at the global level and partly as a result of the discourse on global-ization, recent years have seen a blooming of scholarly and practical interest in the study of social investing, social remittances, and diaspora philanthropy.[2] Although diaspora philanthropy is not a new phenomenon, the study of "philanthropic social investing of new immigrants back to their home coun-tries"[3] is attracting increased attention. There is a sense that we might be wit-nessing a wave of philanthropic giving because many new diaspora communi-ties (particularly Asian diasporas in the USA) have generated enormous new wealth and the forces of globalization have invested them with the desire, the means, and the ability to influence development in the 'home countries'.[4]

Second, as with other Asian diasporas (especially the Chinese and the In-dian), there is a growing feeling within Pakistan and amongst the Pakistani diaspora that Pakistanis abroad could be a source of breakthrough social in-vestments for the country's development. This trend in exemplified by the re-cent writings of Shahid Javed Burki, a prominent Pakistani-American who has been a key and consistent proponent of this view and has articulated various dimensions of this argument in a series of essays published in the Karachi newspaper *Dawn*.[5] Burki forcefully argues that the Pakistani diaspora around the world, and especially in the United States, has a very high potential for transferring investments to Pakistan, and has already been doing so to a signifi-cant degree. He estimates that the aggregate annual income of Pakistanis in North America is around $25 billion, their accumulated wealth around $100 billion, and their combined savings more than $6 billion. Indeed, he has argued that Pakistanis abroad have been a major motor of the recent economic growth in Pakistan, given the fact that in the period 2003-04 the total amount of remittances from Pakistani expatriates was more than four percent of the country's gross domestic product and equal to about one-quarter of the total amount of net investment.[6] Based on such estimates and on the technological ease with which an expatriate can now remain involved with events and investments in Pakistan, he has argued that the Pakistani expatriates should be viewed not as 'lost children' but as an economic and knowledge resource that can be harnessed for national development, including through philanthropic transfers.

Third, for the last many years—but especially in the aftermath of the tragic events of September 11, 2001—Pakistanis in America seem to have themselves become more interested and active in exploring the various dimensions of the diaspora identity both in the United States and in Pakistan. This has included a growing civic engagement within the United States and an enhanced interest in diaspora philanthropy directed towards Pakistan. Conceivably, this might be attributed to the growth and maturation of the community as a whole, the coming-of-age of a second generation of Pakistani-Americans, the recent success of Pakistani-Americans (particularly knowledge professionals), and—more recently—a response to greater scrutiny within American society of all Muslim communities, including Pakistani-Muslims. Whatever the reasons, there is an appreciable mushrooming of Pakistan-related organizations, publications, and philanthropies within the Pakistani diaspora.[7] Although it is difficult to find a literature substantiating this phenomenon, our extensive interviews with Pakistani-Americans suggest that the phenomenon is well-recognized by the Pakistani-American community itself and is validated in subsequent chapters (especially chapter 2).

Finally, and most directly relevant to the genesis of this research, there is an appreciable increase in interest in philanthropy—including diaspora philanthropy—within Pakistan. Although the success of iconic philanthropist Abdul Sattar Edhi and the former cricket superstar Imran Khan are the most widely recognized, there has been a steep increase in the number of institutions and individuals tapping the philanthropic impulses of Pakistanis for social development.[8] This interest in philanthropy became even bigger and more urgent in the immediate aftermath of the 2005 earthquake in Pakistan, which has seen an amazingly vigorous and general response from Pakistani individuals and institutions in the United States. It is too early to say whether this giving enthusiasm will be sustained, but its magnitude has taken even the community itself by surprise.

Key markers that track this growth in interest include the 1999 study on indigenous philanthropy in Pakistan (commissioned by the Aga Khan Development Network). This was followed by the 1999 National Conference on Indigenous Philanthropy, which recommended the creation of a Pakistan Center for Philanthropy (PCP).[9] Created in August 2001, the PCP has since undertaken a number of initiatives to better understand and promote philanthropy in and related to Pakistan, including this research. Simultaneously, various civil society organizations in Pakistan as well as philanthropic initiatives within the United States have been tapping the Pakistani diaspora in the United States with increasing frequency and have begun to realize the potential depth and breadth of the diaspora's philanthropic generosity.[10]

The utility and relevance of this research should be understood within the context of these four concurrent and related trends. This book has multiple audiences. First, it seeks to provide useful information and ideas to organizations in Pakistan or related to Pakistan that wish to tap, encourage and enhance diaspora philanthropy by Pakistani-Americans, particularly for equitable social and economic development in Pakistan. The results of this research should also be of interest to Pakistani-Americans themselves since it is one of the first systematic empirical studies of the institutional life of the diaspora. Finally, the findings of this research should be of value to scholars who are interested in studying either diaspora philanthropy or Pakistani-Americans.

The remainder of this chapter will focus on defining the methodology and research parameters for this book. This will include a discussion of the research design and a summary of the key characteristics of those who responded to our survey instrument and of those who participated in our focus groups. This chapter will conclude by outlining the key caveats and limitations of our results and give the reader a guide to better understanding and interpreting these results. Chapter 2 will present a brief demographic and institutional profile of Pakistanis in America. It will review the history of the Pakistani diaspora in the USA, identify key population centers, and present a taxonomy and exemplars of various types of diaspora organizations that the Pakistani-American community has created. Chapter 3 will present the broad findings in terms of the total giving by Pakistanis in America, including the distribution and key motivations for giving. Chapter 4 will further explore these findings and identify the key trends and tendencies within the giving patterns of the Pakistani diaspora. This will include discussions related to demographic trends, trends related to issues and causes, and trends related to the practical logistics of charitable giving by this diaspora. Chapter 5 will focus on the attitudes and preferences of the diaspora in relation to its philanthropic giving. It will ask key questions in terms of why people give, what makes them give, and whether there is the potential for increased giving to Pakistan-related causes. While Chapters 3 to 5 focus on the results of the survey instruments, Chapter 6 will seek to identify wider community perceptions regarding philanthropy. This chapter will be based on an analysis of various focus group discussions that were conducted as part of this research. Finally, Chapter 7 will try to bring the key findings of the entire book together by identifying the key lessons and recommendations emerging from this research.

Research constraints and design

The genesis of this research predates the events of September 11, 2001, but as with so much else in our 'post-9/11 world' this research was conducted in the shadow of those tragic events and their aftermath. Conceptually, the rationale for this book emerged from the four converging trends that were described in the previous section. Practically, the idea was an obvious outgrowth of the publication of a 1999 study on indigenous philanthropy in Pakistan and the subsequent establishment of the Pakistan Center for Philanthropy.[11] Although conceived well before 9/11, the events of that fateful day not only made the need for such research all the more salient for the Pakistani-American community, but it also imposed significant methodological and design constraints for such research.

Immediately after September 11, immense attention—with sometimes unfair and inappropriate generalizations—began to be lavished on any charity that was related to Islamic causes or to Islamic countries. While some charities that had misused the resources entrusted to them were identified, the official clampdown and media attention was so strong that many Muslims, including many Pakistanis, became fearful of giving to any charity at all just in case their well-intentioned generosity might come back to haunt them. Many believe that these events caused, at least a temporary, 'philanthropic chill' amongst Muslim communities. For example, a community forum of the Illinois Advisory Committee to the U.S. Commission on Civil Rights held in July 2002 found that many Muslim leaders saw the closure of Islamic charities as part of a disturbing trend of profiling Muslim communities and the resulting sense of fear is so high that "seemingly innocuous acts like giving to charity are now done with trepidation at the uncertain ramifications for such acts."[12] Newspaper reports suggested a similar prevalence of fear about giving as well as talking about giving. For example, a report in the *Los Angeles Daily News* (October 30, 2004) used the headline 'Muslims shy away from philanthropy' and quoted one Muslim as saying: "Most people are afraid and confused. They don't wan to give charity to a place and then find out it's financing terrorism."[13] A report in the prestigious Public Broadcasting Service (PBS) news show *NewsHour with Jim Lehrer* (September 12, 2004) spoke similarly of Muslims being afraid of donating to any Islamic charity; one person interviewed on the broadcast pointed out that "they're afraid to give checks because they don't want, in any way, their name to be associated with what the government might consider illegal or suspicious."[14]

In short, by the time the details of this research began to be designed, a very strong climate of fear about all things related to philanthropy was pervasive in all Muslim-American communities, including among Pakistani-Americans. While not all Pakistanis are Muslim, and even though most Pakistan-related charities are not 'Islamic' in their principal focus, the fact that Pakistan is a Muslim majority country and a key player in the post 9/11 'War on Terror' has put strong, and often unfair, pressure on Pakistani-Americans in general and on philanthropy by Pakistani-Americans in particular.

This contextual background is central to the design because it set the *first stringent constraint* on our research methodology. What might have been the obvious strategy of sending out a large number of general survey questionnaires to a large number of Pakistani-Americans across the United States through regular and electronic mail and conducting blind telephone survey interviews with a similar cohort of respondents, was not feasible because of the extremely high levels of apprehension and mistrust that had been generated by the post-9/11 scrutiny of Muslim-Americans. This constraint forced us to design a more personal interaction that began with *a series of 'focus group' meetings* across the country which allowed a more transparent process where participants were able to discuss the issues related to diaspora philanthropy in more general terms, could ask questions and gain a sense of comfort about the nature and purpose of the research, and could contribute to a more nuanced analysis of current and emerging trends. A detailed *survey instrument* was included as part of the methodology, but participants were asked to fill the survey forms *after* the focus groups. Although this could induce some bias on the part of those filling out the forms (since they might reflect the focus group's discussions in their responses), it did have the benefit that respondents were likely to be much more clear on the various specialized terms and concepts used in the survey instrument and came to the exercise with a greater sense of comfort than they otherwise might have.

The survey instrument itself was a fairly detailed questionnaire (see annex) and was finalized after multiple trial runs and reviews. The survey questionnaire focused on general questions about total giving, giving to broad categories, and most importantly on issues related to why people give and what might encourage them to give more. In addition to (and often in preparation for or as follow-up to) the focus group meetings and the survey questionnaires, the research team also conducted a number of *formal and informal interviews* with members of the Pakistani-American community on their own philanthropic preferences, experiences and aspirations. These interviews were often with, but not limited to, individuals who are either philanthropically active themselves or highly active in various Pakistan-related organizations.

In the selection of the focus groups, the survey respondents as well as the people we interviewed, a conscious effort was made to get the views of Pakistani-Americans from across the United States as well as from various economic strata, educational backgrounds, age groups, and professions. This was particularly important because of the *second stringent methodological constraint* that our research design had to incorporate. This constraint came from the total absence of even the most basic data required to construct a baseline for analysis. For example, there is neither data nor good estimates about the income distribution within the Pakistani-American community. Nor are there estimates of the distribution by education or profession within the community. Although there are many anecdotal estimates of the above, these tend to be based on hearsay and are often fanciful; indeed, you can find as many anecdotal estimates as the number of people you speak to. Despite our best efforts, therefore, we were left to make our own estimates about the baseline distributions as the basis of data collection. This also meant that we had to devise appropriate means for data rationalization during analysis (discussed in chapter #3).

Data collection, analysis and presentation

As the previous section points out, the research methodology was influenced by two key constraints: (a) a strong climate of apprehension on the part of the Pakistani-American community about the subject of this research, and (b) a near total lack of baseline data on the demographic and economic characteristics and distribution of the Pakistani-American community.

Responding to these constraints has required a more involved and direct interaction with participants and the design of data gathering instruments that were sensitive to the needs and apprehensions of the community as well as methodologically defensible. As already noted, the 'data' that forms the basis of this research came from three primary sources and was collected and analyzed specifically for this research.

Focus groups

54 focus groups (with a total of 631 participants) were conducted in various metropolitan centers across the United States as the primary source of contact with the Pakistani-American community. The choice of focus group locations was based on (a) our estimate of the size and diversity of the Pakistani-American community in a particular metropolitan area; (b) the desire to interact with different types of Pakistani-American communities (for example, small communities residing in states with relatively few Pakistani-Americans as well as large communities residing in major metropolises with very large Pakistani-American concentrations); (c) a desire to spread the focus groups across the country; and (d) to ensure that Pakistani-Americans from different economic strata, educational backgrounds, age groups, and professions were included in the overall sample.

In terms of the focus group design, the group size was maintained at between 6 and 15. Although there were some focus groups that were larger or smaller than this, we found this range to be the most comfortable for a meaningful dialogue. Each focus group included around 75 to 100 minutes of group discussion followed by time for people to fill out the survey questionnaires. In many cases, the participants stayed on after this for continued, more informal, discussion on the subject. It was also found that groups that were highly diverse (in terms of economic or educational backgrounds) tended to be less communicative and we therefore opted to seek diversity amongst focus groups, rather than within focus groups.

Each focus group was arranged by a local 'host' who used her or his social capital to gather relevant people. This was based on extensive consultation with the project team and to meet project objectives. One means of ensuring diversity in the sample set was to ensure diversity in the hosts who were asked to assist with organizing the focus groups. Each focus group discussion was led by a member of the research team and a standard format of general questions was used.

The essential format of the discussion was to begin with a conversation about the community itself, including its history, its dimensions, and its key features. This was followed by a discussion of the community's perception of the general philanthropic impulses of Pakistanis, both in Pakistan and in the USA. This conversation also included the community's perceptions of how their own philanthropic behavior compared to the philanthropy of other reference communities. This was followed by a discussion on the philanthropic practices within that community with a special focus on specific examples of philanthropy by individuals and organizations in the community. Finally, the focus groups were asked to discuss ways and means by which the quality and quantity of philanthropy directed towards Pakistan could be improved. Within these rather broad areas, the focus group discussions were generally extensive with significant room for the participants to shape the discussion themselves. The research team took notes from each focus group discussion, but without recording any names or any attribution. These notes were then shaped into standardized reports of each focus group discussion. At the end of each focus group discussion, the participants were asked to fill out the survey forms if they wished to.[15]

Survey questionnaires

Although the focus groups formed the backbone of our data collection and provided critical insights and information for this research, much of the raw data reported in this book came from the survey forms that participants filled out. A total of 461 completed forms were analyzed.[16] Not included in this number are the forms that were so incomplete that they were not coded (about 20 forms). Only two respondents indicated that they did not give anything at all philanthropically. The majority of the completed survey forms came from the focus groups themselves. However, a significant minority came independently, either through the PCP website (where the form was placed in electronic form) or through personal invitations from those who had attended the focus groups or were members of the research team.

The forms were collected and coded without attribution or identification that could tie them back to individual respondents. Only one form was collected per household. The survey questionnaire (see Annex) used for this research was developed over multiple iterations and after multiple field tests by a subset of the research team.[17] The questionnaire is structured around three main areas: (a) demographic information relating to the age, education, profession, and other categories of basic information used as the basis of analysis; (b) information about the giving habits of the responding households; and (c) information about the giving motivations of the respondent, including questions about what type of incentives or encouragement might trigger greater philanthropy by Pakistani-Americans.

Interviews and literature review

The third source of data for the research was a series of formal and informal interviews conducted with Pakistani-Americans active in philanthropy or in Pakistan-related organizations. A number of these interviews were conducted in relation to, but independently from, the focus groups. Others were conducted as part of the research to map the institutional life of the Pakistani-American diaspora. Some were arranged specifically with individuals who were particularly active in the Pakistani-American community at large. All interviews were free-form and were conducted for general informational purposes. Along with the focus groups, but even more so, these interviews also served as valuable tools for ground-truthing, validating and verifying the general trends that were emerging from other elements of the research.

Although a detailed literature review was also conducted, the paucity of written sources of information on the Pakistani-American community means that the vast bulk of the information had to be assembled for the first time. While the general literature on diasporas in the United States and journalistic accounts of the Pakistani-American community do give useful pointers, there has been no systematic attempt to create a profile of this community. It is hoped that future scholars will build upon this research to create more detailed and systematic profiles of the demography, economy and sociology of this community.

Presentation of results

Every effort has been made to keep this book data rich but also to ensure that survey numbers do not overwhelm the analysis and are used primarily to corroborate and highlight findings from other sources, especially from in-depth focus group discussions. A similar effort has been made to keep the description and presentation of the data reader-friendly both in its textual description and in its tabular and graphical representation. In order to meet this goal, the following conventions have been applied to data presentation and analysis; readers should be cognizant of these.

◆ All tables and figures in this and subsequent chapters, unless noted otherwise, are based on data from focus groups and survey responses collected for this research. Following standard convention, and to reduce needless repetition, a data source will be mentioned only where data is from outside sources.

◆ For ease in reading, and in order to avoid the presumption of precision, numbers have been rounded off throughout the book, in textual as well as graphical representation. Where data is presented as a percentage, the totals may not add up to 100 because of this reason.

◆ The purpose of the figures and tables is to assist the reader in the analysis and conclusions rather than to simply report the survey results. The figures and tables seek to highlight the most important aspects of the presented data rather than lay out an entire set of survey results. In many cases, therefore, we have chosen to leave out certain categories of responses in questions where percentage responses are being reported (especially in Chapters #4 and #5); unless self-evident, footnotes are used to highlight the missing categories and why the percentages may not add up to 100. For those who do wish to see the entire range of responses, a copy of the survey instrument is attached in Annex and the structure of the original question should allow the reader to estimate the magnitude of the missing categories.

◆ Some of the demographic data collected from the survey was found to be of little analytical significance beyond sample validation and is not reported in the analysis. For example, survey respondents were asked about their employment status, household size, residence status in the United States, and primary responsibility for giving decisions. This data was used to verify the validity of the sample but is not discussed here.

◆ As discussed in Chapter #2, we estimate that there are at least 500,000 Pakistanis in America, and for purposes of calculation, convert that to the equivalent of 100,000 households (a conservative estimate of 5 individuals per household). In the absence of baseline data, a proxy baseline was created to calculate our estimates. Details of the calculations involved are discussed in Chapter #3.

◆ Survey respondents reported their cash and in-kind giving directly in US dollars. They reported their time volunteered in hours per month; the average cumulated time volunteered was then converted into the equivalent of full time

jobs and into estimated dollar cost of time volunteered using standard formula-
tions used in the field and discussed in Chapter #3.

Focus group characteristics

Given the level of anxiety and apprehension amongst Pakistani-Americans in
the post-9/11 environment, organizing these focus groups was no routine task.
It required the identification and support of those who are active in their own
communities and who were willing to build trust between the research team
and their communities. Above all, it required investment in transparency about
the goals of this research, about those who are involved with it, and about its
sponsors. Often, community leaders would seek references and in a few cases
community gatekeepers were not convinced of our purposes. In each case, it
required patience and perseverance.

Indeed, the maximum amount of effort invested into the project went towards this goal. In doing so, we found the Pakistani-American communities to
be remarkably generous with their time and, most importantly, immensely desirous to somehow contribute to Pakistan's development and wellbeing. Once
the initial hesitancy had been overcome and an initial trust established, there
was a strong and evident thirst amongst Pakistani-Americans across the country to talk about, to understand, and to do something about contributing better
to Pakistan and its development. This strong desire to remain meaningfully
involved is itself a key finding of this book, and one that could not have been
derived simply from the survey data.

A total of *54 focus groups were conducted. As many as 631 participants
attended these focus groups, including 435 men (68.9 percent) and 196 women
(31.1 percent).* We sought to keep the size of focus groups between 6 and 15
participants, and most were in this range. The smallest had only 3 people and
the largest as many as 25 (see Table 1).

*Focus groups were held in 17 different states plus the District of Columbia
(DC) capital region.*[18] The choice of location sought to reflect the major concentrations of Pakistani-Americans and to ensure a diversity of economic
strata, educational backgrounds, professions, etc. Seven focus groups, each,
were conducted in New York, California and Texas; states which host three of
the largest populations of Pakistani-Americans. Five each were held in Illinois
and the District of Columbia (the DC focus groups were spread across Maryland, Virginia and DC territory). Four each were held in Florida and New Jer-

Table 1: Focus Group Locations and Participation

Distribution of focus groups by metropolitan area and state, and by participation

	Metropolitan Area	State	Participants (M/F)		Metropolitan Area	State	Participants (M/F)		Metropolitan Area	State	Participants (M/F)
1	Boston	Massachusetts	15 (9/6)	19	Washington	DC	13 (7/6)	37	Newark	New Jersey	9 (8/1)
2	Hartford	Connecticut	12 (10/2)	20	Washington	DC	17 (6/11)	38	New York City	New York	8 (8/0)
3	Chicago	Illinois	14 (14/0)	21	Washington	DC	7 (3/4)	39	Detroit	Michigan	17 (17/0)
4	Chicago	Illinois	15 (13/2)	22	Washington	DC	16 (4/12)	40	Detroit	Michigan	16 (13/3)
5	Chicago	Illinois	9 (9/0)	23	Houston	Texas	9 (8/1)	41	Phoenix	Arizona	8 (8/0)
6	Winston-Salem	North Carolina	4 (4/0)	24	Austin	Texas	15 (15/0)	42	Phoenix	Arizona	14 (14/0)
7	Charlotte	North Carolina	15 (10/5)	25	Providence	Rhode Island	10 (0/10)	43	Poughkeepsie	New York	12 (6/6)
8	Washington	DC	10 (8/2)	26	Houston	Texas	9 (5/4)	44	Tallahassee	Florida	7 (7/0)
9	San Francisco	California	12 (10/2)	27	Houston	Texas	16 (7/9)	45	Los Angeles	California	18 (11/7)
10	San Francisco	California	10 (9/1)	28	Houston	Texas	16 (16/0)	46	Los Angeles	California	16 (10/6)
11	San Francisco	California	11 (8/3)	29	Houston	Texas	9 (5/4)	47	Tampa	Florida	11 (7/4)
12	Los Angeles	California	23 (12/11)	30	Philadelphia	Pennsylvania	6 (1/5)	48	Tampa	Florida	6 (5/1)
13	San Diego	California	7 (6/1)	31	Houston	Texas	14 (9/5)	49	Detroit	Michigan	10 (8/2)
14	Chicago	Illinois	12 (5/7)	32	Philadelphia	Pennsylvania	18 (8/10)	50	New York City	New York	8 (3/5)
15	Chicago	Illinois	5 (5/0)	33	New York City	New York	10 (10/0)	51	Boston	Massachusetts	25 (13/12)
16	Atlanta	Georgia	4 (2/2)	34	Princeton	New Jersey	14 (14/0)	52	New York City	New York	8 (8/0)
17	Birmingham	Alabama	14 (9/5)	35	New York City	New York	5 (5/0)	53	Newark	New Jersey	8 (5/3)
18	Tampa	Florida	3 (3/0)	36	New York City	New York	21 (12/9)	54	Newark	New Jersey	10 (3/7)

sey, while three were held in Michigan. Two focus groups, each, were conducted in Arizona, Massachusetts, North Carolina and Pennsylvania, while one each was held in Alabama, Connecticut, Georgia and Rhode Island, respectively (see Figure 1).

A better way to understand the distribution of focus groups around the country is to plot them by the metropolitan areas they covered. *Our focus groups were spread over 23 different metropolitan areas across the country.* As many as 9 were held in the greater New York City area (6 in the New York City, NY area and 3 around the Newark, NJ area which falls in a different state but is functionally within the greater New York City area). Houston (TX) hosted 6 different focus groups. Five each were held in Chicago (IL) and Washington DC, both of which have major concentrations of Pakistani-Americans. Apart from Newark, NJ (already mentioned), Detroit (MI), Los Angeles (CA), San Francisco (CA) and Tampa (FL) also hosted three focus groups each. Two focus group discussions each were held in Boston (MA),

Figure 1: Focus Group Locations
(Total Focus Groups = 54)

Phoenix (AZ) and Philadelphia (PA). One each was held in Atlanta (GA), Austin (TX), Birmingham (AL), Charlotte (NC), Hartford (CT), Poughkeepsie (NY), Princeton (NJ), Providence (RI), San Diego (CA), Tallahassee (FL) and Winston-Salem (NC). A particular factor in the choice of these locations for the focus groups was to ensure that communities of different characteristics were covered. For example, Atlanta hosts a significantly different Pakistani community from, say, Poughkeepsie; the former is a large city with a large number of Pakistanis living in it, while the latter is a much smaller city with a very small but tight-knit Pakistani-American population. Community dynamics in the two are, therefore, likely to be different.

Analyzing focus groups

The focus groups were consciously structured as a key analytical vehicle and not just as venues from which to collect survey forms. The structured format of the focus group discussion was matched by a similarly structured system of record-keeping and discussion analysis, which, as described in Chapter #6, also includes detailed content analysis of the focus group discussions. However, it is important to clearly understand both the opportunities afforded through such direct participant interaction and the constraints.[19] The strength of the methodology is that it can provide a level of direct interaction, discourse, clarification, detail and nuance that can simply not be derived from survey data alone. This was particularly invaluable in this case because of the lack of any credible baselines. The discussions not only allowed us to validate trends and tendencies that might have been missed from survey data alone, but also provided a regular system of triangulating the emerging findings. Moreover, having the discussion also assisted in developing participant understanding of and confidence in the process, and allowed for more and better responses to the survey questionnaire.

The constraint, of course, is that different groups will invariably have different dynamics that are unique to them. One purpose of focus groups is to recognize these unique dynamics. However, the researcher must remain vigilant to the danger of confusing the dynamics of a particular focus group with the dynamics of that community in general. Focus group data simply cannot allow such inference. The methodology has tried to respond to this by keeping the analysis 'blind' and not identifying particular focus groups within the analysis matrix (see chapter #6).

There is also the issue of selection-bias that can creep in. First, those who take time out to attend a focus group are, by definition, already interested enough in the issue to make such an investment. Second, since focus groups are convened by local hosts, a second layer of selection bias comes in as a reflection of the convener's bias. The first issue implies that extrapolation is limited unless data is also gathered from non-participant populations. The second issue highlights the importance of maintaining diversity within the conveners so that the same diversity is reflected within the focus groups. To the extent possible, we tried to follow both these strategies. Another key factor (discussed in Chapter #6) is that few focus groups can be truly homogenous and in the absence of some voting mechanism the discussion tends to highlight dominant views much better than the distribution of views within the group.

Given the climate of apprehension already discussed, we were careful in neither recording nor reporting the names of the participants. The analysis matrix that forms the basis of Chapter #6 does *not* correspond to the chronological list of locations of focus groups. Hence, the analysis is done on the general characteristics of each group without any reference to its specific location. This not only has the pragmatic virtue of keeping the identity of the group anonymous, it also has the conceptual benefit of keeping the analysis blind, and therefore more honest.

Key characteristics

In terms of focus group characteristics, the notable characteristics were as follows (see Figure 2):

♦ *In terms of age, we were able to get participation from the entire range in the focus groups.* Of the 54 focus groups, 14 were composed predominantly of younger Pakistani-Americans (in their 20s and 30s), 15 were composed predominantly of older Pakistani-Americans, while the remaining 25 had mixed participation from younger as well as older participants.

♦ *In terms of gender, the distribution was skewed and male-biased.* Twenty-five focus groups were predominantly male; a number of these included only men. Another 24 were mixed, but the majority of these also had more men than women. Only five focus groups were predominantly female. This is less than desirable and probably a reflection of the cultural norms of the community.

◆ *In terms of education, a clear majority of focus groups (31) were composed predominantly of Pakistanis with advanced degrees.* This is probably not entirely reflective of the actual community composition but this may not be terribly off the mark for what is generally considered a highly-educated community. Six focus groups were predominantly composed of participants with only basic education (High School level), and 17 focus groups were mixed in their composition by education.

◆ *In terms of income, the focus group composition tended to tilt towards those with higher incomes.* Fully half (27) of the focus groups consisted primarily of participants in higher income brackets. Only one in six (9 focus groups out of 54) were predominantly composed of lower income households. Eighteen focus groups had mixed composition. However, this may not be as skewed as it seems, because the survey data suggests that participants from the full spectrum of income brackets did participate. Indeed, of the four attributes discussed here, diversity within individual groups was probably highest in terms of income ranges represented within individual focus groups.

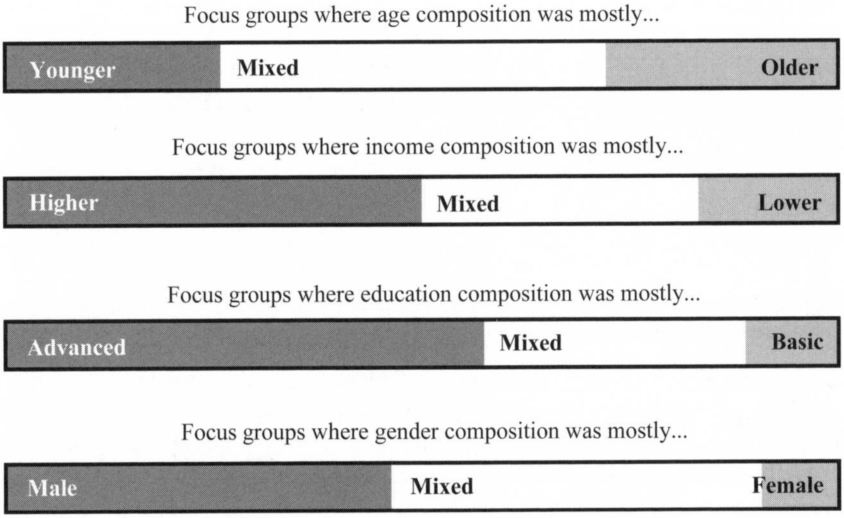

Focus groups where age composition was mostly...

Younger	Mixed	Older

Focus groups where income composition was mostly...

Higher	Mixed	Lower

Focus groups where education composition was mostly...

Advanced	Mixed	Basic

Focus groups where gender composition was mostly...

Male	Mixed	Female

Figure 2: Group Characteristics of Focus Groups

Overall, the focus groups tended to be generally representative of the community characteristics in terms of age, but demonstrated a slight bias towards higher income categories, a more appreciable bias towards more educated participants, and a significant male bias. There was a conscious and concerted attempt to balance for these biases in the collection of the survey forms so that the final sample for analysis was relatively more balanced. For example, a special effort was made to seek more survey responses (independent of focus groups) from less-educated and lower-income households as well as from women, since in both cases (but for different reasons) there was an appreciable hesitancy in being able or willing to attend focus group discussions. Despite these biases, the focus group discussions did represent a deep and detailed insight into a very important subset of Pakistani-Americans in terms of the subject of this study; a subset of more educated, more affluent Pakistani-American households.

Survey respondents' characteristics

A total of 461 valid survey forms were analyzed from across the United States. The bulk of these came from focus group participants, but a significant minority also came from individuals who had not attended the focus groups. The latter group included individuals who were invited directly by the research team as a means to offset the imbalances imposed by the focus group format. For reasons already described, great care was taken to keep the information contained in the survey forms anonymous. No names were asked or recorded and care was taken to ensure that the coding and analysis was in no way linked to individual forms or individual information. The purpose of this section is to outline the key demographic characteristics of our survey respondents.

In terms of national coverage, *the 461 survey forms came from 30 different states across the United States* (see Table 2, Figure 3). The largest number came from New York State (62 forms, 13.45 percent), followed by California (53), Texas (52), New Jersey (44) and Illinois (31). Michigan, Massachusetts, Florida, Arizona and Maryland contributed between 20 and 25 survey forms, while the remaining 20 states on our list contributed less. Some, like Minnesota, Tennessee and Wisconsin, contributed only one each. Although the bulk of the survey forms come from the East coast of the United States, this is not surprising because that is where the major concentrations of Pakistani-Americans are located. As with the focus groups, an effort was made to solicit

Table 2: Distribution of Survey Questionnaires, by State
Total number of valid forms = 461

	State	No. of Surveys (percent)
1	New York	62 (13.45%)
2	California	53 (11.50%)
3	Texas	52 (11.28%)
4	New Jersey	44 (9.54%)
5	Illinois	31 (6.72%)
6	Michigan	25 (5.42%)
7	Massachusetts	24 (5.21%)
8	Florida	21 (4.56%)
9	Arizona	20 (4.34%)
10	Maryland	20 (4.34%)
11	Pennsylvania	14 (3.04%)
12	Connecticut	13 (2.82%)
13	Virginia	13 (2.82%)
14	North Carolina	11 (2.39%)
15	District of Columbia	7 (1.52%)
16	Alabama	7 (1.52%)
17	Georgia	6 (1.30%)
18	Colorado	6 (1.30%)
19	Ohio	5 (1.08%)
20	Rhode Island	5 (1.08%)
21	Washington	5 (1.08%)
22	Missouri	3 (0.65%)
23	Utah	3 (0.65%)
24	New Hampshire	2 (0.43%)
25	Oklahoma	2 (0.43%)
26	Oregon	2 (0.43%)
27	Nevada	2 (0.43%)
28	Minnesota	1 (0.22%)
29	Tennessee	1 (0.22%)
30	Wisconsin	1 (0.22%)

sufficient survey forms from the states with the highest concentrations of Paki-stanis, to get responses from across the country, and from states hosting differ-ent types of Pakistani-American communities. However, no attempt was made to seek direct correspondence between the number of forms received from a state and the estimated population of Pakistani-Americans living there.

As with the focus groups, the even more relevant metric for understanding the distribution of survey responses is to consider the metropolitan centers that respondents identified themselves with. Given the estimates of the demo-graphic distribution of Pakistanis across America (discussed in the next chap-ter), we were able to get responses from most of the major population centers (see Table 3). *Survey forms were received from 39 different Metropolitan ar-eas around the United States.* By far, the largest concentration of Pakistanis in America resides in and around New York City. Fittingly, the largest number of our survey responses (65 forms, 14.10 percent) came from the greater New York City area. This number is forty percent more than the number for the next Metropolitan area on our list, which is Washington DC with 38 forms (8.24 percent). It should be noted that both these regions serve residents of more than

☐ No survey responses   ▦ 6-15 survey responses   ▨ 26-45 survey responses
▨ 1-5 survey responses   ☐ 16-25 survey responses   ■ 46-65 survey responses

Figure 3: Survey Responses by State
(Total Survey Forms = 461)

**Table 3: Distribution of Survey Questionnaires,
by Metropolitan Area**

Total number of valid forms = 461

	Metropolitan Center	No. of Surveys *(percent)*
1	New York City, NY	65 *(14.10%)*
2	Washington, DC	38 *(8.24%)*
3	Houston, TX	36 *(7.81%)*
4	Chicago, IL	31 *(6.72%)*
5	Los Angeles, CA	30 *(6.51%)*
6	Boston, MA	25 *(5.42%)*
7	Detroit, MI	25 *(5.42%)*
8	San Francisco, CA	23 *(4.99%)*
9	Phoenix, AZ	20 *(4.34%)*
10	Newark, NJ	17 *(3.69 %)*
11	Philadelphia, PA	16 *(3.47%)*
12	Tampa, FL	14 *(3.04%)*
13	Austin, TX	13 *(2.82%)*
14	Hartford, CT	12 *(2.60%)*
15	Princeton, NJ	11 *(2.39%)*
16	Charlotte, NC	8 *(1.74 %)*
17	Birmingham, AL	7 *(1.52%)*
18	Atlanta, GA	6 *(1.30%)*
19	Buffalo, NY	6 *(1.30%)*
20	Denver, CO	6 *(1.30%)*
21	Providence, RI	6 *(1.30%)*
22	Seattle, WA	5 *(1.08 %)*
23	Albany, NY	4 *(0.87%)*
24	Miami, FL	4 *(0.87%)*
25	Columbus, OH	3 *(0.65%)*
26	Dallas, TX	3 *(0.65%)*
27	Raleigh, NC	3 *(0.65%)*
28	Saint Louis, MO	3 *(0.65%)*
29	Salt Lake City, UT	3 *(0.65%)*
30	Tallahassee, FL	3 *(0.65%)*
31	Baltimore, MD	2 *(0.43%)*
32	Cleveland, OH	2 *(0.43%)*
33	Las vegas, NV	2 *(0.43%)*
34	Oklahoma City, OK	2 *(0.43%)*
35	Portland, OR	2 *(0.43%)*
36	Poughkeepsie, NY	2 *(0.43%)*
37	Milwaukee, WI	1 *(0.22%)*
38	Minneapolis, MN	1 *(0.22%)*
39	Nashville, TN	1 *(0.22%)*

one state and, therefore, these metropolitan numbers do not correspond with the relevant state numbers. Houston (36), Chicago (31) and Los Angeles (30) were the next three cities in terms of survey forms received. These were followed by Boston (25), Detroit (25), San Francisco (23) and Phoenix (20). This was followed by a string of cities with fewer survey questionnaires, including a large number from where less than 10 questionnaires were received.

Key characteristics

Given what we know about the demography of Pakistani-Americans, the total size of the sample (461) and the distribution of this sample across states as well as across metropolitan areas, we have sufficient confidence regarding the validity of the data set in terms of its geographic distribution. We have sought a similar representativeness within other demographic features of the sample set. Some key aspects of the demographic distributions and characteristics of the sample represented by the survey responses are highlighted here.

The *age distribution* for our survey sample falls very neatly into a bell-shape (see Figure 4). The vast majority (84 percent, 384 respondents) of the respondents were between the ages of 30 and 60, and the single largest age group (in increments of ten) was the 40-50 years old range, comprising of a third of the sample (150 respondents).

The distribution by the *level of educational attainment* was also fairly representative for this highly educated community (see Figure 4). Eleven percent of our sample (53 respondents) had only high school or less of education. However, nearly half of our respondents (224) reported graduate level education, including 23 with Ph.D. degrees.

In terms of *household income*, we also have a proportionately shaped distribution (see Figure 5). Within the under-$200,000 per year income range, the distribution resembles a bell-shape with the peak coming at the $60-80K range (96 respondents, 21 percent) and a healthy tail in the $100-$200K range. This is quite in line with estimates that place the South Asia diaspora as a more prosperous cohort than other immigrant communities in the USA.[20]

The image of our sample as a *highly educated, fairly well-off and generally upwardly-mobile community* is further strengthened by an analysis of the occupations represented (see Figure 6). The original survey form had given respondents a long list of 26 entries to choose from. For the purpose of this analysis we reduced the list to a dozen categories. Not surprisingly, and quite in line with the general self-image of the community, the most common

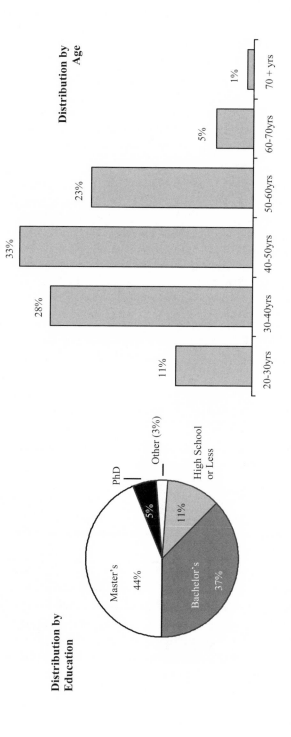

Figure 4: Survey Respondents' Distribution by Education and Age

occupational categories within our survey respondents turned out to be business management (67 respondents, 15 percent; including administrators, business consultants and management executives), information technology (62 respondents, 13 percent), engineering and scientific professions (59 respondents, 13 percent), medical professionals (57 respondents, 12 percent), small business owners (54 respondents, 12 percent; including restaurant/hotel services, retail stores, gas stations, taxi and limousine services, etc.), and finance and accounting (44 respondents, 10 percent).

Of the 461 survey respondents, 341 were men and only 120 were women. This means that *only 26 percent of our survey respondents were female* (see Figure 7). This was despite our efforts to recruit more female respondents outside of the focus groups through direct requests. It should be pointed out, however, that within the focus groups more women participated than filled out the forms, largely because only one form was required per household and very often both spouses would attend the focus groups. Even though the women who did participate in the focus groups were vocal and active in the discussions, the fact that the number of women in those focus groups was itself low, makes the lack of adequate women's participation an important concern.

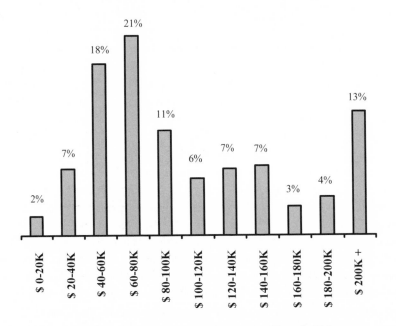

Figure 5: Survey Respondents' Distribution by Household Income

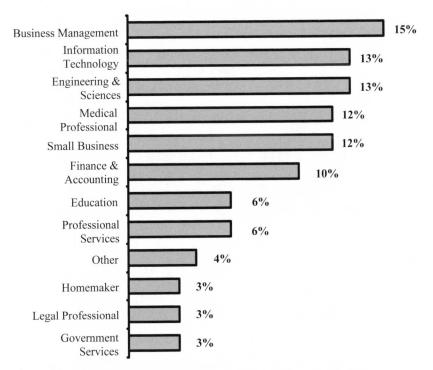

Figure 6: Survey Respondents' Distribution by Occupation

The vast *majority of our respondents were married* (85 percent, 383 respondents) and in many cases couples participated in the focus groups and the filling out of the survey forms together (see Figure 7). Another interesting aspect that emerged from our survey data, and was validated by the focus group discussions, is that those who are married nearly always make their philanthropic decisions together as a couple.

The vast *majority of our respondents were born and raised in Pakistan* (88 percent, 405 respondents). Of the remaining, 11 percent described themselves as being Pakistani by origin but were not raised in Pakistan. Most of the later group were Pakistani-Americans who were born and raised in the United States, but it also included some who were raised outside both Pakistan and the United States (for example, in the United Kingdom or the Middle East). Five forms (1 percent) were filled by non-Pakistanis who are married to Pakistanis and, therefore, are members of Pakistani-American households. Overall, 50 respondents (13 percent of married respondents) reported that one of the two spouses in their household is a non-Pakistani (see Figure 7).

The majority of our respondents came from households where *only one spouse earned an income* (63 percent). The remaining 37 percent reported more than one earning members contributing to the household income. Such a distribution is not the norm within the United States as a whole but may well be close to the norm for Pakistanis living in the United States (see Figure 7).

The *majority of respondents were Pakistani-Americans who have acquired US citizenship* (318 respondents, 69 percent). Another 87 respondents (19 percent) reported US permanent resident status, while 49 respondents (11 percent) had the status of working non-residents. Five respondents (1 percent) reported student status. Based on general impressions within the community, this seems to be a reasonable distribution by status for the Pakistani-American community at large (see Figure 8).

Our sample also shows *a representative distribution in terms of the time spent by respondents in the United States.* Once again, we get a bell-shaped curve with the peak indicated by the 124 respondents (27 percent) who have been in the United States for 10-15 years. This curve corresponds very well with known statistics about the periods when the number of Pakistanis in the United States began increasing rapidly, particularly in the late 1980s and 1990s

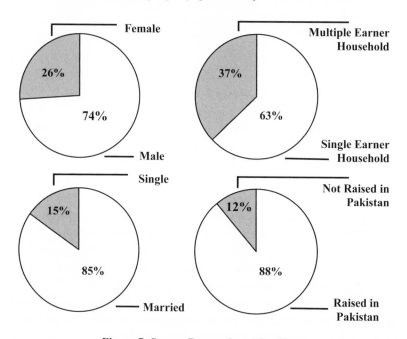

Figure 7: Survey Respondents' Profile

Residence Status in the USA

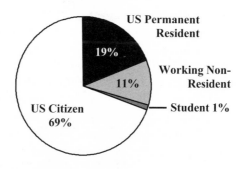

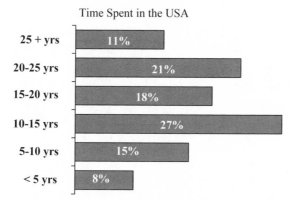

Figure 8: Survey Respondents' Depth of US Identity

(see Chapter #2). The shape of this particular curve is particularly encouraging because it suggests that our sample is reasonably representative of the various 'waves' of immigration from Pakistan to the United States (see Figure 8).

The last two characteristics of the survey sample are interesting not because they assist in gauging the representativeness of the sample, but because they give us a different set of insights into the makeup of our survey sample. The first insight is that although deeply interested in Pakistan and Pakistan's development, *our sample was not overwhelmed by the most active participants in Pakistani organizations.* Indeed, on average, the reported level of involvement in Pakistani organizations tended to be 'moderate to infrequent', with 59 percent of the respondents describing their involvement in these terms. This further corroborates the view that our survey sample does, indeed, have the characteristics of the average within the Pakistani-American community rather

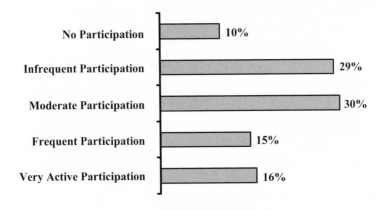

**Figure 9: Survey Respondents' Distribution by Level
of Participation in Pakistani Organizations**

than being dominated by the most active and involved of citizens (see Figure 9).

The final insight is directly related to the previous. Although not the most involved in Pakistani organizations, the people that filled our survey questionnaires tended to be *well-informed about what is happening in Pakistan and have a clear sense of which sources they use to stay in touch with Pakistan.* Given some of our later findings, an understanding of how Pakistanis in America choose to stay in touch with Pakistan is quite critical to reaching them and influencing their philanthropic decisions. Respondents were asked to choose up to three mechanisms by which they stay connected to Pakistan. By far, the most popular choice was through contact with friends and family in Pakistan (317 respondents, 69 percent). This is critical information which we will find repeated in many different ways throughout the survey. The Internet was identified as an important means of staying connected to Pakistan by 46 percent of the respondents, while about 40 percent each mentioned television and newspapers/magazines. Interestingly, as many as 150 respondents (32 percent) consider community events and gatherings to be a primary means of getting information and insight on Pakistan. This would suggest the utility of such gatherings for dissemination of information about philanthropic opportunities. Not surprisingly, only 10 percent noted the radio as a useful vehicle and only 12 respondents (3 percent) mentioned the role of the Pakistan Embassy in the United States. What is quite telling, however, is the fact that only 10 respondents out of 461 (2 percent) stated that they do not stay connected to Pakistan.

Once again, the image we get is of a community that is highly desirous of remaining in touch with the country of its origin (see Figure 10).

Reading the results

Intellectual honesty demands that we clearly state the limits of what can and cannot be said on the basis of our findings and what levels of confidence can be attributed to which set of findings. That being said, we strongly feel that there is great merit in our approach and our findings. The desire to be forthright about the limitations of the methodology must not be confused with a lack of confidence in what we have found, or how we went about finding it.

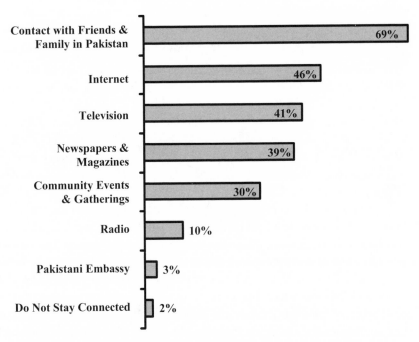

Figure 10: Survey Respondents' Preferred Means of Staying in Touch with Pakistan
Note: The sum of the percentages is greater than 100 because respondents were allowed to choose up to three options.

In this chapter in particular, but generally throughout this book, we have sought to point out the strengths as well as the limitations of the methodology used. These limitations are not unique to this research and are to be found in many survey-based explorations. Given the pioneering nature of this research, we do realize that the approach could be improved. Indeed, we seek to highlight its limitations precisely *because* we want it to be improved upon and added to by future researchers.

Different chapters of this book report on different types of findings. The goal of this section is to provide the reader with a snapshot of how to interpret different findings; some of which are quite definitive, while others are more indicative. Figure 11 provides a visual representation of the levels of confidence that can be attributed to the findings presented in different chapters of this book. The first two chapters are not included in this representation because they present background and contextual information. Chapters #3 through #7, however, present the results of original research.

It is our considered view that the overall conclusions presented in Chapter #7 are robust findings in which we can express the highest level of confidence. This high level of confidence comes because made great effort has been made to ensure that the conclusions are analytically grounded and, importantly, that each finding presented in the conclusion is corroborated by multiple sources and both by survey and focus group results. A similarly high level of confidence can be invested in the results presented in Chapter #5, which reports on survey findings about the philanthropic attitudes and preferences of Pakistanis in America. This to be so because these survey findings were very strongly mirrored in the focus group discussions. Moreover, we feel that unlike other parts of the survey, our respondents were less likely to be apprehensive about sharing their views on questions about their general philanthropic attitudes and preferences. Indeed, during the focus group discussions, there was a perceptible eagerness to talk about such issues which was quite in contrast with the relative unease people felt in talking about the specifics of how much they give to whom, and for what purpose.

It is for exactly this reason that we invest high, but not the very highest, level of confidence in the findings on trends and tendencies presented in Chapter #4. These findings relate to survey results about philanthropic behavior by different demographic categories, by cause and by issue, and by mechanics of giving. We feel that although there might have been hesitancy on the part of some in relation to these questions, in general the survey sample was large enough and each analytical category (for example different age groups or income groups) was represented well enough for the overall results to be generally reflective of reality.

We estimate our level of confidence in the findings emerging from Chapter #3 and Chapter #6 at slightly higher than medium level because both of these chapters present results that are more indicative than definitive. The analysis presented in Chapter #6 is based on the moderators' impressions of

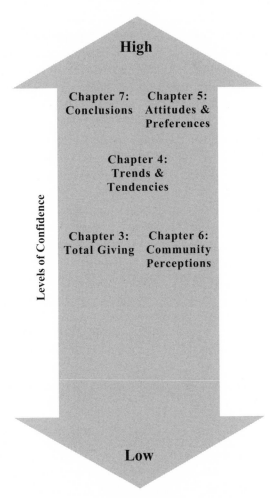

Figure 11: Levels of Confidence, by Chapter

the dynamics of each individual focus group. Although this analysis provides a fascinating and useful backdrop to—and reference for validation of—other results, this analysis is necessarily contextual and therefore not definitive. The key reason for assigning only a comparatively lower level of confidence to the results presented in Chapter #3 (on overall giving patterns) is that these calculations, more than any other in this book, required detailed baseline demographic information, which was missing and, therefore, had to be estimated. Moreover, the only basis of the findings in Chapter #3 is the survey data, which we do not have any means of corroborating from other sources and more generally, survey questions about giving tend to get non-exact responses. We also realize that given post-9/11 apprehensions within the community, the survey questions on which the analysis of Chapter #3 is based were the very ones where our respondents tended to feel the most unease while divulging information.

As the reader proceeds to read on, we hope that this disclosure about our own assessment of the levels of confidence in the various findings will be of help in navigating through the numerous and diverse findings presented in subsequent chapters.

CHAPTER #2

Pakistanis in America

The purpose of this chapter is to provide a brief snapshot of the history, demography and institutional geography of Pakistanis in America. There has yet to be a systematic study of how and why various waves of Pakistani immigrants arrived in the USA, their demographic, economic or professional distribution, or the diversity of the institutions they have set up. There are, however, 'adjacent' studies—especially on Muslims in America or South Asians in America (mostly India-focused)—from which reasonable insights and parallels can be drawn.[21] There is also much by way of anecdotal wisdom. The Pakistani-American community is now large, diverse and organized enough for a systematic enquiry to be conducted. Although we had neither the mandate nor the resources to undertake the type of primary baseline study that is needed, this chapter intends to begin the process by trying to systematically pull together the information that is already available into a basic framework of empirical enquiry that future researchers can build upon. More importantly, the immediate purpose of this chapter is to begin exploring those dimensions of the history, demography and institutional geography of the Pakistani diaspora in the USA that are most useful in making sense of the findings discussed in subsequent chapters.

The following sections will, therefore, explore these three dimensions—history, demography and institutional geography—sequentially. The first is based on a review of the larger literature on immigrant communities in the USA and our analysis of US government statistics to begin piecing together the migration history of this community. The second stems from a recent demographic review on Pakistanis in American conducted by the Pakistan Embassy in Washington, DC, but also draws on other analytical sources, including those of the US departments responsible for the census and immigration. The third section is based on our own original research and seeks to develop a framework for understanding the various types of Pakistani organizations active in the United States, which do, or can, have a bearing on diaspora philanthropy by Pakistanis in America. While the rest of the book was written prior to the 2005 earthquake in Pakistan, this section has been updated to highlight the various ways in which Pakistani-American organizations mobilized their philanthropic instincts to respond to this tragedy.

History

In reviewing the available empirical information about the arrival of various waves of Pakistanis in America, we divide the history into five contiguous phases, each defined primarily by changes in US immigration regulations (see Table 4 and Figure 12). *The first phase is the pre-Pakistan period* that begins with the first wave of Punjabi men (invariably it was just men and they were predominantly from the Punjab) arriving in the mid-nineteenth century and lasts till the 1946 passage of the Luce-Celler Bill in the US Congress that paved the way for Indians—and soon to be Pakistanis—to acquire US citizenship through naturalization. *The second phase continued from 1947 to 1965* and saw a trickle of Pakistanis coming to the US with the beginnings of a distinct 'Pakistani' community in America.

This changed rather dramatically *with the US Immigration and Naturalization Act of 1965, which marked the beginning of the third phase* and triggered a steady and significant growth in immigrants from all over South Asia, including Pakistan. *The fourth phase began in the late 1980s* when favorable immigration laws and educational opportunities attracted large numbers of Pakistanis to the United States. This growth trend of the 1990s got a jolt, as did so much else in the world, with the tragic events of 9/11 and the tightening of immigration rules and practices in its immediate aftermath. *The most current phase in the history of Pakistanis coming to the USA is, therefore, best defined as the post-9/11 phase.*

Phase 1: Pre-Pakistan
The fascinating history of the arrival of the earliest waves of immigrants from British Colonial India (parts of which would later become Pakistan) is of relevance to the future evolution of the Pakistani diaspora in the USA for at least two reasons. First, all available accounts suggest that the vast majority of the early immigrants, right up to 1947, were ethnic Punjabis, many of whom

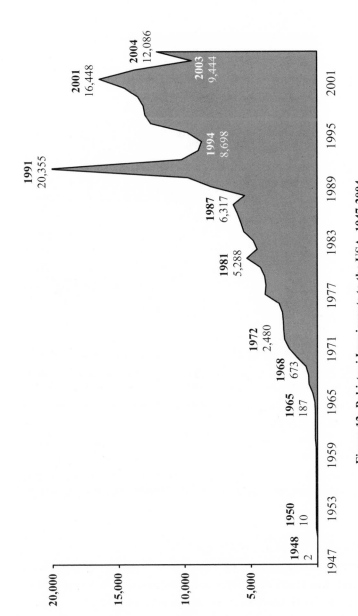

Figure 12: Pakistani Immigrants to the USA, 1947-2004

Numbers in bold are the year with the number beneath showing Pakistani immigrants at that point. *X-axis* = number of Pakistani immigrants; *Y-axis* = time

Table 4: Pakistani Immigrants Admitted by Year

Immigrant aliens admitted for permanent residence

Year	Pakistani Immigrants	Year	Pakistani Immigrants
1947	-	1981	5,288
1948	2	1982	4,536
1949	8	1983	4,807
1950	10	1984	5,509
1951-1960	929	1985	5,744
		1986	5,994
1961-1964	659	1987	6,319
		1988	5,438
1965	187	1989	8,000
1966	347	1990	9,729
1967	646	1991	20,355
1968	673	1992	10,214
1969	851	1993	8,927
1970	1,528	1994	8,698
1971	2,125	1995	9,774
1972	2,480	1996	12,519
1973	2,525	1997	12,967
1974	2,570	1998	13,094
1975	2,620	1999	13,496
1976	2,888	2000	14,535
1977	3,931	2001	16,448
1978	3,876	2002	13,743
1979	3,967	2003	9,444
1980	4,265	2004	12,086

(although probably not the majority) came from areas of West Punjab that would later become part of Pakistan.[22] Second, these early pioneers paved the paths that future immigrants from India and Pakistan would follow by developing the social support systems for these emergent communities and also by actively pushing for legal changes within the US that would enable future generations of South Asians to enter the American mainstream.[23]

Reportedly, the first recorded sighting of a South Asian in the USA comes from Rev. William Bentley in 1790. The unnamed 'Man from Madras' he saw on the streets of Salem, Massachusetts, was a servant of John Gibaut who had brought him along from Madras during a trading mission to India, and probably returned him in May, 1791. As Salem traders began frequenting India in the early 1800s they brought back a number of Indians who were often indentured workers, some of whom did settle in America, and many of whom reportedly became part of the black population of Salem because their darker skins allowed them no other option in what was still a color-based society. While a very small trickle of unskilled laborers from India continued during the 1800s, it was not until the early twentieth century that Indians began coming to the US in more sizeable numbers. Like most other immigrants from Asia, most early Indians came to the Pacific coast, particularly California. The very first batch of university students from South Asia reportedly came in the winter of 1901-02, and by 1906 there were about a hundred students from British India in the USA.[24]

According to Karen Leonard, "the six or seven thousand Indians who came to the western United States between 1899 and 1914 were chiefly peasants from India's Punjab province.... Approximately 85 percent of the early immigrants to the United States were Sikhs, and another 10 or 12 percent were Muslims." However, unaware of religious nuances and wanting to differentiate these newcomers from Native Americans (then called 'Indians'), both the local population and authorities referred to all South Asian immigrants as 'Indian Hindus', even though the vast majority were either Sikhs or Muslims. Leonard goes on to point out that "as Punjabi immigration to the United States increased, growing prejudice made it more difficult to gain admittance [and] there was a rising rejection rate of Asian Indian applicants by the Bureau of Immigration and Naturalization."

The Immigration Act of 1917 formalized the discrimination with its 'barred Asiatic zone' and a 1923 US Supreme Court decision defined them as "aliens ineligible to citizenship" because they were not 'white persons'. Around the same time large numbers of Mexican peasants, displaced by the Mexican Revolution, were also arriving in and around Imperial Valley, California. Unable to return to India to marry, shunned by white America, and desirous of setting down roots in America, large numbers of Punjabi immigrants began marrying Mexican women. This was a fairly widespread phenomenon amongst the early Punjabis (mostly Sikhs but also including Muslims) in California and resulted in a bi-ethnic Indian-Mexican community, especially in and around El Centro in California's Imperial Valley.[25]

Immigration from India came to a near standstill between 1920 and 1940. In addition to new legal barriers there was significant, sometimes violent, public harassment towards a community that was not only visibly 'different' but also becoming more prosperous. Very few Indians were allowed in legally; some 3000 reportedly slipped in illegally via Mexico during this period, but about as many also returned to India, mostly voluntarily.[26] Those who stayed were shunned by their hosts, only heightening their sense of 'Indian community', which caused them to invest in strengthening their cultural, especially religious, identity. They also began demonstrating the entrepreneurial zeal that would characterize future generations of South Asians. Indeed, one might argue that the early Punjabi immigrants to California were the original knowledge workers. The knowledge they brought with them was of irrigated agriculture, something that had just arrived in California but which they had already mastered on the plains of the Punjab. Originally starting as farmhands, their enterprise led many of them to leasing and managing fields of their own. One report suggests that by 1918 over 50,000 acres of rice in California was farmed by Punjabi immigrants, another states that by 1920, they were operating 85,000 acres of fruit orchards and vineyards.[27]

The emergence of a new generation of prosperous Indian farmers in the west and the growing numbers of Indian intellectuals who had come to study in the USA and stayed on, mostly in eastern USA, coincided with the global turn of events including two world wars and independence struggles in British India. The composition of the diaspora was still predominantly Punjabi and Gujrati, but not as much as it had been earlier. The *Indian League of America,* led by Sardar J.J. Singh, was active on the east coast in enlisting the support of US liberals for Indian independence. Mubarak Ali Khan emerged as the American voice of the All India Muslim League, and others such as Anup Singh, Syed Hossain and Taraknath Das were also active in the public arena, including on issues related to US immigration discrimination against Indians. Effort by this first generation of South Asian activists eventually resulted in the signing of the Luce-Celler Bill by President Truman on July 3, 1946, which granted Indians (and soon-to-be Pakistanis) the right to become citizens, own property, and bring their relatives to America on a national quota.[28]

Just as an early generation of East Indians was creating one set of social infrastructure that future Pakistani immigrants would use, multiple generations of non-South Asian Muslim immigrants were creating other elements of that infrastructure. Some suggest that the earliest Muslims to land on these shores might have arrived as part of Christopher Columbus's crew, others suggest that they might even have arrived earlier. Many of the earliest slaves brought to the Americas were certainly Muslims. A much told story relates how one Hadj Ali ('Hi Jolly')—variously described as Syrian or Lebanese—was brought to Arizona by the US government to breed camels, possibly to develop a desert cavalry. The first wave of immigration came in the second half of the nineteenth century when the disintegration of the Ottoman Empire triggered mass movements towards the United States, mostly of Christians but also including significant numbers (some thousands) of Muslims. Reportedly, the first communal prayer was said in Ross, North Dakota in 1900, and the first formal mosque was established in 1915 by Albanian Muslims in Maine. Detroit had an Islamic Association, of Syrian Muslims, by 1912 and a mosque by 1919. By the 1920s a congregation had been established in Cedar Rapids, Iowa, and the mosque that was completed there in 1934 is probably the oldest surviving mosque in the United States.[29]

The oldest Muslim community with clearly Pakistani roots was probably Willows, California (a few hundred miles North of San Francisco). One of the early entrepreneurial Punjabis by the name of Fazal Mohamed Khan arrived here in the 1920s and soon emerged as a successful farmer-businessman, helping establish not only a mosque but also a thriving community of Muslims many of whom, like himself, would later describe themselves as 'Pakistanis'.[30]

Phase 2: 1947-1965

Two nationals of the new state of Pakistan officially immigrated to the USA in 1948, another 8 in 1949, and 10 in 1950. It is not known who these individuals were but they were the precursors of some 1,800 Pakistanis who were granted immigrant status between 1947 and 1965. The Luce-Celler Act had enabled South Asians to immigrate, to gain citizenship and to own property in the USA. However, immigration possibilities were still limited and the new arrivals were mostly the families and relatives of those who were already here or the more entrepreneurial professionals.[31] Students also began trickling in for higher education along with government officials (military and civilian) for training, and many of these would later decide to stay on or return and become immigrants.

The early years of this period are important because the nature of the community began changing dramatically. The pre-1947 population from what had been British India was predominantly male, the immediate response to the Luce-Celler Act was that many of these men brought in their immediate and extended family members. Not only did this change the diversity of the population but now the old immigrants as well as their newly reunited kin could acquire citizenship. The net effect was to broaden the community's social presence as a distinct community while also deepening their roots in their new adopted 'home'. Other factors also helped contribute to a sense of self-confidence within the community. General prejudice against South Asians was finally in decline, the new laws on property ownership allowed greater prosperity, and a new generation of more educated professionals began arriving. Importantly, the emergent 'South Asian' community was rapidly acquiring the reputation of being a community of 'achievers. This was not an undeserved reputation, some early examples of successful Pakistani-Americans include:[32]

♦ In the world of business, Fazal Mohamed Khan, mentioned above, was a business and community leader in the Sacramento region of North California, and the new ownership regulations allowed him to expand his holdings to nearly 2,500 acres of rice fields. He and his family became major patrons of the nascent and emerging Pakistani community in the USA.

♦ In the world of performing arts, Sabu Dastagir was playing lead roles in Hollywood; his credits include, *Elephant Boy* (1937), *The Drum* (1938), *The Thief of Baghdad* (1940), *Jungle Book* (1942), *Black Narcissus* (1947), *The End of the River* (1947), *Sabu and the Magic Ring* (1957), *A Tiger Walks* (1964), etc. Although he was born in South India and immigrated to the United States well before 1947 Sabu Dastagir claimed Pakistan as his mother country. During World War II he enlisted in the US Army Air Force and was awarded the Distinguished Flying Cross.

♦ In the world of the professions, Fazlur Rahman Khan, a young engineer from what was then East Pakistan, arrived in 1952 on a Fulbright Scholarship to study engineering at the University of Illinois. He would soon become the premier engineer for efficient high-rise construction and is best known for his innovative engineering designs for Chicago's 100-storey high John Hancock Tower and the 110-storey Sears Tower (then the tallest building in the world).

Even as these early pioneers were attracting the attention and admiration of their American neighbors, more Pakistanis were arriving in America. Not only was there a jump in the annual inflow of immigrants from Pakistan in the

1950s (see Table 4), there was also a growing traffic of non-immigrant visitors from Pakistan who came as a consequence of deepening political and military alliances between the two countries. Of those who came for education and training, many would stay on to work and obtain immigrant status later. In the earliest years, the community was still seen largely as an extension of the pre-partition 'East Indian' community. However, by the early 1960s there were numerous Pakistanis in America and the triangular politics of Pakistan-USA-India had become intricate to the point that talking about a single 'East Indian' community was no longer meaningful.[33] Moreover, by this time the Muslim community had also grown significantly across major urban centers in the USA and Pakistanis had begun seeing themselves as, and were being seen as, part of the larger Muslim community more than a just subset of the South Asian diaspora.[34] Importantly, although very much a part of the South Asian and the now Muslim diasporas in the USA, a distinct and identifiable 'Pakistani' community was beginning to become evident and active in the United States.

Phase 3: 1965-1987

The passage of the 1965 Immigration and Naturalization Act was one of the most significant events in US immigration policy and like for so many other immigrant groups it dramatically changed both the number and nature of Pakistanis immigrating to the USA. The new law was one of the many civil rights initiatives of the 1960s and was a critical milepost for all Asian communities because it not only reversed decades of discrimination but also created conditions favorable to Asian immigrants.[35] The new law adopted high limits for each country (20,000 per year) and issued immigrant visas under seven different preference categories, including preferred occupational skills, family reunification and vulnerability to political and religious persecution.[36] The law, which became fully effective in 1968, had a dramatic effect on the intake of immigrants from all over Asia, but especially from South Asia.[37]

In the case of Pakistan, the immigrant intake into the USA had averaged about 100 per year during the 1950s, which was close to the allowed quota for immigrants from Pakistan. It had risen gradually in the early 1960s reaching 187 admits in the year 1965. By 1968 when the new rules came into force, it had jumped three-and-a-half times to 673 immigrants. By 1970 that had more than doubled, and as many as 1,528 immigrants were officially admitted. The number of immigrants jumped by 70% between 1970-75 (despite the breakup of Pakistan, which meant that the population base they were coming from was reduced by half), reaching 2,620 Pakistani immigrants in 1975. It went up by similar proportion in the next five years, reaching 4,265 immigrants in 1980 and crossing the 5,000 mark following year. In 1985, as many as 5,744 immigrants of Pakistani birth were admitted and by 1990 the number of new admits had grown to 9,729. In short, the 25 year period between 1965-90 saw the number of annual immigrants admitted from Pakistan jump from 187 to 9,729; an increase of over 50 times.

Cutting off the demarcation of this phase of Pakistani immigration at 1987 is largely a decision of convenience and seeks to incorporate the second order changes to the 1965 Immigration Act that the US Congress started enacting in the late 1980s and into the 1990s. What is significant, however, is that the 1965 law enabled not just more Pakistanis to immigrate, but encouraged different types of Pakistanis to seek their fortunes in the United States. If the Punjabi agriculturalists moving into California in the late nineteenth century were the original knowledge-workers from South Asia, those coming in the late 1960s and 1970s were the second wave of knowledge-immigrants. It is not coincidental that the discourse in South Asia, including Pakistan, was focused on the concept of 'brain drain'.[38] Those immigrating to the USA during this period included a disproportionate number of physicians, engineers, scientists, and other highly trained professionals. Some immigrated directly because their professions were in high demand in America, others poured into US universities and found enticing opportunities upon graduation.

Members of religious minorities also arrived in significant numbers. For example, relative to their numbers within the overall population in Pakistan, there are disproportionately large communities of Pakistani-Christians and Pakistani-Zoroastrians (*Parsis*) living in the USA. A number of Pakistanis with less educational qualifications also came during this period, often using the preference categories for relatives. Many immigrants from this last group flocked towards the large urban centers like New York City, Chicago, Houston, Los Angeles, etc. These three categories of Pakistani immigrants came from distinct socio-economic backgrounds within Pakistan and those distinctions were, for most part, maintained in the USA. The total number of Pakistanis, even within these different groups, was large enough by the 1970s for distinct Pakistani institutions to begin emerging in the large urban centers. Some of the oldest Pakistani associations, for example, date back to the early 1970s.

Phase 4: 1987-2001

Although there is no particular reason to choose 1987 as the marker for this particular phase of Pakistani immigration into the USA, it is quite clear that from the late 1980s into the early 1990s a number of changes had converged and a new page had been turned in the evolution of the Pakistani-American community.

First, the accumulated number of Pakistanis that were residing in the United States by the late 1980s had grown, particularly in major urban centers, into viable 'Pakistani-American' communities. They were now able to serve as meaningful support groups that could assist immigrants to assimilate in their new surroundings and not feel totally lost and alone in a new country. Strong kinship networks in Pakistan meant that new immigrants arriving in a major US city from Pakistan could feel assured that they either already knew someone who lived there, or had a reference from someone they knew, or would find enough people from their home base in Pakistan. Equally, Pakistanis no longer seemed as 'new and different' to host communities as earlier generations might have been; this also made assimilation easier. All of this combined to make immigrating a less frightening proposition than it had once been.

Second, various advances in the technology and economy of air travel and modes of communication (television, telephone and later the internet) had begun to shrink the world dramatically. The presence of so many Pakistanis in the US, more familiarity with what to expect while here, and the various technological advances not only meant that life in a different continent would be less different than it might have been for earlier immigrants, but also that technology had made the USA less 'distant' from Pakistan than it had once been.

Finally, a series of immigration innovations – especially the Immigrant Visa Lottery introduced in 1990 and the Special Agricultural Worker (SAW) clause within the 1986 Immigration Reform and Control Act (IRCA) of 1986 – coupled with better availability of information within Pakistan on US immigration enabled larger numbers of Pakistanis to seek residence in the United States.

All of this meant that as many as 62 percent of all the Pakistanis who have acquired immigrant status in the US between 1947 and 2004 (range of available data) have done so in the fifteen years between 1987-2001 (more on this later). This period saw the most active growth in the number of Pakistanis immigrating to the United States. A key determinant of this growth was the set of changes in US immigration regulations. For example, the Immigration Reform and Control Act (IRCA) passed by the US Congress in 1986 included a Special Agricultural Worker (SAW) clause (phased out in 1994) which was used to legalize a large number of Indian, Pakistani and Bangladeshi workers in agriculture.[39] This mostly explains the uncommonly large jump in the number of immigrants from all these countries in 1991, a year which saw the number of official Pakistani immigrants jump more than a hundred percent to 20,355.[40]

Over the next few years the Pakistani immigrant intake stabilized around the 9,000-10,000 per year level, and then began rising again in 1995. This coincides with the operationalization of the Immigrant Visa Lottery (also known as the 'green card lottery') for Pakistan. The lottery was part of a 1990 law but began in 1995; which is also when we see a new wave of increased growth in Pakistani immigrants (since 2001 Pakistan is no longer included in the list of countries that can utilize this scheme). The purpose of the lottery was to introduce diversity into the immigrant pool and was open to citizens of countries sending low number of immigrants to the USA. The lottery attracted large numbers of applicants from across the economic and educational strata because it had no pre-requisites except twelve years of education and recent work experience in a profession that requires at least two years of training. Between 1995 and 2001 the number of Pakistanis jumped some 70 percent, from 9,774 immigrants in 1995 to 16,448 immigrants in 2001. A significant proportion of this were the 'winners' of the 'green card lotteries'.[41]

The mix of Pakistanis immigrating to the United States in this period included, as before, a large number of highly trained professionals as well as significant numbers of less-skilled workers. The first group came, as before, because they had the preferred professional skills; this included medical professionals, engineers, information technology specialists, academics, etc. A large proportion of this group first came to the US for education and training and then returned (in the case of physicians) or stayed on to seek employment and immigrant status. This period saw a high proportion of knowledge workers migrate from Pakistan to the United States, especially engineers and (later) professionals in the information technology field.

Many of the less-skilled workers came as a result of the lottery as well as other immigration channels and were immediately absorbed into the US labor force. Most amongst this latter group found employment in small businesses, including retail stores, gas stations, taxi services, etc. Many amongst them have gone on to own their own businesses. Because of their very different socioeconomic backgrounds, these two groups tend to interact rather infrequently, except on religious or national celebrations. However, it should be noted that they do socially interact much more frequently here in the USA (especially around Pakistan-centric events and causes) than they might have in Pakistan.

Phase 5: Post-9/11

Whether the world changed with 9/11 or not, it is quite clear that US immigration policy and practice did. It did so most perceptibly for Muslims coming in and out of the US, including Pakistanis and those of Pakistani descent. The tragic events of 9/11 are clearly a pivotal point in the evolution of the Pakistani diaspora in the USA and mark a new phase in its evolving history. While the pre-9/11 immigration history of Pakistanis in America could be largely understood within the context of Pakistan being a South Asian country, the post-9/11 history of Pakistanis in America is being, and will be, defined much more within the context of Pakistan being a predominantly Muslim country. However, while it is evident that the events of 9/11 will impact the future of Pakistanis in America; it is not yet evident exactly how it will do so. The nature of the impact will depend, in fact, not only on the current and future decisions by the US government but also on the Pakistani-American community.

In terms of immigration dynamics, there is much apprehension that pervades the community. One constantly hears of examples of the mistreatment of Pakistani-Americans already living in America as well as of those visiting from Pakistan. One also hears examples to the contrary. It is not always clear which stories are real and which have been repeated so often as to take on an unwarranted sense of authenticity. What is empirically clear from this research is that like Muslim-Americans in general, the Pakistani diaspora lives with a very high degree of apprehension about their own future in the USA and that of future immigrants.[42] Although there are not yet enough data points for post-9/11 immigration data for meaningful analysis, the available data does point towards two issues, one more conclusive than the other (see Figure 13).

First, it is quite clear that in the immediate aftermath of 9/11 there was a significant clamping down on Pakistanis coming into the USA. The number of Pakistani immigrants admitted for permanent residence in 2001 was 16,448. This slid down to 13,743 in 2002 and to 9,444 in 2003; a nearly 40 percent reduction in a span of two years. The drop in the number of all non-immigrant visas issued to Pakistan was even more dramatic. 2001 was, in fact, a peak year with 72,982 non-immigrant visas (including visit, work, business, pleasure, student, and all other forms of non-immigrant visas). By 2002, however, only 46,735 such visas were issued to Pakistanis and by 2003 this number had slid

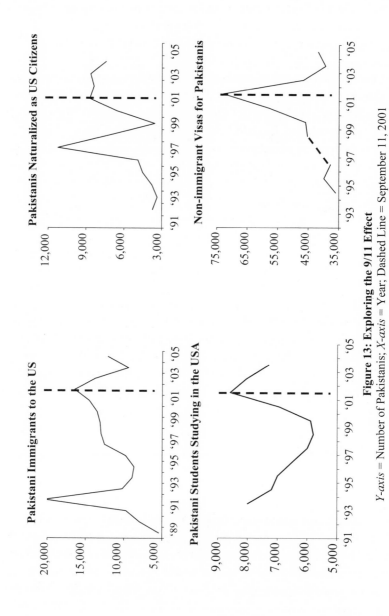

Figure 13: Exploring the 9/11 Effect

Y-axis = Number of Pakistanis; *X-axis* = Year; Dashed Line = September 11, 2001

further down to 39,429; a drop of 45 percent over two years. There does not seem to be a similarly significant dip in the number of Pakistanis granted naturalized US citizenship, but that may be because citizenship is a multi-year process and changes in practice need more time to show up in the data.

The number of Pakistani students studying in America is also a result of multi-year decisions, which probably explains why the dip is not as dramatic as for immigrant and non-immigrant entries. An upward trend in the years preceding 9/11 had taken the number of Pakistani students studying in the USA to 8,644 for the academic year 2001/02. For the academic year 2003/04, this number is down to 7,325. While exact causality is difficult to determine and although some of this may be explained by the hesitancy of those within Pakistani to venture into the United States given post-9/11 apprehensions, the evidence from data on immigrants admitted, non-immigrant visas granted and students studying in the US suggests that the inflow of Pakistanis into America did slow down in the immediate aftermath of 9/11.

Until we get more recent data, it is not clear whether this slowdown is permanent and there is some fledgling indication that it may not be. The number of immigrants admitted as well as the number of non-immigrant visas issued to Pakistanis for the year 2004 was, each, greater than that for 2003. It cannot be determined whether this is a once-off increase or the beginnings of a reversal of the slide. Moreover, data for 2004 naturalizations or 2004/05 students studying in the USA is not yet available. All in all, it is clear that the immediate response to 9/11 was a marked slowdown in the number of Pakistanis admitted into the USA; however, it is too early to say whether this will be a lasting trend or not.

Demography

Pakistanis in America are a relatively new and relatively young community of immigrants. It is a community that has large numbers of highly trained professionals and is economically well off, with higher household incomes than the national average. Immigrants of Pakistani descent can be found across the length and breadth of the United States, but are mostly concentrated in a handful of states and a few major urban centers. Based on a recent study by the Pakistan Embassy in Washington, DC, we estimate (rather conservatively) that there are about half a million Pakistanis living in America today. This section will explore these and related issues, in reverse order, beginning with the question of the overall populations of Pakistanis in America.

As we have noted earlier, there is no single authoritative source for all essential baseline demographics (population size and distribution, income, age, gender, etc.) on Pakistanis in America. However, a recent study conducted by the Pakistan Embassy in Washington, DC, provides the single best estimate of the total number and distribution of Pakistani-Americans across the United States.[43] The Embassy's pioneering study, coordinated by Mohammad Sadiq, is the first enquiry of its kind and uses a robust methodological approach and data from multiple sources to construct a reasoned estimate of the total number and distribution of Pakistanis living in America. The Embassy estimated the 2002 Pakistani-American population to be around 480,000. Our current research has extrapolated and rounded this number to an even half million; based on our further corroborations of the Embassy's numbers, we estimate there to be at least 500,000 Pakistanis living in the USA today. Given that our calculations are made in 2004, this makes our estimate even more conservative than the Embassy's.

Simply estimating the size of the diaspora can sometimes turn into a heated discussion within the Pakistani-American community. It is sometimes claimed (often based on reasonable inductive arguments) that the total number of Pakistanis in America may be closer to one million (twice our estimate).[44] Based on an extensive review of the available data and relevant literature, our conclusion is that while our own (and the Embassy's) estimate may be on the cautious and conservative side, the actual number is much more likely to be closer to the half million mark than one million.

There are a number of reasons for this assessment. First, the Pakistan Embassy's estimate is based on actual data, including data from US immigration and the Embassy's own consular records. Second, our own analysis of data from US immigration records corresponds closely to the Embassy's estimates. Third, our straw poll of various Pakistani communities' assessment of their own size (as opposed to their assessment of the size of the overall Pakistani population in the USA) corresponded reasonably well with the Embassy's estimate. Finally, a very similar result is produced when calculations are made independent of the Embassy's study by using the total Muslim population in the United States as the basis of assessment. Although the estimates of the Muslim population in America vary widely (and sometimes wildly), the most recent and robust analysis suggests that it is in the range of around 3.5 million Muslims in America; this analysis further suggests that around 27 percent of these Muslims hail from South Asia and some 15 percent from Pakistan. If correct, these estimates would suggest a population of around 525,000 Pakistanis; a number that is remarkably close to our estimate.[45]

There is also the issue of illegal and undocumented Pakistanis in America. While it is not possible to get any official estimates on the number of undocumented Pakistanis residing in the United States, it is quite clear that this group has, at various points, comprised a sizeable number. However, it has been suggested that *the proportion of undocumented Pakistanis in America might have significantly gone down in recent years.* Community leaders suggest that, on the one hand, the increased scrutiny of non-documented immigrants in the post-9/11 environment has forced large numbers (especially in the New York area) to move out of the USA. On the other hand, changes in US immigration laws in the 1990s allowed large numbers of undocumented immigrants to get legal immigrant status. In particular, the spike in immigration numbers in the early 1990s may partly be explained by this conversion. The study from the Pakistan Embassy on which our estimate is based, reports that its data "includes all kinds of visa-holders, visa over-stayers and those who entered the US without any documentation."[46] It should be noted, nonetheless, that any discussion of this subject can only be speculative and it is likely that the presence of undocumented Pakistani-Americans makes our estimate of the total population all the more conservative.

Before leaving this subject, some mention should be made of why US Census data was not used to estimate the Pakistani population in America. The 2000 US Census included a question (number 6) about 'race,' which included 'Asian Indian' as one of the explicitly stated options and additionally allowed respondents to write-in their preference. Slightly more than 200,000 respondents choose to write in 'Pakistan' or 'Pakistani' as their race. An additional question (number 10 in the 2000 census) sought information on 'ancestry'. In 1990 some 100,000 respondents had written in 'Pakistan' as their ancestry and this number had increased by 150 percent in the 2000 census to just over 250,000.

However, these numbers are likely to be undercounts because (a) the question is open-ended and requires the respondents to self-identify the appropriate category, (b) census documents themselves point out that Pakistanis can fall into multiple categories (including 'Asian Indian'), therefore it is quite likely that only a sub-set of Pakistani-Americans would have actually opted to write in 'Pakistani' voluntarily, (c) significant number of Pakistanis who are still students or temporary workers may not fill the census, (d) identification of

multiple ancestries are allowed, and (e) the large difference between the
'Pakistani' responses to the two questions does not encourage a high level of
confidence in responses to these questions.[47] Like other analysts,[48] our conclusion is that these numbers severely undercount the number of Pakistani-
Americans and possibly assign large numbers of them to other adjacent categories (most importantly as 'Asian Indians').

Pakistanis across the 50 States

In terms of the distribution of Pakistanis across America, the study from the
Pakistan Embassy presents some fascinating numbers (see Figure 14, Table 5).
In the few communities where we were able to ask our focus group participants

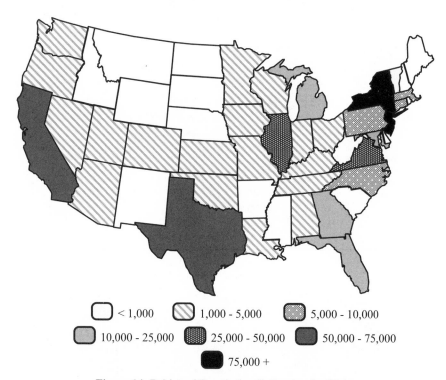

Figure 14: Pakistani Population Estimates, by State
Based on estimates by the Pakistani Embassy, Washington DC
Note: the states of Alaska and Hawaii have just over 100 Pakistani
residents each

Table 5: Estimated Distribution of Pakistani Population in the USA, by State
Based on 2002 estimates by the Pakistan Embassy, Washington DC

	State	Foreign-born Residents & Citizens	US Born Citizens	Others/ Non-citizens	Total
1	New Jersey	51,055	19,758	23,996	94,80
2	New York	51,055	19,735	23,978	94,76
3	California	28,978	11,214	13,620	53,81
4	Texas	26,981	10,442	12,681	50,10
5	Illinois	19,616	7,591	9,220	36,42
6	Virginia	13,489	5,220	6,340	25,04
7	Florida	9,011	3,487	4,235	16,73
8	Maryland	7,183	2,780	3,376	13,33
9	Georgia	6,009	2,325	2,824	11,15
10	Michigan	5,731	2,218	2,694	10,64
11	Pennsylvania	4,160	1,610	1,563	7,333
12	Massachusetts	3,660	1,416	1,236	6,312
13	Connecticut	3,317	1,284	1,100	5,701
14	North Carolina	2,987	1,156	1,000	5,143
15	Ohio	2,553	988	978	4,519
16	Washington	1,975	764	754	3,493
17	Minnesota	1,651	639	635	2,925
18	Missouri	1,599	619	600	2,818
19	Wisconsin	1,337	517	599	2,453
20	Indiana	1,306	507	580	2,393
21	Arizona	1,285	497	574	2,356
22	Louisiana	1,276	494	550	2,320
23	Oklahoma	1,151	445	549	2,145
24	Nevada	1.090	422	545	2,057
25	Colorado	1,019	394	540	1,953
26	Kansas	999	387	539	1,925
27	Tennessee	899	348	530	1,777
28	Utah	749	290	520	1,559
29	Oregon	692	268	519	1,479
30	Delaware	593	229	518	1,340
31	Kentucky	585	226	516	1,327
32	Alabama	521	202	510	1,233
	District of Columbia	508	197	502	1,207
33	Iowa	456	176	401	1,033

Table 5 (continued)

	State	Foreign-born Residents & Citizens	US Born Citizens	Others/ Non-citizens	Total
34	South Carolina	422	163	399	984
35	West Virginia	363	140	315	818
36	New Hampshire	322	125	300	747
37	Mississippi	301	116	299	716
38	Arkansas	276	107	270	653
39	New Mexico	273	106	260	639
40	Rhode Island	256	99	243	598
41	Nebraska	174	67	160	401
42	Maine	160	62	154	376
43	Alaska	115	45	113	273
44	Hawaii	113	44	100	257
45	North Dakota	68	26	59	153
46	Idaho	39	15	30	84
47	Vermont	46	18	16	80
48	South Dakota	36	14	13	63
49	Montana	22	9	10	41
50	Wyoming	18	7	12	37

to estimate the size of the Pakistani population in their state, we found reasonable correspondence to the Embassy's numbers.

The reader should be careful, however, not to assume precision in these numbers. Despite being seemingly exact, these are only *estimates*. Estimates of state populations are more likely to be imprecise than the cumulated population for the entire USA because the rate of inter-state relocation, especially job-related relocation, can be fairly high and such relocation is difficult to capture in the data. Moreover, while such relocation does not change the number of Pakistanis living in America, it can impact the calculation of how they are distributed across states.[49] Even if the exact number is not precise, this data is useful in providing an indicative sense of the general concentration of Pakistani-Americans in various parts of the country. An analysis of the distribution of Pakistanis by state, as estimated by the Pakistan Embassy in Washington, DC, leads to a number of interesting insights.[50] Here we will highlight a few of the salient points that emerge from an analysis of this data:

◆First, and quite strikingly, *Pakistani-Americans are to be found in each one of the 50 states plus the District of Columbia.* What emerges here is the picture of a community beginning to spread across the land and the emergence of a large number of much smaller Pakistani communities, away from the major metropolitan centers.

◆However, *the vast bulk of Pakistanis in America are still concentrated in a handful of states.* Indeed, two out of every five (40 percent) Pakistanis in America live in only two states: New Jersey and New York. By similar to-ken, over 60 percent of Pakistanis in America are concentrated in four key states: New Jersey, New York, California and Texas. Over 90 percent of Pakistanis in America reside in only 15 out of the 50 states.

◆*Pakistanis in America are still predominantly an 'East Coast' community with 60 percent of them to be found along the Atlantic coast, but the new growth is towards the West and South of the country.* More precisely, however, it is a 'mid Atlantic' community with about half of all Pakistanis living in the Eastern corridor from around New York City to Washington, DC. Some 15 percent are to be found along the West Coast, mostly in California. Slicing it differently, we find that although the majority of Pakistanis in America are still in the northern States (North of the Mississippi River), just under 40 percent of all Pakistanis in America now live in the southern states. Some 13 percent live in the mid-western states, with the major concentration being in Illinois and a sizeable one in adjoining Michigan.

◆Looking at individual states rather than regions, *the five states with the most Pakistanis are New Jersey (94,809), New York (94,768), California (53,812), Texas (50,104) and Illinois (32,427).* However, as we will later discuss, a special case should be made for *the states adjoining the Washington, DC, area (Virginia, Maryland, Delaware) which between them have some 41,000 Pakistani-Americans*; a number that would place them ahead of Illinois's population of Pakistani-Americans. The states with the fewest number of Pakistanis include Wyoming (34), Montana (41), South Dakota (63), Vermont (80) and Idaho (84).

Pakistanis in urban America

While the Embassy's study does not provide any numbers on the population of Pakistani-Americans by metropolitan centers, we are able to derive some insights based on the state-by-state population data and the conventional wisdom from our own focus group discussions.

It is evident that *the single largest concentration of Pakistanis anywhere in America is in and around New York City*. The 'Big Apple' as it is sometimes called has been attracting immigrants from all across the world for centuries and remains a magnet for immigrants today, including those from Pakistan. The mega city is composed of multiple communities rather than just one community. Coney Island, for example, boasts of a very large community of Pakistani shop owners and small businesses, all concentrated in one location, which gives it a physically 'Pakistani' feel. However, the NYC footprint is much larger than the concentration of Pakistanis in its five boroughs. Large numbers of Pakistanis live in suburbs across the state line in New Jersey but operate very much in the greater NYC radius. Some estimate that half of the Pakistani residents of New Jersey and a significant number of the Pakistani residents of Connecticut work in and around the greater NYC area. It is difficult to place an exact number on how many Pakistani-Americans live in and around New York City, but *estimates of around 120,000 or more Pakistanis in the Greater New York City area would not be unreasonable.*

The suburbs in and around Washington, DC, the greater Houston area, and 'Chicagoland' are all good candidates for being host to the second largest concentration of Pakistanis in America. Each city probably has around 35,000-40,000 Pakistanis living in and around them. While Houston and Chicago have historically had a high number of Pakistani-Americans, the Washington, DC, area has seen a particularly steep growth in the number of Pakistani-Americans in recent years and may well surpass them soon. Although only slightly more than a thousand Pakistanis actually live in the District of Columbia, most of those who live in Virginia and Maryland and some of those in Baltimore actually operate in the 'Greater DC' area.

Chicagoland, which is a name given to the great Chicago Metropolitan area, includes nine suburban communities in Illinois, Wisconsin and Indiana. The bulk of those living in these three states live in Chicagoland. While other cities may have seen a greater growth in the number of Pakistanis in recent years, Chicago still has one of the most active and established Pakistani communities. Outside of New York City, it has the largest number of Pakistani organizations, its famous Devon Street (pronounced by Pakistanis as 'Dewan Street' is one of the most famous locations for authentic Pakistani cuisine in America, and its calendar of Pakistan-focused social events probably rivals even that of New York City. The Pakistani population in Texas is more spread out than it is in many states (with the exception of California). For example, significant populations of Pakistani-Americans are to be found in Dallas, Austin and other Texas cities. However, the largest concentration is in Houston. Like Chicago, Houston boasts of an active Pakistani community, many Pakistani organizations and even a significant local Pakistani press that publishes a number of newspapers in Urdu.

As a state, California has the third largest Pakistani-American population, and it is a population that is growing rapidly. However, *California's Pakistani population is divided between two major metropolitan centers; one of which is concentrated in and around Los Angeles, and the other in and around San Francisco/San Jose.* Los Angeles is certainly the larger of the two, with 30,000 or more Pakistanis, but the Greater San Francisco area (known as the 'Bay Area' and inclusive of San Jose and its suburbs) has seen much more rapid growth in recent years, especially as engineers and information technology specialists from around the world, including Pakistan, flocked there through the 1990s and beyond.

While *New York City (NY), Washington (DC), Houston (TX), Chicago (IL) and Los Angeles (CA) are quite clearly the five largest metropolitan areas in terms of their Pakistani-American populations* a large number of cities with significant and growing Pakistani populations are now to be found across the country. Metropolitan areas with between 5,000 and 10,000 Pakistani-Americans include, for example, Detroit (MI) in the Midwest; and Philadelphia (PA) in the Mid-Atlantic; Atlanta (GA) and Orlando (FL) in the Southeast; and Boston (MA) as a hub in the Northeast/New England. In other regions, cities that have smaller, but quite active, Pakistani communities include Seattle (WA) in the Northwest, Phoenix (AZ) in the Southwest, etc.[51] The key point to be made is that *although the vast majority of Pakistanis are still concentrated in half a dozen major metropolitan centers, growing and growingly active Pakistani communities are to be found across the country.*

Pakistani-Americans: A young community

Our analysis highlights two important characteristics of Pakistani-Americans as an immigrant community in a country full of immigrant communities.

First, Pakistani-Americans are here for the long-term and have developed deep roots in America. Using the Pakistan Embassy's estimates, we find that just under 75 percent of Pakistanis living in America already have US citizenship (through naturalization or birth) or permanent residence status. In short, despite the fact (as we have seen earlier and will discuss later) that Pakistani-Americans are extremely eager and active in maintaining their links to Pakistan, this is a community that is also eager to make the US its permanent (as opposed to temporary) home. There is no necessary contradiction in this; especially now that dual citizenship is permitted by both countries. While the challenges of balancing multiple identities can be difficult, as we shall find later, this situation also translates into an eagerness within the community to act as a bridge-builder between their two homes, and is evident in the philanthropic behavior of the Pakistanis in America.

Second, despite the fact that people from areas that now constitute Pakistan have been arriving in the US for well over a century, as immigrants, Pakistani-Americans are a fairly recent and still fledgling immigrant community. For example, three-fourths of Pakistani-Americans (just over 75 percent) have themselves immigrated to the USA ('first generation immigrants') and only 25 percent are US-born citizens. Much more significantly, in reviewing the historical data of immigrants from Pakistan who have been officially admitted with permanent residence, we find that of all the Pakistanis who have immigrated to the United States in the 57 years between 1947-2004, 75 percent have immigrated in the last 17 years (since 1987). Indeed, half of all Pakistanis who have immigrated between 1947-2004 did so during or after 1993, and one in every four (25 percent) has arrived in the last five years (during 1999-2004). Another way to read the numbers is that of all the Pakistanis who have obtained immigrant status between 1947 and 2004, only one percent did so prior to 1965 and only ten percent did so prior to 1978 (see Figure 15).

What this means is that even though a significant proportion of the community is now well-settled in America, the majority is composed of relatively recent arrivals who (a) still have deeper links to, and relationships with, their friends and families living in Pakistan, and (b) are still in the process of adapting and adjusting to the demands of translocation into a new society.

Demographic characteristics

Direct evidence of demographic characteristics—distribution by age, gender, income or occupation, etc.—is even more scarce than other forms of baseline information. However, significant insights can be derived from available information with reasonable levels of confidence. Based on the available data, especially data on the demographic characteristics of Pakistanis who have recently received permanent residence or naturalized citizen status, and on the insights derived from our focus group discussions, we can highlight the following key conclusions (see Table 6).

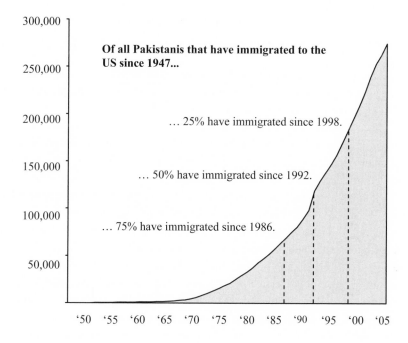

**Figure 15: Cumulative Number of Pakistani Immigrants to the US,
1947 - 2004**

In terms of age, *Pakistani-Americans are a relatively young group*. The simple fact that most Pakistanis who have immigrated to America have done so quite recently, suggest that this is a relatively youthful group. Immigration data for the fiscal year 2003 supports the proposition that this is a community of younger immigrants with a large sub-population still in the late-20s to early-40s age group. The overall population of Pakistani-Americans is likely to be younger than the data on immigrant Pakistanis suggests because about a quarter of all Pakistanis in America are US-born citizens who, as children of earlier Pakistani immigrants, are likely to be younger, and often of college-going age or recent college graduates. What this means is that *a large majority of Pakistani in America are either already in the productive labor force with many more years of work ahead of them, or are about to join that labor force.*

It is also worth noting that, although still small in size, *the first generation of Pakistani 'retirees' is also becoming evident.* This is an important group of

Table 6: Demographics of Immigrating Pakistanis, 2003

Information on Pakistanis granted Legal Permanent Residence and Naturalization

Characteristics	Permanent Resident, 2003			Naturalizations, 2003		
	Total	*Male*	*Female*	*Total*	*Male*	*Female*
Total	9,4	4,652	4,762	7,4	3,6	3,739
Age						
Under 18 years	2,5	1,294	1,262	D	D	D
18-24 years	1,3	600	771	1,1	57	526
25-34 years	1,9	1,058	921	2,1	92	1,253
35-44 years	1,4	675	754	2,0	1,0	984
45-54 years	971	483	488	1,0	53	486
55-64 years	693	320	372	408	22	188
Over 65 years	416	222	194	D	D	D
Unknown	--	--	--	430	22	202
Marital Status						
Single	3,9	2,157	1,766	1,4	95	507
Married	5,1	2,429	2,721	5,4	2,4	2,986
Other	334	64	270	355	16	192
Unknown	7	2	5	120	66	54
Occupation						
Executive and Managerial	525	497	28	495	38	114
Professional and technical	613	489	124	804	56	243
Sales	93	80	13	542	31	231
Administrative Support	40	27	13	214	95	119
Farming, Forestry, Fisheries	162	162	--	6	6	--
Operators, Fabricators, Laborers	58	53	4	354	29	61
Precision Production, Craft, Repair	30	25	5	64	D	D
Service	516	450	66	249	12	123
Military	--	--	--	24	D	D
No Occupation	5,7	1,975	3,766	2,0	45	1,554
Unknown	1,6	894	743	2,6	1,3	1,284
Major Class of Admission						
Family-sponsored Preferences	3,3	1,774	1,583			
Employment-based Preferences	1,4	734	689			
Immediate Relatives of US	4,1	1,884	2,290			
Diversity Programs	8	3	5			
Refugees and Asylee Adjust-	365	192	173			
Other	88	65	22			

Pakistanis who immigrated during the early years (1947 into the 1960s), who have lived long and worked hard in America, who have often done well economically, and who are now   deciding to retire in the USA. This is a potentially significant group for diaspora philanthropy because the confluence of the impulse to give (accentuated with age), the ability to give (because of large savings), and the incentive to give (because of US inheritance tax laws) can result in relatively large and targeted giving by these senior citizens.

The gender balance within the Pakistani-American community seems to be quite even. For example, 2003 data shows that in terms of permanent residence as well as naturalization, slightly more women than men received the nod from the US immigration service. Marriage is a key dynamic here. Pakistanis who acquire permanent residence are more likely to be married than not, and those who acquire citizenship are even more likely to be married; in both cases they are likely to be married to other Pakistanis. Moreover, single Pakistanis given permanent residence or naturalization status in 2003 were more likely to be men than women. While this would suggest that a large number of Pakistani women who immigrate to the United States do so after marriage, the numbers do show that this may no longer be the predominant reason. Large numbers of single women are now acquiring permanent residence status and citizenship by naturalization. These include many highly skilled women joining the US workforce as knowledge workers.

In terms of income and occupation, conventional wisdom within the community suggests that *Pakistanis in America are a generally affluent community; a large proportion is in high skill professions such as engineering, information technology, healthcare, and business management; and another large proportion owns, or works in, small service-related businesses.* We find no reason to doubt this assessment, and enough evidence to support it. Our own observations, our focus group discussions, and comparisons to other reference groups supports this assessment. Immigration numbers are of little use because the categories they use are very broad and, more importantly, because the two most common occupational categories for Pakistanis granted permanent residence or naturalization are 'no occupation' and 'unknown.' However, of those who do state an occupational category, 'executive and managerial' and 'professional and technical' are amongst the more popular categories, as are 'sales' and 'service.'

In terms of economic affluence, the US Census calculates the mean household income for all US households in 2002 as $57,852 per year; it also notes that this number is $70,047 for Asian households.[52] Within Asian households, South Asian households are generally considered to be the most affluent; it would not be unfair to suggest that *the average household income of Pakistanis in America is probably similar to or higher than the average for Asian households; i.e., more than $70,000 per year.* Given that the profile of Indians in the USA has been similar to that of Pakistani-Americans, one can extrapolate from the literature on South Asians in America, including that on Indians, to suggest that Pakistani-Americans are a community with higher than average income, higher than average educational attainment, higher than average rates of savings, and higher than average representation in high skill professions.[53]

Institutions

The goal of this last section is to review the key categories of institutions that have evolved to serve the social and cultural needs of the Pakistani diaspora in America; to do so with a particular focus on those institutions that are particularly 'Pakistani'; and to highlight the role that such institutions do or can play in philanthropy by Pakistanis in America. Like many other immigrant communities, Pakistanis in America have created a whole array of institutions that serve as support groups for the expression and nourishment of the Pakistani aspects of their identity.

Of course, all people have to juggle multiple identities; immigrant communities often more so than most others. In the case of Pakistani-Americans, the 'Pakistani-ness' they seek to nurture is often accompanied by 'American-ness', by professional identities, identities based on the locality where they live, by class identities, and in many cases by religious identity. Different institutions serve the purpose of nourishing different identities. We will focus here only on those institutions that are primarily Pakistani in nature and which serve to express and nourish this particular aspect of the identity needs of Pakistanis in America.

The world of Pakistani institutions in America is large, complex and dynamic. For a community of only half a million, *the sheer number of institutions we find is impressively large and points towards an active and involved community.* The immense investment of time and resources that keep these organizations alive is itself a form of community giving that provides essential identity support systems to Pakistanis in America. However, it is difficult to capture the dimensions of this institutional landscape not only because there are many institutions but also because they are complex institutions that are difficult to empirically classify. Moreover, this institutional landscape tends to change very fast and many organizations tend to be transitory. There is a quick turnover of organizations, often because many are structured around a few dynamic individuals who either move on to other things or whose dynamism fades over time.

For all these reasons, trying to produce a definitive list of Pakistani organizations is not only difficult but of rather limited temporal value. We will focus, therefore, on categorizing the major types of 'Pakistani' institutions and highlight their characteristics by using examples of particularly active or archetypical organizations within that genre of institutions. We have identified five distinct, but sometimes related, categories of institutions that are commonly found within and across Pakistani diaspora communities in America and which serve to maintain and enhance the 'Pakistani' aspects of these communities. The five categories of organizations we have identified, include: (a) cultural identity and civic organizations, (b) professional and business associations; (c) religious institutions; (d) information and advocacy platforms; and (e) charitable and development initiatives.

Cultural identity and civic organizations

Most cities and regions with sizeable Pakistani populations have one or more Pakistani Associations serving as focal points for Pakistan related cultural activities in that vicinity. These associations are often the primary institutional face of their communities and play an indirect as well as direct role in facilitating philanthropic events and initiatives.

Some areas, like Raleigh, NC, Phoenix, AZ, and Boston, MA, have a single large organization with a long history of continuous service and a diverse portfolio of activities. Other areas—particularly in locations with large Pakistani populations like New York, Chicago or Los Angeles—have a number of organizations, many with long histories, and often focusing on a particular aspect of that community's cultural life. New York, Chicago and Los Angeles, for example, each have over a dozen Pakistani cultural associations each. Also included in this category are student organizations that are designed to serve the cultural and identity needs of Pakistani students at specific educational institutions. The defining characteristics of all these organizations is that (a) they are locality-oriented, (b) they provide a regular space and opportunities for Pakistanis in that community to interact socially, and (c) their activities are designed to provide opportunities for Pakistani-Americans to express their cultural affinities. Such organizations are particularly active around events of Pakistani significance and their activities tend to be geared towards reinforcing Pakistani cultural aspects, including those related to music, food, dress, and the arts.

The list of Pakistani civic associations and their activities is long, but they fall into some similar patterns. For all such organizations the most important priority is creating a sense of community amongst Pakistani-Americans in a particular geographic area and serving their cultural needs. They do so through a variety of activities. For example, the *North Carolina Pakistani-American Anjuman* (PAA, www.ncpaa.org) has been publishing a newsletter that focuses on community news and on general interest articles about Pakistani culture. The *Pakistan Association of Greater Washington* (PAGW, www.geocities.com/pakistan_association) also produces a newsletter as one of its regular activities. One of Chicago's numerous Pakistani associations, the *Pakistani American Association of North America* (PAANA, www.pakwatan.com/main/pana) has outlined plans to establish a 40,000 square feet community center in Chicago. In Phoenix, Arizona the *Pakistan Information and Cultural Organization* (PICO, www.pakistaninformation.org) is particularly innovative in its events to mobilize the Pakistani community; its docket of recent activities not only includes Eid, Muharram, and Milad-un-Nabi events and a Pakistan Independence Day festival but also music galas, a Basant Festival, a white water rafting outing and community excursions to major league baseball games. Recently, the Pakistani Organization of Arizona (POA, www.pakistaniarizonian.org) has emerged with the goal of serving as an umbrella organization of the various Pakistani initiatives in the state.

Although their primary goals are to serve the cultural needs of the Pakistani community, these organizations also play an important role as cultural ambassadors of Pakistan within American neighborhoods. In both Chicago and New York, the annual Pakistan Independence Day parade has now become a regular feature of those cities' cultural calendar. Although these parades have sometimes been marred by frictions within the Pakistani community they do attract local and national politicians and large attendance by Pakistanis and non-Pakistanis. New York's Pakistan parade has been an official city event since the 1980s, is held on Madison Avenue, and has reportedly attracted as many as 50,000 people. Reputedly, the parade was founded by Inayat Shaikh, a lawyer from Attock, who has been in the US for over three decades and was recently appointed a judge in the Taxi and Limousine Commission's court in

New York. Chicago's parade began in the late 1980s, takes place along a portion of Devon Street that has been officially designated as the Mohammed Ali Jinnah Way by the City of Chicago, and attracts around 15,000 people. Both events are usually accompanied by separately organized Pakistan Day Festivals.

Such festivals are held, at smaller scales, all across the country by the various Pakistani associations. Recent Pakistan Day events organized by the *Pakistan Association of Southern New England* (PAASNE, www.paasne.com) exemplify a recent trend of designing these festivals as outreach events meant to showcase Pakistani culture for non-Pakistanis.

While these civic organizations are themselves not philanthropic in their primary intent, they are often key facilitators for organized philanthropy by the communities they serve. For example, when Imran Khan was raising funds for the *Shaukat Khanum Hospital* project the leadership of Pakistani civic associations in various cities (sometimes in their personal capacity) often played central roles in mobilizing support and organizing fund-raisers. In other cases the charitable intent is directly built into their activities. For example, the *North Carolina Pakistani-American Anjuman* recently held a Tsunami relief fund raiser dinner as a response to the calamity in the Indian Ocean. The charitable activities of the *Pakistani American Association of Connecticut* (PAACT, www.paact2000.org) have included raising funds for drought victims in Thar (Pakistan) and for Earthquake victims in Gujarat (India) and donating computers to under-privileged girls' schools in rural Pakistan.

Based in Phoenix, Arizona, the *Pakistan Information and Cultural Organization* takes its mission as 'Pakistan's ambassadors of goodwill' particularly seriously and one of its stated goals is to encourage community volunteering by its members. PICO keeps a detailed record of hours volunteered by its members for a wide variety of causes, which have included the Paz de Cristo Community Center, the St. Vincent de Paul Society, Habitat for Humanity, St. Mary's Food Bank, Salvation Army, the Phoenix Zoo, the Phoenix Art Museum, group volunteering for the local affiliates of National Public Radio (NPR) and much more. PICO has received official commendations from the city and state for its volunteering activities. In addition, PICO has also been sponsoring deserving students in various schools and colleges in Pakistan.

The tragic 2005 earthquake in Pakistan has dramatically changed the focus of just about every Pakistani organization in USA, and especially civil and community organizations. While it is too early to say whether this is a long-term shift or just an immediate response, it is quite clear that every one of the

Pakistani Associations launched some initiative to raise funds for or initiate efforts in repose to the earthquake. In Boston, for example, the *Pakistan Association of Greater Boston* (PAGB, www.pagb.org) joined with a number of other organizations and created a 'zalzala group' (earthquake group) to facilitate coordination amongst the various Pakistani organizations in the Boston area working on earthquake relief. In Arizona, PICO reports have raised over $85,000 and over 2 tons of food for the effort. Similar reports pour in from all across the US. What is clear is that this tragedy has galvanized community organizations into become philanthropic organizations, at least in the short term.

Surprisingly, *there are very few associations dedicated to a particular region or ethnicity within Pakistan.*[54] There are, however, some exceptions. For example, the *Sindhi Association of North America* (SANA, www.sanalist.org) has been very active since the mid-1980s, has held regular annual national conventions since the mid-1990s, and has a number of active chapters in major population centers across America. National and regional chapter events have a strong focus on cultural aspects of Sindhi identity including Sindhi nationalism, particularly on issues related to the Sindhi language. Philanthropically, SANA created the Dr Feroz Ahmed Memorial Fund in memory of a US-based Sindhi academic who died in 1997. The fund has been providing stipends to deserving students in Pakistani universities and medical colleges.

As a generation of Pakistani-American children born and raised in the United States has grown and reached young adulthood, there is a perceptible shift in the activities of many groups, with an increasing emphasis on activities that speak to the interests and concerns of younger Pakistani-Americans, and relatively less on the needs of newly arrived immigrants. A number of organizations have started creating special programs for this purpose. For example, the *Pakistan Association of Greater Boston* has a special affinity group called *Young American Pakistani Professionals* (YAPP, www.pagb.org/pagbweb/yapp.html) and has also launched an Urdu conversation group that is attracting younger members. The Pakistan Embassy has been actively promoting its *Rising Leader Initiative* (www.palc.us/risingleaders) which supports Pakistan-focused activities for younger Pakistani-Americans.[55] Such initiatives are a manifestation of the changing demography of the Pakistani-American community and the increasing importance of younger Pakistani-Americans who were raised here in America.

An important implication of this trend is that the Pakistani student populations in US Universities now have increasing proportions of Pakistanis born and/or raised in the United States. This is beginning to change the nature of activities of the *Pakistan Student Associations (PSAs)*. PSAs are to be found on most university campuses with a dozen or more Pakistani students on average.[56] Many smaller PSAs tend to be erratic and transitory, withering away once the few students who invest their energy in the PSA move on. There have been numerous attempts in the past to form a nationwide association of PSAs, most recently by the Pakistan Embassy in Washington, DC, which has facilitated the creation of a *National Pakistani Student Association*,[57] hosted its first national meeting and supported a regional PSA conference organized by Pakistani students at the *University of California in Los Angeles* (www.bol.ucla.edu/~psa).

The Pakistani students at *Columbia University* claim that one of the first PSAs (www.columbia.edu/cu/ops) was formed there. *Massachusetts Institute of Technology* (www.mit.edu/activities/paksmit) also has an independent and long-standing PSA that has operated continuously over a long period of time and became the precursor of the Pakistan Association of Greater Boston. Like many PSAs in relatively smaller communities, the one at *Rensselaer Polytechnic Institute* (paksa.union.rpi.edu) also provides a forum for Pakistan-based interaction for the Pakistani community in the region. PSAs also tend to become forums for Pakistan-related outreach events, host visitors from Pakistan including civil society and philanthropic leaders, and occasionally raise funds for charitable causes.

For example, a recent concert organized by the Pakistani students at *Stanford University* (www.stanford.edu/group/pakistan) raised funds for The Citizens Foundation in Pakistan, and the PSA at *Stevens Institute of Technology* (www.stevens-tech.edu/paksa) -- from whose campus the twin towers in New York were directly visible – organized a special event to raise money for the World Trade Center Relief Fund soon after 9/11. As with other Pakistani organizations, PSAs became extremely active in the aftermath of the 2005 Earthquake in Pakistan and a quick survey of their recent activities suggests a major shift at just about every campus towards raising awareness and funds for the earthquake victims. Indeed, it is noteworthy that in a very large number of cases the earthquake related events on campuses were organized in conjunction with non-Pakistan-related student organizations, especially including South Asian organizations.

Professional and business associations

Some of the best-known, most active and influential Pakistani organizations in the USA are professional and business associations. The primary purpose of Pakistani professional and business associations is to serve as a professional support network for Pakistanis from a particular professional category. Although many such organizations are location-based, their activities are filtered by the professions of their members, rather than by geography. In addition to networking, most of them also focus on the cultural needs of their constituencies, and many of them have active initiatives on public affairs and on philanthropic giving.

As one of the largest, most established, and most affluent professional group amongst Pakistani-Americans, it is not surprising that Pakistani physicians are also one of the most organized. The *Association of Pakistani Physicians of North America* (APPNA, www.appna.org) was established in 1977 under the leadership of Dr. Zaheer Ahmed from Detroit; a parallel and similar organization launched by Dr. Bunyad Haider on the East Coast later merged with APPNA.[58] Since then, APPNA has grown into a conglomerate of affiliated organizations and initiatives. These include a host of regional chapters, various alumni associations, a *Young Pakistani Physicians Resource Center* (YPPRC, www.ypprc.org); and affiliated organization for spouses, school going children, and college going children of APPNA members (APPNA Alliance, CAPPNA and SAYA, respectively). APPNA's annual convention—in 2005, a 4-day extravaganza of professional seminars, networking opportunities, socio-political discussions, and cultural events—has become the preeminent regular event on the Pakistani-American calendar and attracts large numbers of Pakistanis from all across America and an array of invited guests from Pakistan. From its earliest years, APPNA has sought to influence US public and policy opinion on matters related to Pakistan, and in 1990 it established a *Pakistani-American Public Affairs Committee* (PAKPAC; www.pakpac.net) as a separately registered entity that can donate money to political campaigns in the United States.

APPNA's charitable activities have a long history, rooted in its constitution, which defines one of its aims to be participation in "… charitable activities both in Pakistan and in North America." In 1989 *APPNA-Sehat* (www.appnasehat.org.pk) was launched as an integrated health education project in Pakistan; this went on to spur the creation of the *Human Development Foundation of North America* (HDF, www.yespakistan.com; discussed later), which also has its roots in APPNA. In 2005, plans for an *APPNA Charitable Foundation* were approved which will serve as an umbrella organization for APPNA's various charitable projects including its free clinics in the US, educational scholarships for Pakistani-Americans, etc. APPNA also has indirect philanthropic impacts through its members and affiliates. Its conventions are regularly frequented by those raising funds for charitable causes in Pakistan. Moreover, its members tend to make important individual and informal philanthropic contributions to Pakistan, especially in the health sector, and these are often influenced by the network opportunities provided by APPNA. Importantly, many of its affiliate alumni organizations have their own philanthropic initiatives. For example, the *King Edward Medical College Alumni Association of North America* (KEMCAANA; www.kemcaana.org) actually predates APPNA and pioneered formal programs for Pakistani physicians in America to return to Pakistan to provide professional training and services to hospitals and medical colleges.[59] In 2005, the *DOW Graduate Association of North America* (DOGANA, www.dowalumni.com) created an endowment fund for DOW Medical College, Karachi, called EnDOW, and have now raised a total of one million US dollars to seed this fund which will provide financial support to DOW medical college and to Civil Hospital, Karachi. Other alumni associations have become similarly active in giving back to their alma maters.

Not surprisingly, the APPNA and especially its affiliated regional organizations were extremely active in the relief efforts related to the 2005 earthquake in Pakistan. In the first few weeks after the earthquake, various APPNA-related organizations raised nearly $1.8 million in cash support for the relief effort and were instrumental in collecting corporate donations for more than $10 million worth of medical and surgical supplies. This effort was mostly centered around the various regional chapters of APPNA. In New England, for example, the *Association of Pakistani Physicians New England* (APPNE; www.appne.org) organized a major fundraiser in association with the *Indian Medical Association of New England* (IMANE), raised $200,00 and launched a program of assisting first responders in the Hazara region of the Northwest Frontier Province (NWFP). Similar efforts were also mobilized in Connecticut, Illinois, Texas, and other parts of the country. Probably even more than the monetary and in-kind contributions, the largest impact of APPNA on the earthquake relief efforts has been the very large number of Pakistani physicians who have visited and volunteered their services in the areas devastated by the earthquake.

Representing a new breed and a different model of the Pakistani professional association is the *Organization of Pakistani Entrepreneurs of North America* (OPEN, www.openglobal.org), which has emerged as one of the most dynamic, innovative and organized of the Pakistani professional associations. Created in 1998 by a Boston-based group of entrepreneurs and technology professionals, the organization is now the premier platform for Pakistani-American entrepreneurial leaders in high technology sectors. OPEN has a highly decentralized structure with independent chapters in New England, Silicon Valley, New York, and Washington, DC. The emphasis of OPEN's activities is on networking, mentoring of young entrepreneurs and professionals, and information and knowledge sharing. One landmark initiative by OPEN-New England was its 2002 $50,000 Business Plan competition for aspiring Pakistani entrepreneurs from North America.[60] OPEN events regularly bring together high achieving Pakistani professionals as well as high profile American experts and executives. Amongst Pakistani organizations, OPEN is one of the leaders in the growing trend towards trying to integrate the American mainstream into the activities of these diaspora organizations. OPEN's response to the 2005 earthquake in Pakistan has concentrated on trying to leverage its networks with corporate America to raise awareness and support for the relief effort.

The list of Pakistani professional and business organizations is long and diverse and we can only cite a few examples here. The *Association of Pakistani Scientists and Engineers of North America* (APSENA, www.apsena.org) has a long history and recently convened its twenty-first annual conference in Washington, DC. The *Old Ravians Association* and the *Karachi University Alumni Association* have had a presence in America for many years but operate at a fairly low-key level. Two relatively new organizations that have sought to meet the needs of younger Pakistani-American professionals are *DASTAK-Network of Pakistani Professionals* (www.dastak.org) and the *International Organization of Pakistani Women Engineers* (IOPWE, www.iopwe.org). Both aspire to be support groups but, importantly, each has a commitment to philanthropy imbedded in its charter and has actively sought to mobilize the charitable spirit amongst its members. There are a large number of organizations that seek to encourage greater business links between USA and Pakistan including, for example, the *Pakistani American Business Executive Association* (PABE, www.pabe.org) and the *Pakistan American Business Association* (PABA, www.pabausa.com). Both include a focus on encouraging investment in Pakistan, by Pakistani-Americans as well as by international companies; PABA also serves as a career development support group for Pakistanis in America.

A different, very local, type of business association is to be found in cities with a concentration of Pakistani-owned small businesses. These operate as support groups for Pakistani small business owners and often have a significant social welfare component to their activities. For example, the *Pakistani Merchant Association of Coney Island* has a special fund to support the needy within its own community, including widows and their children. *Chicago's Pakistani Business Association*, whose members are mostly storeowners in the famed Devon Street, has been running a free clinic for some years where the majority of patients are from other minorities living in the Devon Street vicinity.

Amongst the most influential of these local organizations is *New York's Pak Brothers Yellow Cab Drivers Union*, which lists more than one thousand of New York's Pakistani taxi drivers as its members. The organization primarily serves as an advocacy group for Pakistani-American cab drivers and, like most other Pakistani organizations in New York, was particularly active in working towards the safety and rights of this vulnerable group in the immediate aftermath of 9/11. This is a particularly important group because the majority of taxi drivers in New York City are from South Asia and within this group Pakistani Yellow Cab drivers make up one of the largest, most organized, and very often influential interest group.

Religious institutions

It is conceptually difficult to give national identity to religious institutions, because "the ecumenical is always in tension with the national and ethnic."[61] This is particularly true for Islam (the dominant religion amongst Pakistani-Americans) with its claim of universality—with the mosque being a place for the congregation for all Muslims, irrespective of nationality or ethnicity. However, as a practical matter, it is quite clear that particular religious congregations in America do end up serving believers from a particular nationality more than those from another. This can stem from the demographics of the community, the identity of those who established the institution, or the dominant nationalities within the leadership.[62] While many of the religious institutions that serve the needs of Pakistani-Americans cannot really be called 'Pakistani' institutions, it is clear that some are more Pakistani in the sense that they tend to serve the needs of large numbers of Pakistani-Americans, or Pakistani-Americans are a major and/or dominant presence in them. The focus here is on these institutions. However, before discussing such institutions, a few general words about religion and philanthropy.

A 2002 study on *Faith and Philanthropy* in America found that about 60 percent of all households in the US give to their religious congregations, that those who actively give to their congregations are also likely to be actively involved in secular causes, and are likely to be more generous in their giving. The study concluded that, "the power of faith-based giving and volunteering is clear, compelling, and measurable" (p. 8).[63] At the same time, Williams (p. 11) suggests that religion plays a critical role in the lives of most immigrant communities: "Immigrants are religious—by all counts more religious than they were before they left home—because religion is one of the important identity markers that helps them preserve individual self-awareness and cohesion in a group.... In United States, religion is the social category with clearest meaning and acceptance in the host society, so the emphasis on religious affiliation and identity is one of the strategies that allows the immigrant to maintain self-identity while simultaneously acquiring community acceptance."[64] What is true for Americans in general and immigrants in general also seems true for Pakistani-Americans. Like other immigrant groups before them, Pakistanis in America have been active in establishing places of worship, which nearly always also serve as social gathering places and community centers, in some cases with an identifiably 'Pakistani' flavor.

Faith-based philanthropy by Pakistani-Americans takes two dominant forms. First, giving to congregations is predominantly for the establishment and maintenances of their places of worship. Second, faith acts as an important motivator for giving. The obligation to be charitable, to help the poor and assist the needy, is central to Islam through the concepts of *zakat* and *sadaqah*.[65] Such giving happens specifically for the purpose of meeting one's religious obligation, but the giving itself is not necessarily directed to religious organizations; instead, the bulk of this faith-motivated charity is direct giving to those who are poor and in need, most often through individual and kinship networks. In Islam, the religious injunction specifically places priority on direct giving to the needy within one's own community. However, some have argued that, particularly in the US context, such giving can also be directed to the building of mosques because they are community support institutions.[66] Although the 1990s saw the emergence of organized Muslim charities engaged in welfare and humanitarian activities in Muslim countries as well as organizations seeking support for broader Muslim causes—including those in hotspots such as Palestine, Bosnia and Kashmir—our survey results and focus group discussions suggest that the bulk of faith-motivated giving by Pakistani-Americans has been, and remains, focused on the establishment of places of worship and direct giving to individuals in need.

It has been estimated that there are more than 1,200 mosques in America.[67] Many of them are called 'Islamic Centers' because they incorporate a wide array of social and community services which range from schools, seminar series, inter-faith discussion groups, marriage counseling, wedding facilities, burial services, assistance to the poor within the community, prison programs, soup kitchens and food support initiatives, anti-drug and anti-crime programs, day care and pre-school support, substance abuse initiatives, voter registration, to community gatherings and in some cases even sports.[68] None proclaim to be solely Pakistani, but Pakistani-Americans contributed critical resources for the establishment of many of these Islamic Centers and many have predominantly Pakistani leadership and congregations. Most mosques in America are open to all Muslims, however, given the demographics of the larger Muslim community in the US, most are non-denominational or Sunni. Many Shi'a congregations—including Ithna'Ashari, Bohra Ismaili and Nizari Ismaili *jamaats*—also have large proportions of Pakistani-Americans (such congregations are found across the country, particularly in population centers like Houston, Chicago, New York, and Los Angeles).[69]

Islamic Centers and mosques in America are invariably community-run initiatives, most without any full-time paid employees at all. Their survival and operation depends on community volunteers even more than on monetary donations. The single largest investment by Pakistani-Americans in these institutions is through volunteered time. Along with Pakistani civic associations, and possibly much more so, Islamic Centers are the focus of the vast bulk of time volunteered by Pakistani-Americans. Given the growing size of the Muslim population in America, most communities have more than one mosque and each is usually managed independently by volunteers from its congregation. In a few cases, large Muslim communities have established umbrella groups to manage various religious institutions within their region. One of the most comprehensive of these is the *Islamic Society of Greater Houston* (ISGH; www.isgh.org), a large proportion of whose leaders and volunteers are Pakistani-Americans. The ISGH manages seventeen Islamic Centers within the Houston area. Managed through an elaborate structure of volunteer committees, ISGH activities include education, religious and social services. Its recent activities have included a packed calendar of seminars and discussions, sponsorship of the basketball 'hoopfests' with the *Muslim Youth Basketball Asso-*

ciation (MYBA, www.mybausa.org), a program for feeding the homeless, and a series of events for children. ISGH also operates a funeral home, manages a section in the local cemetery, maintains a bookstore, and runs a library. Its regular annual reports and website details its activities, including its active *zakat* program which has a focus on helping the needy within the Houston community and distributes about $3,000 every Friday for rent assistance, food coupons, bus passes, and other support to the poor. It also provides free medical services through its *Al-Shifa Medical Services Center.*

The largest annual gathering of Muslims in America is the annual convention of the *Islamic Society of North America* (ISNA, www.isna.net). In 2005, ISNA held its 42nd Annual Convention in Chicago with an attendance of some 40,000 Muslims from across the USA and Canada, especially younger Muslim-Americans raised in America, and also including a significant number of Pakistani-Americans. ISNA came into being in the 1960s and has evolved into an umbrella group for a number of Muslim organizations (some of which pre-date it) including the *Muslim Student Association* (MSA, www.msanational.org), the *Association of Muslim Scientists and Engineers* (AMSE, www.amse.net), the *Association of Muslim Social Scientists* (AMSS, www.amss.net), and the *Islamic Medical Association of North America* (IMANA, www.imana.org). The annual ISNA gathering has a very strong cultural and social thrust to it, including an international trade fair, a food festival, entertainment programs, an art exhibition, and a number of matrimonial events. ISNA also holds a series of regional conferences, is involved in public affairs advocacy and interfaith coalition building, publishes a magazine called *Horizon*, runs a popular matrimonial match-making program, provides *halal* food certification, and has a number of community building initiatives.

A second major umbrella group of Muslim Americans is the *Islamic Circle of North America* (ICNA, www.icna.org). ICNA also describes itself as a non-ethnic, non-sectarian Islamic organization but was originally started in the 1970s by South Asian Muslims and tends to attract large numbers of Pakistani-American-Muslims, especially to its annual convention. Many of ICNA's activities and goals are similar to ISNA (the ICNA magazine is called *Message*) but its focus tends to be more focused on deepening religious understanding and practice than on being a social support network.

Importantly, ICNA has a large relief program called *ICNA Relief-Helping Hand* (www.reliefonline.org), which operates humanitarian relief and development programs in a number or Muslim and non-Muslim countries, including both the USA and Pakistan. For example, they collected over $1.5 million for victims of the 2005 Tsunami in Southern Asia, and operated relief work in Sri Lanka, India and Indonesia. The ICNA website also reports a program in Darfur, Sudan. Not surprisingly, the recent earthquake in Pakistan became a major fundraising cause for ICNA and according to its website as much as $6 million in cash and another $4 million in kind was raised for the earthquake relief efforts in Pakistan. Prior to the earthquake, their programs in Pakistan included a number of projects on education, health-related initiatives, clean drinking water, handicap rehabilitation, and various welfare programs for the poor, especially widows and orphans.

Pakistan is a predominantly Muslim country (95 percent), as are Pakistani-Americans. However, there are a significant number of non-Muslims in Pakistan (approx. 5-8 million) and there are also a significant number of non-Muslim Pakistani-Americans, mostly concentrated in a set of tight-knit non-Muslim Pakistani-American communities (especially in New York, Los Angeles, Houston and Chicago), and generally having low degrees of interaction with Muslim Pakistani-Americans. Data on population distribution by religion is not available, but Christians probably constitute the largest non-Muslim community within the Pakistani diaspora in America. Although larger Christian-Pakistani communities exist in New York and California, a particularly active community of Pakistani-Christians resides in and around Philadelphia, which has regular church services for Pakistani Christians, publishes a regular magazine, the *Pakistan Christian Post* (PCP, www.pakistanchristianpost.com) and has a number of active Pakistan-focused organizations including the *Pakistani-American Christian Association* and the *Christian League of Pakistan*. These community support institutions for the Pakistani-American-Christian community are strongly Pakistan-focused in their activities, with a passionate interest in the human rights of minorities in Pakistan.

A thriving Zoroastrian (Parsi) community also exists in the USA with strong community institutions in most major metropolitan centers and a national *Federation of Zoroastrian Associations of North America* (www.fezana.org). Significant concentrations of Parsis with roots in Pakistan are to be found in Houston, New York and Chicago, including one of the most famous Pakistani-Americans, author Bapsi Sidhwa, a Parsi now settled in Houston. Many Parsi-Americans of Pakistani-origin keep close contact with Pakistan. Reportedly, a small number of Hindus from Pakistan also migrated to America. During the course of this research we met at least one Jew of Pakistani origin who grew up in Karachi and later migrated to Israel.

Information and advocacy platforms

In terms of sheer numbers, the most abundant Pakistani institutional entities to be found in the USA today are information and advocacy platforms. These can be found in large numbers and diverse variations, they include ethnic Pakistani media outlets, their presence is particularly profligate on the Internet (many are Internet-only platforms while some have more traditional institutional structures) their rates of demise tend to be high (but the rate at which new platforms are spawned is even higher), and their primary focus areas include information provision, image-building, advocacy and policy discussions related to Pakistan. Pakistan-related information and advocacy platforms have important implications for Pakistan-related philanthropy because they can strongly influence the information available and perceptions about charitable initiatives and opportunities in Pakistan. These platforms have been, and can be, important means of providing information about philanthropic options and initiative and motivating more giving by Pakistani-Americans. The philanthropic importance of such internet-based platforms became especially evident in the aftermath of the 2005 Pakistan earthquake.

Many professional and civic organizations also play an important advocacy and information function, most seek to enhance Pakistan's image within the larger American society, and some are also forums for intellectual discussions on pressing socio-political issues. However, for some organizations this is the *principal purpose* of all their activities. For example, in Chicago, the *Indus Society of North America* has been focusing specifically on these goals through its events and discussions for nearly twenty years. In California, the *Council of Pakistani American Affairs* (COPAA) has similar goals and initiatives. Such place-based organizations often resemble more general civic organizations. In Boston, a different model has developed with a formal group evolving for the sole purpose of organizing annual *Pak-Millennium Conferences* (www.pakistan2000.org) since 1999, with each theme-based conference focusing in depth on an issue of current relevance to Pakistan and Pakistani-Americans.

There are, of course, a number of universities in the USA with a special interest in Pakistan. The *American Institute of Pakistan Studies* (AIPS, www.pakistanstudies-aips.org) has served as an umbrella group for these initiatives since 1973. Another notable initiative is the new *SAIS Pakistan Fund* at the School for Advanced International Studies (SAIS) at Columbia University for strengthening the School's Pakistani-related offerings. This is notable because the idea and the initial contributions to the fund have come from Pakistani-Americans. On a different dimension of advocacy are organizations whose goal is to advance Pakistan-USA relations by lobbying US decision-makers; these organizations are also built upon the philanthropic contributions of Pakistani-Americans. These include, for example, the *Pakistan American Public Affairs Committee* (PAKPAC, pakpac.net), the *Pakistani American Congress* (PAC, www.pacus.org), and the *Pakistani-American Liaison Center* (PALC, www.palc.us).

The advent of the Internet has led to a proliferation of information and advocacy platforms and also dramatically changed the nature and scope of their activities. Notable amongst those taking advantage of the new digital opportunities is the *Association of Pakistani Professionals* (AOPP, www.aopp.org), which focuses primarily on building a positive image for Pakistani-Americans by focusing on the anti-Pakistan bias in US media. Another innovative initiative is the *Virtual Think Tank Pakistan* (VTTP, www.vttp.org), which seeks to mobilize the knowledge resources of Pakistanis, especially including Pakistani-Americans, for practical projects that can benefit Pakistan. The Internet has also allowed the Pakistan Embassy (www.embassyofpakistan.org) to change the nature of its interaction with the Pakistani-American community, especially through the use of email to keep the community informed of its activities. The Embassy has also recently launched a plan to establish a *Jinnah Center* to act as a public information and advocacy think tank and is seeking financial support from the Pakistani-Americans to establish and operate it.

The list of information and community discussion websites on Pakistan is long and the quality of these sites is variable. Many are personal initiatives of individual Pakistani-Americans or Pakistani students in America. The most recent phenomenon is the mushrooming of *Pakistan-related blogs*. Any search engine query will reveal page after page of Pakistan related informational sites and blogs. Notable amongst such blogs related to Pakistan are: iFaqeer.blogspot.com, Pakistaniat.com (All Things Pakistan) and wantandost.blogspot. com.

However, the universe of such initiatives changes fast and many sites are ephemeral. What is important, however, is to note the phenomenon and to highlight the fact that these sites and blogs have the potential of being important sources of information for Pakistani-Americans, including on worthy charitable initiatives. The philanthropic power of these websites and blogs was most evident in the aftermath of the 2005 earthquake in Pakistan, These sites became the source of choice for Pakistani-Americans not only to remain informed with events but also for getting advice on who to give their charitable contributions to and how (see, www.saquake.org, www.pakquake.com, pakistan.wikia.com, www.risepak.com, etc.)

The premier discussion forum on Pakistan-related issues, including frequent discussions on topics related to charitable and development giving to Pakistan, remains *chowk.com* which started in 1997 and reports that it has "over 2000 published articles, 10,000 registered users, 150,000 moderated discussions, and innumerable forum style impromptu responses." Starting as a forum for discussions on all-things-Pakistani in the pre-blog era, chowk.com has evolved into a South Asian forum but is still principally focused on Pakistan.

The websites of Pakistan's major newspapers remain the principal source of information on Pakistan for Pakistani-Americans. However, there is also a thriving Pakistani ethnic media in the USA. This is in addition to the mainstream Pakistani television channels now available on cable and satellite, and includes a host of locally-produced and broadcast ethnic television and radio shows in cities with major Pakistani populations, including New York, Chicago, Houston, Washington, DC, and Los Angeles. Many cities also have a large number of local Pakistani newspapers, mostly weeklies and mostly in Urdu, that provide local news, information on local events, and advertisements for Pakistan-related services such as Pakistani restaurants, *halal* food shops, travel agencies, etc. They also often include information on and advertisements about charitable causes in America and in Pakistan. The best-established weekly publication focused on Pakistanis in America is *Pakistan Link* (www.PakistanLink.com) which is published weekly and is now also widely read on the internet. *Chowrangi* (www.chowrangi.org) is a recent initiative to produce a high-quality feature magazine in English focusing on the lives and concerns of Pakistani-Americans but targeting an audience broader than just Pakistani-Americans.

Charitable and development organizations

The last decade has seen the emergence of a number of Pakistan-focused charitable and development initiatives by Pakistani-Americans. The trend of creating and supporting charitable and development-focused institutions—particularly on issues related to education—seems to have been further bolstered in the aftermath of 9/11. The recent earthquake in Pakistan was instrumental in the coming of age of many of these organizations and also in the creation of more new ones.

A range of these charitable and development initiatives of varying size and structure are to be found across the country. Many are independent organizations while others are related to existing community or professional associations. Some include fund-raising in the USA as well as designing and operating new development interventions in Pakistan. Others focus only on raising philanthropic support for existing initiatives in Pakistan, without being involved in the creation or management of new interventions. In all cases, the scale can vary from the very large to the very small.

There are a number of groups whose purpose is to raise philanthropic support for specific charitable organizations in Pakistan. For example, the *Edhi Foundation* (www.edhifoundation.com) runs its own fund-collecting affiliate (The *USA Edhi International Foundation*) based in New York. Given the great reputation and recognition of Abdul Sattar Edhi (called the "most venerated man in Pakistan" by Reader's Digest),[70] the Foundation is able to attract support from Pakistani-Americans without formal fund-raising activities. After the 2005 earthquake in Pakistan the Edhi Foundation was by far the charity of choice that Pakistani-Americans gave to. Although exact figures are not available, an outpouring of donations were sent to the Foundation through its USA-based arm, through a variety of more regionally focused pass-through organization, or directly through individual donations.

The establishment of the *Shaukat Khanum Memorial Cancer Hospital and Research Center* (www.shaukatkhanum.org.pk) by cricketer Imran Khan is an inspiring story of how celebrity can be channeled for the public good and used to mobilize the philanthropic impulses of large numbers of people; in this case, over one million individual donors, worldwide, helped raise the $22 million for the hospital. The effort to raise funds for the hospital also represented a pivotal moment in the evolution of diaspora philanthropy by Pakistani-Americans, by demonstrating the philanthropic potential of Pakistani-Americans, not only in mega-cities but also in middle-sized Pakistani communities. It also demonstrated that given the right cause, large number of Pakistani-Americans who had not previously donated to organized humanitarian and development charities could be mobilized to do so. The Hospital continues to raise funds through regular fund-raising by the *Imran Khan Cancer Appeal, Inc.*, which was set up in the USA for this specific purpose. This initiative has since evolved into the Imran Khan Foundation (www.imrankhanfoundation.org) which has also been very active in raising support in the United States for the 2005 earthquake in

Pakistan, both through its own efforts and by partnering with other Pakistani organizations (for example, OPEN).

Amongst the earliest initiatives in Pakistan that were able to generate and sustain support from Pakistan-Americans was the *SOS Children's Villages of Pakistan* (www.sos-childrenvillages.org), which works for the welfare of orphaned and abandoned children and operates seven SOS children's villages, six youth homes, seven schools, four vocational centers, two medical centers, and one emergency program. A dedicated and loyal set of Pakistani-Americans, particularly in the Washington DC area, have been regularly raising funds for SOS villages in Pakistan for many years now. Another example is the *United Fund of Pakistan* (UFP), registered in the USA for the purpose of raising support for the *Layton Rahmatulla Benevolent Trust* (LRBT, www.lrbt.org.pk), which provides comprehensive free eye-care services to the poor in its 12 hospitals and 26 clinics in Pakistan, has treated over 11 million patients, and in 2004-05 performed over 135,000 surgeries which was about a quarter of all cataract surgeries done in Pakistan. The UFP raises funds for LRBT through two annual gala events, one in New York and one in Washington. In Houston, *SIUT North America* (www.siutna.org) has been active for five years in raising philanthropic support for the *Sindh Institute of Urology and Transplantation* (SIUT, www.siut.org). SIUT provides comprehensive medical and surgical facilities in urology, nephrology and transplantation free of cost to all patients and in 2003 provided treatment over 300,000 patients, including nearly 73,000 dialyses.

In recent years, *TCF-USA* (www.tcfusa.org), a volunteer group registered to raise funds for *The Citizens Foundation* (TCF, www.thecitizensfoundation.org), has been quite innovative and dynamic. In Pakistan, TCF runs a network of purpose-built schools in urban slums and rural areas providing high-quality primary and secondary education to low-income communities and is operating 224 school units in 26 locations, with over 30,000 students, nearly half of them girls. TCF-USA raised over $300,000 for TCF schools in 2004. TCF-USA also changed the focus of its fundraising to immediate earthquake relief and rehabilitation after the 2005 earthquake in Pakistan and one feature of its very successful campaign has been a transparent web-based discussion and information forum on the relief progress (tcfquake.blogspot.com) TCF-USA has also been able to mobilize Pakistani student and alumni communities to raise support for TCF schools. Groups of Pakistani alumni of the University of Texas at Austin and of Grammar School, Karachi, have each pledged to 'adopt' individual TCF schools. Many other similar initiatives – most of them informal and some at quite small scales—of Pakistani-Americans organizing in small groups across the US to raise support for a particular charitable organization in Pakistan.

Over the years a new breed of Pakistani-American philanthropic initiatives have developed where Pakistani-Americans have a much greater role in not just raising funds for, but also in designing and sometimes managing humanitarian and development programs in Pakistan. The premier philanthropic institutions in this mode is the *Human Development Foundation of North America* (HDF, www.yespakistan.com/hdf), which grew out of the community of APPNA and Pakistani physicians but has since mushroomed into probably the most recognized and respected philanthropic enterprise of the Pakistani-American diaspora. Over the years, HDF has developed a system of regular fund-raisers arranged by volunteers in different communities across the United States. HDF's recent tax statement reported one of its best fund-raising years with over $1.30 million collected from direct public support in 2004.

The key goal of HDF's *'Project Pakistan'* is to establish holistic human development initiatives amongst underprivileged communities in Pakistan as models that can be scaled up and scaled out by others. Their 2005 report to the community reported that HDF now has programs in every region of Pakistan and has helped set up 980 development organizations (each serving a 'unit' of 1000 households), with a membership of 12,558 with 40 percent female participation. In these communities, HDF was providing extensive *health services* including community health centers, vaccination programs, nutritional monitoring, pre- and post-natal care and annual health screenings; the *educational programs* include nearly 200 non-formal schools, 5 secondary schools, 190 parent-teacher associations, and 180 adult literacy workshops; the *micro-enterprise program* had trained over 6000 people and issued 6,351 loans for a total of Pak. Rs. 71.85 million. In addition, the *physical infrastructure program* had invested in the construction of two dams and three link roads, lining 19 water courses and installing 194 hand-pumps.

HDF recently decided to launch its *'Project USA'*, which will focus on Pakistani-Americans. Useful and detailed expositions of HDF's achievements and activities are available on the Internet, at its general-purpose Pakistan web portal www.yespakistan.com, which is a very useful source of information of development giving directed not just to HDF activities, but to Pakistan in general. HDF was already working in many of the areas hit by the 2005 earthquake in Pakistan and launched a large fundraising, relief and rehabilitation operation for the earthquake immediately. Apart from partnering with other relief organizations in the area, HDF also directed its efforts towards establishing a field hospital in the affected areas.

Another highly-regarded philanthropic initiative by Pakistani-Americans is *Developments in Literacy, Inc.* (DIL, www.4dil.org) which was launched in 1997 in southern California by a group of Pakistani-Americans, mostly women, with the objective of promoting literacy in rural, underdeveloped areas of Pakistan, particularly female literacy. DIL has management offices in Los Angeles and Islamabad, and chapters in Los Angeles, New York, San Francisco, Washington, Houston, San Diego, Ottawa and Singapore, which focus on fundraising. DIL has been extremely successful in raising funds across the USA and elsewhere. For example, a single fundraiser in New York in 2005 raised $325,000 for DIL, another in Los Angeles raised $275,000. The DIL model is significantly different from others and instead of running its own projects DIL partners with existing NGOs in Pakistan, financially supports their activities and closely monitors the finances, content and quality of their programs. Since its inception, DIL has helped establish and operate some 200 schools in impoverished areas in Pakistan, working with various local partners.

Another interesting example in this genre of organizations is the *Promotion of Education in Pakistan Foundation* (PEP, www.pepfoundation.org) based in New York and founded in 1994. PEP foundation has been successful in mobilizing a large number of high profile Pakistanis around its programs, which include a fellowship program that has funded over 300 graduate students in Pakistan and a visiting faculty program. More recently, the Foundation has focused its activities around setting up a new national university in Pakistan.

What is quite striking is the upsurge in the desire amongst Pakistani-Americans, particularly young Pakistani-Americans, to find means to be directly involved in development and charitable initiatives in Pakistan. Many of these initiatives are still fledgling and many might not survive. However, a new generation of Pakistani-Americans, led by young professionals, is clearly taking the lead in creating new initiatives and bringing new ideas and enthusiasms to diaspora philanthropy by Pakistani Americans. For example, in Pennsylvania we found *Ibtida* (www.ibtida.org) which seeks to invest its philanthropic energies in quality education for underprivileged communities in Pakistan. In Minnesota, students about to graduate from University set out to establish the *Global Council of Pakistan* (www.gcpak.org) as a means to channel the knowledge and resources of the Pakistani diaspora for Pakistan's development and have raised funds for a few small projects in the education and health sectors. In California, *Koshish Foundation* (www.koshish.org) has chosen to focus on technical, especially computer-related, education amongst low-income communities. From the East Coast of the United States come a set of young professionals and entrepreneurs who have pooled their skills and knowledge to create the *Pakistan Literacy Fund* (www.pakfund.org) as a one-stop clearinghouse of diverse initiatives related to education and literacy in Pakistan, giving donors information about credible initiatives in Pakistan and the opportunity to channel their philanthropic contribution into the initiative that best meets their priorities.

One of the most dynamic of this breed of young organizations run by young Pakistani-American professionals is the *Association for the Development of Pakistan* (ADP, www.developpakistan.org). Set up in Massachusetts to support social innovation for locally-driven and participatory development in Pakistan, ADP began as a 'pass through' fundraiser for existing projects in the areas of education, prison welfare and sanitation. It came into its own with the 2005 earthquake in Pakistan, when there was a surge in desire amongst Pakistani-Americans to find a convenient and trustworthy way to send money to legitimate organizations doing good work on the ground in Pakistan. ADP's already had a system in place and immediately mobilized it towards raising support for earthquake relief. In this process it raised nearly half a million US dollars, the bulk of which were channeled to the Edhi Foundation, some to the Pakistan President's Earthquake Relief Fund, and some towards ADP's own initiatives.

Individual giving

Although the focus of this entire section is on Pakistani-American institutions, it needs to be underscored (as we will discuss later) that the vast bulk of giving by Pakistani-Americans, especially to causes in Pakistan, happens not through established institutions but through individual, kinship and non-organizational networks. These can be difficult to analyze, precisely because they are individual, kinship-based and non-organizational. Indeed, even in the Pakistani-American response to the 2005 earthquake, the vast bulk of support was mobilized and deployed individually rather than institutionally. Indeed, one hears of many instances where social and family gatherings became impromptu fundraisers for earthquake relief.

However, in our research we found many powerful examples of individual giving by Pakistani-Americans, to causes in America as well as those in Pakistan. For example, in 2004, a Pakistani couple from California, Sara and Sohaib Abbasi, made headlines by announcing a $2.5 million gift to Stanford University to help establish a program in Islamic Studies. Earlier, the couple had already endowed a named professorship and the graduate Fellowship in Computer Science at the University of Illinois at Urbana-Champaign, where Sohaib Abbasi had studied before he became a senior executive at the computer software giant, Oracle. Sara Abbasi also happens to be one of the leading forces behind DIL. Earlier, in 1995,

Malik and Seeme Hasan gave a $2 million gift to the University of Southern Colorado, Pueblo, for the establishment of what became the Malik and Seeme Hasan School of Business. Dr. Hasan, who was the CEO of Health Systems Inc., has also been active in political and public affairs while Seeme Gul Hasan has been a long standing patron of the arts, and especially classical music, in Colorado.

Safi Qureshey, one of the founders of AST Research, has invested significant philanthropic contributions in innovative Pakistan-related causes through the *Safi Qureshey Foundation* (www.sqfoundation.org), most notably supporting the 'Alif project' which brought to Pakistan Television an Urdu version of the popular children's educational program Sesame Street. Zia Chishti, Chairman and CEO of The Resources Group and formerly of Align Technology, has also been an active philanthropist giving to a number of Pakistani and Pakistani-American causes.

An interesting trend that our focus groups alerted us to was the growth of charitable trust funds being established by Pakistani-Americans as earlier generations of the diaspora start reaching retirement. A combination of the desire to give something back, which can sometimes be enhanced with age, and US tax laws that encourage the creation of charitable trusts seems to be leading to an increase in the creation of individual and family trusts. We found numerous examples of older Pakistani-Americans who had set up such trusts and all indications suggest that this trend will continue to grow as the population ages. It is quiet likely that such individual and family trust funds will play an even greater role in the philanthropic giving of the Pakistani diaspora in the United States in the future.

These, of course, are a few of the better-known examples amongst the many affluent Pakistanis who give in large amounts or to a large number of causes. Many do not wish to talk about their giving and prefer to do it quietly. Many Pakistani physicians, for example, give generously of their time and expertise to hospitals and medical colleges in Pakistan, regularly volunteering their skills and knowledge. Some Pakistani academics and researchers in

America are equally generous with their expertise and time to causes in Pakistan.

The largest net individual giving, however, comes in the form of the sum of the very large number of fairly small individual contributions to individual causes. During our focus groups, we found a large number of individuals who had contributed to a school, a dispensary, a mosque in their ancestral village or made a sizeable individual donation to an institution in Pakistan. For example, in Staten Island, New York, we met a group of workers (none particularly high-income) all of whom came from the same village in the Murree Hills area and who had pooled their otherwise meager charitable resources to purchase an ambulance for their village and pay the expenses of a full-time driver who can take the sick to hospital in Rawalpindi, when needed. In Chicago we found a small shop owner who has been (for five years then) underwriting the entire textbook and school supplies expenses of all the children in his village school. In Washington, DC, we found a taxicab driver who had been bearing the entire expenditure of a girls school in outside Quetta, in the Baluchistan province. Inspiring Pakistani-Americans like these are littered all across the USA.

CHAPTER #3

Total Giving

This, along with the next two chapters, will present the results of the analysis of the survey responses received. These three chapters are based mostly on the analysis of the 461 household survey questionnaires that were collected as part of the research for the book. The analysis is based on 2003-04 data and we expect that the giving would have been significantly higher is 2005 because of the devastating earthquake in Pakistan.

In deriving the lessons from these results our discussion has been guided by the views that we heard during the focus groups themselves and what makes intuitive and logical sense in the context of the interviews we conducted and the review of the larger literature. In essence, we have been guided by the quantitative results of the survey analysis, but have tried hard not to be enamored by these numbers. Instead, we have sought to carefully gauge the deeper implications and rationale behind these results and to draw from them larger lessons about the giving practices of Pakistanis in America. We invite the reader to adopt similar caution in interpreting these results.

Calculations and categories

One of the biggest challenges faced in conducting this research was the deep sense of fear and anxiety that Muslim communities (including most Pakistanis) in America feel in the post-9/11 world. This has also generated a deep distrust of survey instruments on an issue as sensitive as charitable giving. This posed a serious methodological hurdle that was partially tackled by conducting face-to-face focus groups instead of using impersonal (and, in the current circumstances, more suspicious) telephone or Internet questionnaires. A different conceptual hurdle was that the type of detailed data on income and demographic distribution required a truly scientific sampling, which is simply not available for Pakistanis in America.

Based on our estimates of approximately 500,000 Pakistanis living in America (Chapter 2) and a household size of 5, we approximate a total of 100,000 Pakistani-American households. However, not knowing the distribution of income or other demographic variables within this universe meant that we could not easily assume that our sample was reasonably representative of Pakistanis in America. In fact, the research team's own assessment is that the sample had an *under-representation* of households on the lower end of the economic scale ($40,000 per annum or less) and an *over-representation* of households on the higher end of the economic scale ($200,000 per annum or more).[71] This meant that simply taking the average giving per household as reflected in our survey findings was likely to give erroneous (and exaggerated) results. However, within any given income category we had enough survey responses to have reasonable confidence that we could estimate the appropriate average giving for Pakistanis in that *particular income category*. We, therefore, needed a baseline for the likely income distribution of Pakistanis in America around which to normalize our findings.

In searching for a census category that was likely to have a somewhat similar income profile to Pakistanis in America, we selected the income distribution of all Asian communities in the USA. This is a good benchmark to use because the US Census Bureau collects and analyzes race information on Americans of Asian descent and detailed data is available on the income distribution of this subset of Americans.[72] Asians in America, including Pakistanis, tend to be a relatively more affluent community than other categories of Americans.[73] It is further assumed that within the larger Asian category, the income profile of Pakistanis in America is more similar to that of Indians in America. If so, calculations made by the Indian diaspora suggest that the average income of Asian Indians in America is higher than that of all Asians in America.[74] This means that selecting the income distribution of Asian-Americans as the baseline is not only a reasonable choice; it is a conservative assessment.[75]

To arrive at the estimates of philanthropic giving by Pakistanis in America, we normalized the raw survey results by assuming that the 'real' income distribution of Pakistanis in America is similar to that of Asians in America, but the giving patterns of households within any given income category is reasonably represented by our survey results. The impact of this assumption is that our giving estimates are significantly *less* than what they would have been if we had simply assumed the distribution reflected in our survey responses as the correct distribution. We believe that this baseline adjustment allows better conformity to the real distribution.

Definitions

The survey instrument asked questions about different types of philanthropic contributions and about the different causes to which these were directed. These categories were built upon standard definitions in the literature but adapted to the special features of giving by the Pakistani diaspora in the US. Importantly, it should be noted that we have adopted a broader definition of philanthropic giving than is sometimes used, particularly in the USA. We have included all forms of giving and volunteering (in cash, in kind and in volunteered time) and our results are best compared to broad surveys of giving and volunteering, such as those conducted in the United States by *Independent Sector*.[76] Philanthropy, of course, is a culturally constructed concept and one insight that was repeated across our focus groups related to how giving to individuals (rather than just institutions) is an integral part of upholding the 'public good' in societies where state and non-state institutions are incapable or uninterested in providing the necessary social safety nets.

Building on the definitions provided in the survey forms and the explanations provided during focus groups, the key terms should be understood as follows:

♦ *Volunteering:* Giving time and services, without remuneration, to organizations and events related to philanthropic causes. For example, this would include time volunteered for events organized by Pakistani associations in the US, time volunteered by US-based professionals such as doctors on their visits to Pakistan, etc.

♦ *In-kind Giving:* The giving of goods that have monetary value to the recipient. For example, this would include donation of books, materials, clothes, computers, etc.

♦ *Monetary Giving:* This includes the giving of money to individuals or to organizations.

♦ *Faith-motivated Giving:* This refers to monetary giving motivated by faith-based charitable obligations (such as *zakat* or *sadaqah*).[77] However, it should be noted that this refers to the motivation for giving and not to the use that the contribution is put to. Hence, faith-motivated giving is not to be confused with giving to religious causes. For example, this would include giving monetary assistance to the poor, either individually or through civic organizations, as part charitable obligations motivated by injunctions of one's faith.

♦ *Issue-motivated Giving:* This refers to monetary giving motivated by specific issues of interest to the giver, rather than by injunctions of faith. For example, this would include giving money to support a cultural event related to Pakistan, or to an issue such as environmental protection, etc.

♦ *Pakistani Causes Based in Pakistan:* This includes causes that not only related to Pakistan but are also based in Pakistan. For example, this would include giving to civic organizations or to needy individuals based in Pakistan.

♦ *Pakistani Causes Based in the US:* This includes causes that are related to Pakistan but are based in the United States. For example, this would include giving to community organizations either of Pakistanis or related to Pakistan, including the Pakistani associations that operate in different US cities, or asso-

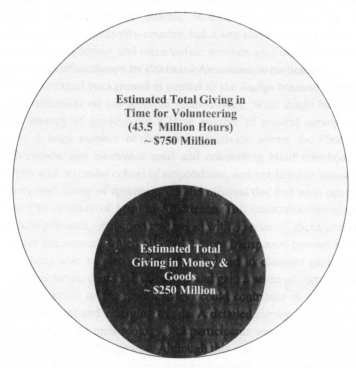

Figure 16: Estimated Total Giving by Pakistanis in America
Giving in money, goods and time; Total = ~$1 Billion

ciations of various Pakistani professional groups.

♦ *Causes Unrelated to Pakistan:* This includes causes located in the US or other parts of the world that are not directly related to Pakistan. For example, this would include causes such as human rights, world hunger, the arts, religion, etc. when they are <u>not</u> focused specifically or primarily on Pakistan.

Total estimated giving

We estimates that the average giving—in terms of money and goods—for Pakistani households in America is around $2,500 per household per year. It also estimates that the average Pakistani household in America contributes around 435 hours per year of volunteer time. As discussed earlier, we estimate that there are a total of 100,000 Pakistani households in America (based on an estimated population of 500,000 Pakistani-Americans), which suggests that *Pakistanis in America donate approximately a total of $250 million in cash and in-kind and the equivalent of $750 million in volunteered time; or an estimated total of $1 billion in cash, in kind and in time volunteered* (see Figure 16).

Before discussing the details, it should be stressed that any gross numbers based on an opinion survey need to be interpreted with a measure of caution. Philanthropy studies in general are not suited to exactitude. However, recognizing the various limitations discussed earlier, and understanding that our results are only as good as the survey responses we received, we have reasonable confidence that the numbers presented in this chapter represent a realistic estimation of the general levels of philanthropic giving by Pakistanis in America.[78]

Given the above caveat, there are a number of features of the estimated total annual giving by Pakistanis in America that should be highlighted (see Figure 17).[79]

♦ Of the $250 million that we estimate as the total annual giving in cash and in-kind, *about 80 percent ($200 million) is given as monetary contributions and the remaining 20 percent ($50 million) as an in-kind philanthropic contribution* of goods.

♦ In terms of what motivates this giving, *the total amount is split nearly evenly between faith-motivated and issue-motivated giving.* Each category amounts to an estimated total annual giving of around $125 million.

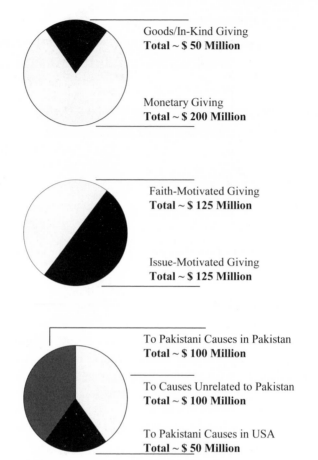

Goods/In-Kind Giving
Total ~ $ 50 Million

Monetary Giving
Total ~ $ 200 Million

Faith-Motivated Giving
Total ~ $ 125 Million

Issue-Motivated Giving
Total ~ $ 125 Million

To Pakistani Causes in Pakistan
Total ~ $ 100 Million

To Causes Unrelated to Pakistan
Total ~ $ 100 Million

To Pakistani Causes in USA
Total ~ $ 50 Million

Figure 17: Distribution of Total Estimated Annual Giving
(Monetary + In-Kind)
Total ~ $ 250 Million

◆ A third way to cut the same pie is to note that *around $100 million (40 percent) of this contribution goes directly to Pakistani causes in Pakistan.* Another $50 million (20 percent) goes to Pakistani causes in the United States and the remaining 40 percent ($100 million) goes to causes unrelated to Pakistan.

◆ *The monetary value of the estimated 435 hours of volunteered time per Pakistani household in America comes out to be around $750 million.* While this is an impressive figure, translating volunteered time into a direct monetary value is conceptually problematic.[80] A better way of understanding the value of

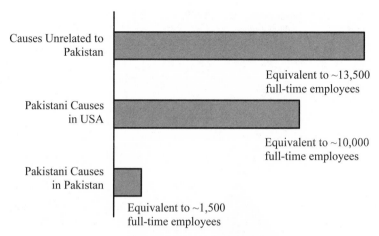

**Figure 18: Value of Total Estimated Volunteered Time in Equivalent
Annual Full-Time Employees**
Total ~ 25,000 full-time employees per year

volunteered time is to convert it into the equivalent full-time employees that
the volunteers replaced with their contributions. Using this measure, *the total
43.5 million hours per year volunteered by 100,000 Pakistani households
represents the equivalent of over 25,000 full-time employees.*[81] This is a very
significant volunteering contribution for a community of this size and without
it the wide multitude of organizations that represent the various community
interests of Pakistanis in America (see Chapter #2) could not possibly function.
Much of this volunteered work may well be supplemental labor and it is clear
that volunteers fill in for work that would be otherwise done by paid workers.
However, it is also clear that the vast network of Pakistan-related organizations
(Chapter 2) could simply not operate without this massive investment of volunteered time by Pakistanis in America. (See Figure 18)

♦The *time volunteered by Pakistani households in the USA to causes unrelated to Pakistan is an equivalent of around 13,500 full-time employees* (54
percent of volunteered time). Although a majority of this goes into the maintenance of mosques and other places of worship, this also includes volunteering
by Pakistani-Americans to secular non-Pakistan-related causes such as soup
kitchens, community groups, school associations, and other charitable organizations. Another 40 percent, or an equivalent of some 10,000 full-time employees goes to Pakistani causes in the USA, including social, cultural and philanthropic organizations run by Pakistanis. Not surprisingly, only a small frac-

tion—6 percent of the total volunteered time, or an equivalent of 1,500 full-time employees—goes to Pakistani causes in Pakistan. However, this last category is noteworthy since a significant proportion of this represents highly skilled Pakistani professionals in America (e.g., physicians) contributing their time and expertise to causes in Pakistan as they did, for example, in the aftermath of the 2005 earthquake in Pakistan.

The overall findings suggest that Pakistanis in America are remarkably generous and active as a community. Moreover, it suggests that while the community retains a deep commitment to 'Pakistani' causes, their philanthropic interests are not confined to causes in Pakistan. Like the rest of America, faith is an important motivator of the giving habits of Pakistani-Americans; but even more significantly, issue-motivated philanthropy constitutes an equally large proportion of their giving.

Although it is very enticing to focus on the total quantum of giving, such numbers are necessarily broad estimations rather than exact measurements. It is more meaningful to parse these numbers down and look at the patterns and trends that underlie them at the level of giving per households. This is because too many 'averages' are operating within the calculation of total giving and also because more operational insight can be derived in this manner from the patterns of giving by households. With the above caveats in place, there are a number of important findings that can be derived by focusing on the distribution of giving by this stylized 'average household'. Three sets of findings, in particular, seem noteworthy. These relate to (a) the distribution of giving, (b) the motivation for giving, and (c) the level of giving by 'average' Pakistani-

Table 7: Estimated Giving Profile (Annual) of Average Pakistani Household in America

Total ~ US$ 2,500 per hear per household

	Pakistani Causes in Pakistan	Pakistani Causes in USA	Causes Unrelated to Pakistan	Total Giving
Monetary Giving (Faith-Motivated)	$450	$200	$350	$100
Monetary Giving (Issue-Motivated)	$390	$230	$380	$100
In-kind Giving	$190	$85	$225	$500
Total Giving	$1030	$515	$955	$2,50

American household. The rest of this chapter will discuss these three aspects in turn.

Distribution of giving

To the extent that one can conceptualize the average Pakistani-American household as an artifact of our results, its broad giving patterns are described in Table 7.

The numbers, of course, are by now familiar to us because the calculations of the aggregate quantum of giving were based on them.[82] However, what is more interesting here is the proportion by which these contributions are distributed. Although we use the same rounded-off numbers in Table 7 that our aggregate numbers were based upon, this table provides a little more texture in terms of looking at the distribution of the overall giving in terms of the type of giving (monetary giving motivated by faith, issue-motivated monetary giving, in-kind giving) and also in terms of the causes that people give to (Pakistani causes in Pakistan, Pakistani causes in the USA, and causes unrelated to Pakistan). Since the numbers are based on survey results and since they have been already averaged out across a rather wide range to arrive at a stylized 'average household', the table is more indicative of the proportion of giving that goes to various causes or to various kinds of giving, than as a measure of precise flows.

Monetary and in-kind giving
A first and immediate reaction to this table is its striking sense of symmetry. We had already noted that overall about 40 percent of the total giving goes to Pakistani causes in Pakistan, another 40 percent to causes unrelated to Pakistan, and the remaining 20 percent to Pakistani causes in the USA. Interestingly, these proportions remain roughly similar even when one looks at any sub-component of the aggregate. Beyond this consistency, a close examination suggests that there are at least three noteworthy findings about the distribution of household giving.

First, *the bulk of the total monetary and in-kind giving by Pakistanis in America does go to Pakistani causes* (around 60 percent). Second, *a very significant portion of this (around 20 percent) is directed to Pakistani causes in America* and these contributions are critical to maintaining the elaborate and multi-faceted set of Pakistani activities and organizations that were described

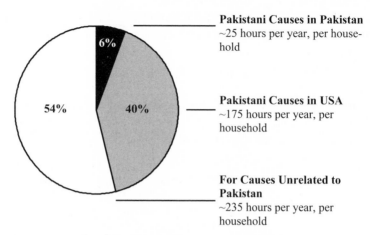

Pakistani Causes in Pakistan
~25 hours per year, per household

Pakistani Causes in USA
~175 hours per year, per household

For Causes Unrelated to Pakistan
~235 hours per year, per household

Figure 19: Distribution of Volunteered Time
Total ~ 435 hours per year, per household

in earlier chapters. Third, *a very significant proportion (around 40 percent) of the giving by Pakistani households in the USA is directed to causes that are not related to Pakistan.* This giving relates to the non-Pakistani facets of identity of the Pakistani diaspora, including their faith-motivated identity as well as their adopted identity as residents (and often citizens) of the United States.

These findings points towards an emerging portrait of Pakistani-Americans as a generous community that retains a commitment to its Pakistani roots both through its giving to Pakistan and its focus on nurturing Pakistani causes in the USA. Yet, it is also a diaspora that has significant additional pulls on its philanthropic impulses; in particular, those stemming from other facets of its identity—including faith-related identity and its adopted American identity.

Volunteering

Understandably, the contributions of volunteered time are not distributed along the same proportions as monetary and in-kind contributions (see Figure 19). The obvious constraint here is physical presence. Only 6 percent of the time volunteered goes to Pakistani causes in Pakistan. It is reasonable to assume that in fact most Pakistani households do not give any volunteered time to causes in Pakistan and this 6 percent is an artifact of that minority of households which do, in fact, give a much greater proportion of their own volunteered time to causes in Pakistan. This volunteered time includes the time contributions of highly skilled expatriate Pakistanis (for example, physicians, professors, and other professionals) and those who are very active in setting up their own philanthropic initiatives or in supporting existing nongovernmental organizations in Pakistan.

A much greater proportion of this volunteered time (around 40 percent or 175 hours per year per household) goes to Pakistani causes in the USA. This includes various Pakistani community associations that operate across the major cities and states in the US as well as a variety of diverse groups that focus on particular aspects of the Pakistani identity. Indeed, without this very serious investment of time by Pakistani volunteers, the vast network of Pakistani organizations in the USA could not possibly function.

Finally, and not surprisingly, the largest proportion of the volunteered time (around 54 percent or 235 hours per year per household) goes to causes unrelated to Pakistan. Our focus group discussion and interviews suggest that the vast bulk of this time contribution goes to faith-related institutions (such as mosques and churches). Again, this massive contribution of volunteered time is critical to the functioning of these congregations which, in most cases have religious as well as social purposes. Like other immigrant communities before them, Pakistanis have tended to turn their places of worship into social and cultural congregations which play a vital role in maintaining and nurturing the community identities of the diaspora.[83]

Arguably, the very sizeable contributions that Pakistanis in America make through their volunteered time is a critical—possibly *the* critical—element in maintaining and nurturing the network of identity organizations (whether Pakistan-focused or faith-focused) that have sprung up to service the social and identity needs of the Pakistani diaspora.

Faith as a motivation to give

Our key finding with respect to faith-based motivation for giving is that although there may be differences in detail, at the general level, the role of faith as a motivation for giving by Pakistanis in America is not very different from the role of faith as a motivation for giving by Americans at large. In this regards at least, the Pakistani-American household is strikingly similar to its American neighbor.[84]

Interestingly, a fairly consistent 'half-and-half principle' seems to emerge from survey results. Focusing only on the monetary contributions for the moment,[85] not only is it about evenly divided between faith-motivated and issue-motivated giving, but this pattern remains consistent even when we break down the numbers for giving to Pakistani causes in Pakistan, to Pakistani causes in America, and to causes unrelated to Pakistan.[86] The significance of this consistency suggests that about half the giving by Pakistani-American households is motivated by faith-based obligations to be charitable, while the other half is motivated by more issue-based motivations. Moreover, this general half-and-half rule is consistent across categories of giving (across different age groups, different education levels, different lengths of stay in the US, and different income levels). *The surprise here is not that faith is a major motivation for giving; what is noteworthy is that our respondents report that issues are an equally important driver of their giving decisions.*

Given the sensitivity of the subject, one must point out that faith-motivated giving is not to be confused with giving to religious causes; it refers to the *reason that motivates people to give, rather than to the destination of their contributions.* Indeed, although faith is a major motivation for giving, religion is not the most important issue that Pakistanis in America give to. The decision to ask our survey respondents to differentiate between their faith-motivated and issue-motivated monetary giving was driven by the need to accommodate the special status of the obligation to be charitable as enshrined in concepts such as *zakat* and *sadaqah.* Our focus group discussions suggest that people do make a clear distinction in their mind between contributions that are motivated by religious obligations and those motivated by a more general charitable impulse. However, the focus group discussions as well as various survey results (discussed later) demonstrate that much of the faith-motivated giving goes to non-faith-related causes, especially to direct assistance for the poor and needy. As such, this question focused not on *who* the contribution is made to, but on *why* it is made.

Despite the rather unique way in which we had posed our survey question, the findings are quite consistent with what is found in surveys of giving patterns of the general population in the United States. Indeed, the result of the most recent survey by the organization *Independent Sector* found strikingly similar results. According to their survey, American households that contributed to fulfill religious obligations gave on average slightly more than twice as much as given by other households.[87] This seems to suggest that the half-and-half principle evident in our results is not inconsistent with the general American norm.[88]

For example, a recent US report on *Faith and Philanthropy* concludes that "faith-based generosity, whether measured in terms of dollars or time, is real, measurable, and carries considerable impact" (pg. 36) and that for all Americans "religious belief is without question one of the most important factors [that influence levels of giving] independent of economic status" (pg. 8); importantly, and again consistent with out findings, the same US report also finds that those who respond to a faith-motivated charitable impulse also demonstrate "high levels of generosity to other causes as well" (pg. 8).[89] In this respect, as in many others, the motivations that propel the giving patterns of Pakistanis in America are quite similar to the impulses that motivate their American neighbors.

While Pakistanis in America seem to share with other Americans a strong sense of charitable duty based on their faith, it does seem from our survey that Pakistanis in America give *less* to religious organizations than do Americans in general. According to the already-mentioned US-survey conducted by *Independent Sector*, religious organizations are by far the single largest beneficiary of giving by Americans in general: 53% of all the charitable contributions in America go to religious organizations.[90] By contrast, religious organizations are not amongst the top beneficiaries of philanthropy by Pakistanis in America (the top beneficiaries, quite decisively, are individuals who are poor and in need). Our survey of Pakistanis in America finds that only 7.5% of our respondents report giving most (50% or more) of their overall contributions to religious organizations and as many as 53% of our respondents reported that they either gave nothing or less than 10% of their overall contributions to religious organizations.

It is, of course, conceivable that this particular finding is induced by the climate of fear that has been created for Muslims in America, including many Pakistani-Americans, in the aftermath of the tragedy of 9/11. However, the results from our focus group discussions clearly corroborate this result and show that needy individuals remain the primary focus of faith-motivated giving. The focus group discussions also stressed that giving to religious organizations primarily means giving for the purposes of building and maintaining places of worship which, in the context of most diaspora communities in the United States,[91] also serve a dual social function as community centers.

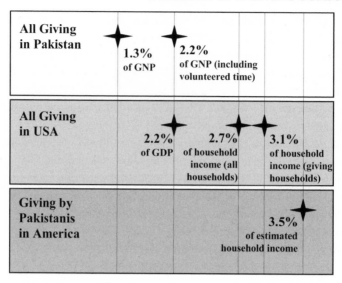

**Figure 20: Rough Comparisons of Giving
Patterns for Related Groups**

Philanthropic comparisons

While it is very difficult, and not necessarily useful, to get precise comparisons
with the giving profiles of other related populations (for example, Pakistanis *in*
Pakistan, or all givers in the USA), rough comparisons suggest that that the
overall giving by Pakistanis in America compares favorably with these cohorts.

Key comparisons

A major conceptual problem with such comparisons is that different cohorts may have very different income profiles and different reports tend to use
different methodologies and baselines for their analyses. Indeed, the calculation of what is included in 'philanthropy' or 'giving' may also vary from report
to report, even within the same country. Any comparison with the giving patterns of other groups of givers should be cognizant of these issues and the
reader is advised caution. Having said that, let us (very cautiously) indulge in
some very rough comparisons (see Figure 20).

A 1999 study estimated that indigenous philanthropy in Pakistan totaled
the equivalent of about Rupees 70.5 billion per year (including volunteered

time), of which around Rupees 41 billion was monetary or in-kind giving.[92] Although the study did not report its findings in terms of household incomes it did estimate that indigenous philanthropy amounted to 2.2 percent of Pakistan's gross national product (GNP) if the value of volunteered time was included. This means that the monetary and in-kind contributions amount to around 1.3 percent of Pakistan's GNP. This study included individual giving, giving in kind and in time in its calculations.

The nearest estimates available for giving in the US (by all Americans) suggest that total US giving in 2003 amounted to $241 billion, or 2.2 percent of US gross domestic product (GDP).[93] However, the numbers are not directly comparable because the US calculations include institutional giving (by endowments, etc.), it is based on tax data, it does not include the value of volunteered time, and calculates on the basis of GDP rather than GNP. However, a 2000 survey-based estimate which used household income as the yardstick for analysis found that the giving by all US households amounted to 2.7 percent of their household incomes and that this number shot up to 3.1 percent when calculated only for households that do contribute, either in cash, kind or in time.[94] This study is the most comparable to our in terms of methodology and scope.

Our estimates for giving by Pakistanis in America (including monetary and in-kind but *not* including volunteered time) suggests that this group gives around 3.5 percent of its household income to philanthropy. While the spread between this number and the percentages cited above for all giving in Pakistan and in the USA, respectively, is quite wide, the real difference may well be less wide. First, the US numbers suggest that total giving is a significantly smaller percentage of GDP than it is as a percentage of household income. If the same is true for Pakistan then one would expect the giving in Pakistan to be significantly more than 2.2 percent of household income. Second, our overall estimate of Pakistanis in America giving 3.5 percent of their household income to philanthropy is based on using the average income of all Asians in America ($70, 047 per year). As we have suggested earlier, it is quite likely that the average income of Pakistani households in America is, in fact, more than this. If so, the proportionate giving as a percentage of that higher income would be slightly less.

In short, although we cannot be fully sure whether, and by how much, the percentages discussed here would converge if the appropriate adjustments are applied, the one conclusion we can make with confidence on the basis of our rough comparison is that Pakistanis in America are no less, and possibly more,

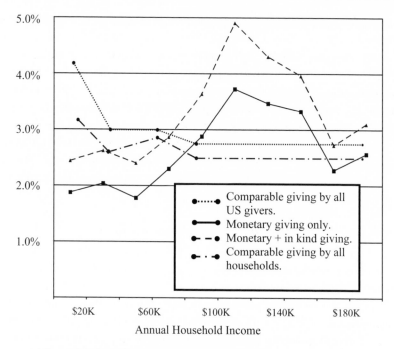

**Figure 21: Giving by Income for All-USA Giving and for Giving
by Pakistanis in America**

generous in their giving habits than their compatriots in Pakistan and their
neighbors in America.

Another, possibly better, way to compare the giving patterns of Pakistani
households in America with the giving patterns of all US givers in general is to
compare the percentage of the household income that is given in monetary and
in-kind contributions per year. Figure 21 compares the findings of the 2000
national survey of trends in giving and volunteering in the USA to our own
estimates.[95] Although the income brackets for which figures are reported for
the two are slightly different, these are more comparable figures because the
income baseline used for our survey numbers are the actual reported income
brackets rather than an estimation based on data for Asians in America. Two
sets of numbers are reported for US givers; giving by all US households and
for US households that do report some form of philanthropic giving. The data
from our survey (representing the monetary plus in-kind giving) is best compared to the giving by philanthropically active US households because our

survey methodology was not random and attracted individuals who were active givers.

An interesting finding from Figure 21 is that for lower and middle income groups (up to around $40,000 per year household income) Pakistani households in America give a significantly smaller percentage of their household income, however, for higher income groups ($75,000 to $100,000 and possibly above) they give slightly more than the all-USA population. Although there is a noticeable peak for giving by Pakistanis in America in the $100,000 to $200,000 range, the difference is probably not as pronounced as this peak because the US data averages out the giving for all income groups greater than $100,000 while our data does not.

A misplaced sense of philanthropic inferiority

The point of making these comparisons is to get a sense of how Pakistanis in America compare in their philanthropic generosity to the two peer groups most important to them: Pakistanis in Pakistan and Americans in America. While we do caution against overly precise comparisons between these numbers (all of which are wide averages), the point to be made here is simply that the general level of overall giving by Pakistani households in America is quite similar to the level of giving by American households.

This is a meaningful, and even surprising, finding because during our focus groups when this question was posed to the participants, the most common response was an insistence that Pakistanis in America do *not* give as much as other communities in America and probably give less (proportional to incomes) than Pakistanis in Pakistan. Interestingly, our survey results suggest that the philanthropic impulses of Pakistanis in America compare very favorably with both these reference groups.

This becomes important, as we shall see in Chapter #6, because the Pakistani-American community seems to have a low self-image of its own giving patterns and the general view within the community is that it is not as giving as other relevant population groups in the USA or in Pakistan. The mismatch between the community's perception of its own giving levels, of the giving levels of other communities, and the reported giving by this and other communities is intriguing. It is probably a factor of an exaggerated sense within the community of how much other communities give as well as an underestimation of the charitable impulses of their own community as a whole. Some, but certainly not the entire extent of this mismatch, may also be explained by the differences in how various reports on giving have defined and measured the total giving by a community.

CHAPTER #4

Trends and tendencies

In the last chapter we began analyzing on our findings by estimating the overall quantum of philanthropic giving and volunteering by Pakistanis in America. We then explored the giving patterns of the stylized average household in relatively greater detail. This allowed us to explore some important aspects of the giving patterns of the Pakistani-Americans. Lastly, we compared the average giving by Pakistani-American households with the giving patterns of Pakistanis in Pakistan and all Americans to get a sense of contrast with two key reference groups.

In this chapter, we 'open up' the various dimensions of giving by Pakistanis in America and focus our attention on how different variables such as income, age, education, length of time in the United States, and level of participation in the Pakistani community impact the philanthropic decisions of different households. This will allow us to more closely examine the trends and tendencies that underlie the broader giving patterns of Pakistanis in America that have been highlighted earlier. We will also look at how the giving by Pakistani-Americans is distributed by different causes and different issues. Finally, we will focus on a number of issues related to how the giving actually takes place; that is, the mechanics of giving.

The demographics of giving and volunteering

Let us begin by looking at how the total household giving relates to key demographic variables. Based on our survey design, the total household giving is understood to have three components: giving in money, giving in goods, and giving in time.

For our analysis, giving in money includes both faith-motivated and issue-motivated monetary giving.[96] Giving in goods (in-kind giving) is measured in US dollars per household, as is giving in money. For giving in time, we calculate the total time volunteered by the household and report it here in number of hours per year. For our current discussion we will focus on these three components of household giving and how they correspond to five key variables: age of respondent, education level of respondent, household income, how long the respondent has lived in the USA, and the level of participation in Pakistani community organizations and events. Table 8 presents this information for relevant categories within each variable. All numbers in the table have been rounded off.

Figure 22 is derived from this data and presents a set of five graphs (one for each of the five variables), which report the total giving (monetary giving plus giving in goods) in the form of vertical bars (left-hand y-axis) and simultaneously depict the trends in terms of time volunteered by the household (right-hand y-axis) through the trend-line. This set of graphs tell a much more interesting story in terms of how each of the five variables impacts the trends and tendencies in total household giving and household volunteering.

A number of noteworthy trends and tendencies that emerge from these graphs. The first, most obvious, and entirely unsurprising conclusion that emerges from these numbers is *that total giving (monetary and in-kind) tends to rise with increasing income.* The giving tends to rise sharply for income levels under $100,000 per year but then tends to flatten out for the $100,000-$200,000 per year range. This flattening and the slight dip one notices at the $160,000-$180,000 range may be partly explained by the lower number of responses received in these income ranges. Similarly, the sudden rise in average giving for households earning more than $200,000 per year is explained by the fact that this included respondents with a very wide range of income levels (going up to households with incomes of more than $1 million per year). The point to note here is that, in general, the curve for household monetary giving as a function of household income is fairly smooth and validates the expected correspondence between rising income and a concurrent increase in total household giving.

What is much more noteworthy, and somewhat surprising, in terms of the influence of income levels is that there is no apparent concordance between rising income and the amount of time devoted to volunteering by the household. Indeed, to the extent that one can identify a trend-line within the fluctuating distribution, it would be a rather flat trend-line. This would suggest that *the amount of time volunteered by a household is not significantly influenced by the household's income level.* However, it does suggest (and the accompanying table validates) that lower-income households tend to contribute a much

Table 8: Average Household Giving by Kind and by Demographic Variables

		Giving in Money (Dollars/Year)	Giving in Goods (Dollars/Year)	Giving in Time (Hours/Year)
Age	20-30 years	$ 1,476	$ 323	264 hrs
	30-40 years	$ 2,747	$ 780	326 hrs
	40-50 years	$ 3,828	$ 829	488 hrs
	50-60 years	$ 3,670	$ 773	533 hrs
	60+ years	$ 3,117	$ 642	612 hrs
Education	High School or less	$ 1,062	$ 207	432 hrs
	Bachelors degree	$ 2,249	$ 595	454 hrs
	Masters Degree	$ 4,379	$ 1,000	410 hrs
	PhD and Other	$ 4,440	$ 701	554 hrs
Income	Under $20,000	$ 188	$ 52	558 hrs
	$20,000-$40,000	$ 612	$ 175	279 hrs
	$40,000-$60,000	$ 893	$ 307	425 hrs
	$60,000-$80,000	$ 1,612	$ 393	428 hrs
	$80,000-$100,000	$ 2,597	$ 676	400 hrs
	$100,000-$120,000	$ 4,104	$ 1,292	324 hrs
	$120,000-$140,000	$ 4,518	$ 1,075	551 hrs
	$140,000-$160,000	$ 5,002	$ 937	552 hrs
	$160,000-$180,000	$ 3,884	$ 747	339 hrs
	$180,000-$200,000	$ 4,889	$ 1,000	377 hrs
	Over $200,000	$ 8,491	$ 1,723	540 hrs
Years in the United States	Under 5 years	$ 993	$ 454	282 hrs
	5-10 years	$ 591	$ 343	332 hrs
	10-15 years	$ 1,143	$ 572	421 hrs
	15-20 years	$ 1,638	$ 734	431 hrs
	20-25 years	$ 2,342	$ 1,078	513 hrs
	Over 25 years	$ 2,702	$ 1,235	594 hrs
Participation in Pakistani Community	No Participation	$ 1,197	$ 661	190 hrs
	Infrequent	$ 995	$ 350	312 hrs
	Moderate	$ 1,607	$ 861	415 hrs
	Frequent	$ 1,964	$ 676	525 hrs
	Very Active	$ 2,441	$ 1,303	774 hrs

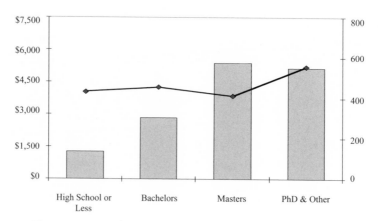

Figure 22a: Impact of Education Level on Trends in Total Giving
Left axis = Household Giving ($/year); *Right axis* = Household Volunteering
(hours/year)

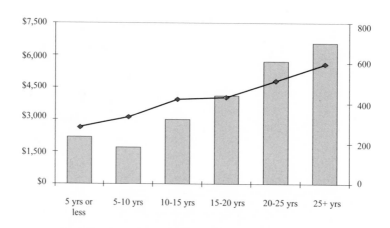

Figure 22b: Impact of Time in USA on Trends in Total Giving
Left axis = Household Giving ($/year); *Right axis* = Household Volunteering
(hours/year)

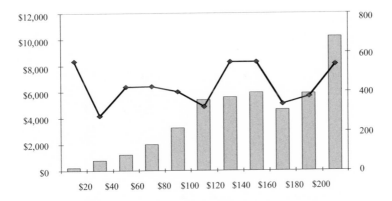

Figure 22c: Impact of Income on Trends in Total Giving
X axis = Household income, in thousands $US/year; *Left axis* = Household
Giving ($/year); *Right axis* = Household Volunteering (hours/year)

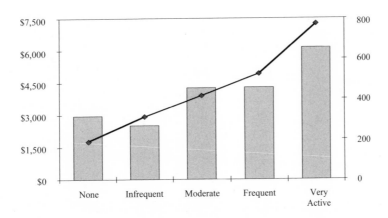

**Figure 22d: Impact of Participation within the Pakistani Community on
Trends in Total Giving**
Left axis = Household Giving ($/year); *Right axis* = Household Volunteering
(hours/year)

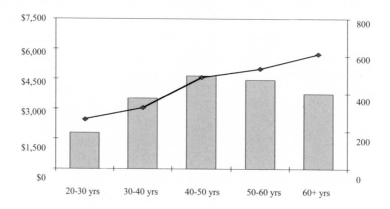

Figure 22e: Impact of Age on Trends in Total Giving
Left axis = Household Giving ($/year); *Right axis* = Household Volunteering
(hours/year)

greater proportion of their overall philanthropy in time rather than in terms of giving money and goods.

Higher levels of education do tend to correspond with higher levels of giving but, once again, there is no apparent correlation between and level of education. Based on insights from the focus groups, it might be suggested that the level of education is so closely associated with income in our sample that the level of education simply becomes a surrogate for income and therefore mimics the latter.

The unsurprising conclusion in terms of the influence of age on giving patterns is that *the level of giving increases steadily up to the 40-50 years range and then declines.* This trend is likely a function of the 40-50 years age range where the earning potential is the highest. What is more interesting to note here is the clear trend line in terms of household time devoted to volunteering. *The amount of time volunteered steadily increases with age.* This suggests that Pakistani-Americans of retirement or near-retirement age are a particularly important asset as volunteers because they combine a high level of experience and expertise with a high desire to give their time and energies to charitable and philanthropic causes, and particularly to the management and activities of Pakistani-American organizations and initiatives.

Our results suggest that *increasing levels of involvement and participation in Pakistani community organizations corresponds with greater total giving.*

This finding is important because it suggests that those who are active in the Pakistani-American community are also likely to be active givers in general and are likely to be responsive to calls for giving to causes in Pakistan as well as to causes unrelated to Pakistan. Not surprisingly, households which are more active in Pakistani community activities are also considerably more active as volunteers.

Arguably the most interesting result emerging from this general analysis of trends and tendencies is that *households with Pakistani-Americans who have lived in the United States longer tend to give more as well as volunteer more than those who have been here shorter durations.* In some cases this may be partly attributable to income increases that can come with longer time periods spent in the US; however, this can only be a partial explanation since longer periods of stay in the US do not always correspond with increasing income. One might speculate that this result is also to be explained by other factors, possibly including a heightened desire to 'return' something to Pakistan as it becomes clear to the immigrant household that they are now less likely to return themselves and developing habits of giving, especially institutional giving and volunteering, based on their host society's trends in America.

Taken together, these findings suggest that while income is an obvious indicator of who is likely to give more, it is also important to look beyond income. Indeed, the level of participation in the Pakistani community, the length of time that a person has been in the United States, and age may all have positive impacts on the time and resources that a household can devote to philanthropy.

Giving by cause

While the trends that we have discussed relate to total giving, let us now turn our attention to how this giving is distributed between causes related to Pakistan (in the United States and in Pakistan) and to those not related to Pakistan.

A first and clear result to report is that *Pakistan and Pakistani causes remain a major focus of giving by Pakistanis in America,* although there is a small but not insignificant minority that shies away from giving to Pakistani causes, or to Pakistani causes in Pakistan. An overwhelming majority (over 90 percent) of our respondents direct some proportion of their philanthropic giving to Pakistani causes—either in Pakistan itself or in the US. Over 80 percent of the respondents give some proportion to causes in Pakistan and as much as

Table 9: Average Household Giving by Cause and by Demographic Variables

For survey respondents; N=461

		Pakistani Causes in Pakistan (Dollars/Year)	Pakistani Causes in the USA (Dollars/Year)	Causes unrelated to Pakistan (Dollars/Year)
Age	20-30 years	$ 821	$ 302	$ 676
	30-40 years	$ 1,530	$ 758	$ 1,239
	40-50 years	$ 1,798	$ 1,093	$ 1,767
	50-60 years	$ 1,489	$ 1,053	$ 1,900
	60+ years	$ 1,403	$ 754	$ 1,602
Education	High School or less	$ 673	$ 125	$ 471
	Bachelors degree	$ 1,055	$ 676	$ 1,112
	Masters Degree	$ 2,112	$ 1,214	$ 2,053
	PhD and Other	$ 1,794	$ 1,216	$ 2,132
Income	Under $20,000	$ 125	$ 63	$ 56
	$20,000-$40,000	$ 488	$ 64	$ 234
	$40,000-$60,000	$ 528	$ 181	$ 491
	$60,000-$80,000	$ 763	$ 346	$ 895
	$80,000-$100,000	$ 1,349	$ 759	$ 1,165
	$100,000-$120,000	$ 1,982	$ 1,249	$ 2,165
	$120,000-$140,000	$ 2,248	$ 917	$ 2,428
	$140,000-$160,000	$ 2,332	$ 1,075	$ 2,533
	$160,000-$180,000	$ 1,794	$ 1,197	$ 1,640
	$180,000-$200,000	$ 2,631	$ 1,507	$ 1,751
	Over $200,000	$ 3,635	$ 2,893	$ 3,686
Years in the United States	Under 5 years	$ 1,146	$ 630	$ 417
	5-10 years	$ 927	$ 296	$ 478
	10-15 years	$ 1,298	$ 551	$ 1,148
	15-20 years	$ 1,653	$ 967	$ 1,497
	20-25 years	$ 1,985	$ 1,296	$ 2,431
	Over 25 years	$ 2,016	$ 1,708	$ 2,823
Participation in Pakistani Community	No Participation	$ 1,289	$ 501	$ 1,170
	Infrequent	$ 1,105	$ 221	$ 1,184
	Moderate	$ 1,439	$ 973	$ 1,854
	Frequent	$ 1,854	$ 1,172	$ 1,260
	Very Active	$ 2,328	$ 1,859	$ 1,946

65 percent give only to Pakistani causes, and not at all to causes unrelated to Pakistan. There were, however, about 9 percent of our respondents who did not report giving anything at all to Pakistani causes, and just under 13 percent who gave nothing to Pakistani causes in Pakistan.

To delve deeper into these trends, let us begin by looking at the same five variables (age of respondent, education level of respondent, household income, how long the respondent has lived in the USA, and the level of participation in Pakistani community organizations and events), but instead of focusing on the type of giving we will focus on how the total giving (monetary and in-kind) is distributed between causes related to Pakistan in Pakistan, to causes related to Pakistan in the United States, and to other causes. The numbers used in Table 9 aggregate the total giving (monetary plus in-kind) and then report on how this giving is distributed between these three types of causes. Once again, all numbers have been rounded off.

To facilitate a discussion that focuses on the distribution of the giving along the three broad causes we will focus only on the total giving (monetary plus in-kind) that goes to each cause. Of particular interest is how much of the total contribution goes to Pakistani causes as opposed to causes unrelated to Pakistan; and also within the contribution going to Pakistani causes, how much goes to causes in Pakistan and how much goes to Pakistani causes in America.

Obvious as it might be, the very first conclusion that is immediately apparent is that for each variable and for each category within each variable, Pakistani-Americans distribute their overall giving across the three broad categories. A closer examination of the data shows that the vast majority of our respondents do, in fact, give to all three types of causes. This is significant because *it demonstrates the portrait of a community that is comfortable in maintaining, and in contributing to, its multiple identities.* It presents us with an image of a diaspora that continues to feel the pull of its original homeland (as demonstrated through its giving to Pakistani causes in Pakistan), is eager to serve as an ambassador for that identity (as evidenced by its giving to Pakistani causes in America), and is also active in the civic life of its new adopted home.

In terms of the influence of income levels on the distribution of total giving by cause, it is difficult to identify any strong trend or tendency. What may be more interesting here is the trend that is not apparent in the distribution. Contrary to what one might have assumed, the proportion of giving to Pakistani causes in general and to Pakistani causes in Pakistan in particular does *not* go down with increasing income levels. Indeed, it seems that for a very large segment of our respondents (all income levels upwards of $40,000 per year) about 40% of their total contribution is directed towards Pakistani causes in Pakistan. Although there are appreciable fluctuations in how the total giving gets divided between the three causes, it is noteworthy that there are no massive shifts from one type of cause to another with increasing income levels. This becomes more apparent as one looks at the underlying numbers presented in the accompanying table.

Two important observations emerge from looking at the distribution by levels of education of the respondent. First, there is a difference between the giving behavior of those who have a college education and those who do not. Pakistani-Americans having a college education (Bachelors, Masters, PhD or other professional degrees) tend to behave very similarly, indeed, nearly identically. About 40% of their total giving goes to Pakistani causes in Pakistan, another 20% to Pakistani causes in America, and the remaining 40% to causes unrelated to Pakistan. What is striking about the distribution of giving for respondents without college education (high school or less) is that it is both different and similar to the giving by more educated respondents in interesting ways. It is different in that much more of their contributions (more than 50%) go directly to Pakistan; it is similar in that about the same proportions (around 40%) goes to causes unrelated to Pakistan. The real difference, then, is that *less educated respondents tend to give far less to Pakistani causes in America than their more educated compatriots.*

No dominant trend seems to be evident in terms of the impact of age on the distribution of total giving. By and large, the distribution of giving remains consistent across different age-groups. Although there is a very slight increase in giving directed to causes unrelated to Pakistan for respondents aged 50 years and above, the numbers available to us do not suggest a clear trend. Again, the big news here might just be the consistency: that age does not influence the distribution of giving, and Pakistani-Americans of all ages seem to be fairly consistent about how they distribute their total giving between Pakistani causes in Pakistan, Pakistani causes in the USA, and causes unrelated to Pakistan.

A more differentiated picture emerges when one considers the influence of the level of participation in the Pakistani community and its events on the distribution of giving. *Households who participate more vigorously in community activities not only tend to give more (as noted earlier) but also tend to give more to causes related to Pakistan, than those who are less active.* Not surprisingly—since the participation being measured is in Pakistani organizations in the US—a greater proportion of their giving for Pakistan-related causes is directed to Pakistani causes in America (as opposed to those in Pakistan). However, since respondents who are more active in the Pakistani community are also giving more in real terms, the net impact is that even though a larger proportion of their overall giving goes to Pakistani causes *in the US*, the amount going to Pakistani causes *in Pakistan*, as well as the amount going to causes unrelated to Pakistan, is also greater for this group than for those who are less active in the Pakistani community.

This trend is better illustrated in Figure 23, which plot the amounts given for each cause, rather than the proportion given. An interesting element in this particular picture is that at the other end of the spectrum the level of giving for respondents who reported no participation at all in Pakistani community organizations is higher than one might have expected. Based on our focus group discussions, this may be explained by the fact that our sample included a small number of very affluent and high-value givers who were very interested in giving to Pakistani causes, but not particularly active in the Pakistani community. Although we are unable to statistically verify this, our assessment is that although the number of such households is fairly small, their impact can be quite large because they tend to be extremely affluent and demonstrate a tendency for high-value giving.

The clearest trend in this discussion relates to the duration of time that the respondents have been living in the United States. Our data quite clearly suggests that *although the overall level of giving increases proportionally with the duration of time that a respondent has lived in the United States, the proportion of this amount that goes to causes that are not related to Pakistan also increases.* It is quite clear that the pull of causes other than those related to the 'mother country' increases with time. As people get more comfortable in their adopted country, raise families in the communities they have migrated into, and become more familiar with their new neighbors and more rooted in their neighborhoods, they also enlarge the areas and issues that they are philanthropically interested in.

In plotting the real amounts going to each of the causes, we find that even as the *proportion* of contributions going to causes unrelated to Pakistan increase, the actual amounts going to Pakistan-related causes (in Pakistan and in America) does *not* decrease (see Figure 23). Again, this is principally because there is a trend for the overall giving to increase with the duration of time that a respondent has lived in the United States. In short, more and more of the additional amount of giving is directed towards causes unrelated to Pakistan, but the amount directed to Pakistan-related causes tends not to decrease.

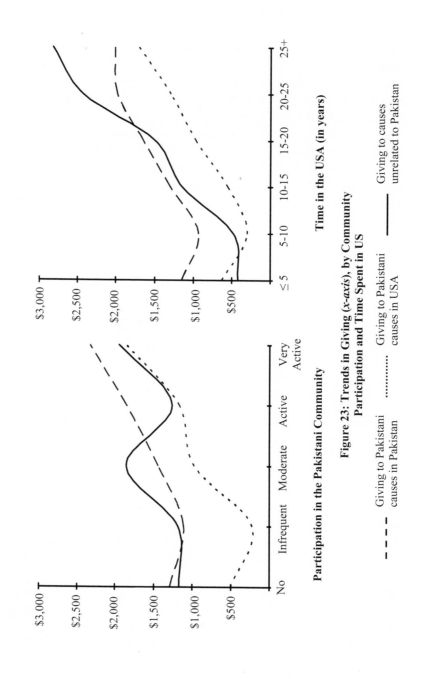

Participation in the Pakistani Community

Time in the USA (in years)

**Figure 23: Trends in Giving (x-*axis*), by Community
Participation and Time Spent in US**

Giving to Pakistani
causes in Pakistan

Giving to Pakistani
causes in USA

Giving to causes
unrelated to Pakistan

Giving by issues

Let us now turn our attention to the issues that inspire the giving patterns of Pakistanis in America. What are the types of issues that Pakistanis in America tend to support with their philanthropic giving? Are the issues they support through their giving in Pakistan different from the issues they support through their giving outside of Pakistan? (See Table 10)

Our survey asked respondents to identify the three most important issues that they usually contribute to. An overwhelming result that emerges is that *social issues—including poverty reduction and helping the needy, education, health, etc.—are by far the most important issues for Pakistanis in America.* Looking first at overall results for the entire sample, we find that the issue of poverty and helping the needy emerges as the top priority for Pakistanis in America, with 29 percent of our respondents including it as one of their top three most important issues.[97] Each of two issues—civil and human rights and religion—are identified by about a quarter of our respondents as amongst the most important issues that they contribute to. It should be noted that here they are referring to religion as an issue that they give to rather than as a motivation that inspires them to give. Following closely behind are the issues of education and literacy and of community development, which are identified by 21 and 18 percent, respectively, as being amongst their top three most important issues in terms of philanthropic giving.

What is even more interesting, however, is how this list gets shuffled when we try to look at the most important issues by cause.

Pakistani causes in the United States

It is not surprising at all that community development (meaning the development of the Pakistani community in the USA) is identified by 36 percent of our respondents as amongst the most important issues in terms of their giving to Pakistani causes in the US. Like many other immigrant communities, the desire to maintain a sense of cultural and community identity and to impart that sense to one's future generations is a paramount goal for Pakistanis in America.

What is more interesting is that as much as 34% of our respondents list civil and human rights as one of their most important issues in this category. This is quite obviously a result of the post-9/11 climate of fear that Muslim-Americans find themselves in and the mounting threats that they perceive to

Table 10: Issues that Pakistanis in America Consider Most Important

Percentage of respondents who considered this to be one of

their three most important issues

(Totals add up to more than 100 because each respondent was allowed three choices)

Pakistani causes based in the US	Pakistani causes based in Pakistan	Causes unrelated to Pakistan	TOTAL (across causes)
#1. Community Development (36%)	#1. Poverty/ helping the Needy (62%)	#1. Religion (51%)	#1. Poverty & Helping the Needy (29%)
#2. Civil and Human Rights (34%)	#2. Education and Literacy (39%)	#2. Civil and Human Rights (39%)	#2. Civil and Human Rights (25%)
#3. Poverty/ helping the Needy (18%)	#3. Health (27%)	#3. Community Development (17%)	#3. Religion (25%)
#4. Political Mobilization (17%)	#4. Human Development (12%)	#4. Poverty/helping the Needy (16%)	#4. Education and Literacy (21%)
#5. Arts, Culture & Sports (14%)	#5. Religion (11%)	#5. Political Mobilization (15%)	#5. Community Development (18%)

their civil and human rights.[98] Also of interest in this list is the issue of political mobilization that is considered important by 17 percent of our respondents and comes in at fourth place. Based on the discussions we heard during our focus groups, it is clear that this is a reflection of the perceived need by Pakistani-Americans to become more active citizens in the US political process.

Pakistani causes in Pakistan

When one looks at the issues identified as being most important in terms of Pakistani causes based in Pakistan, the most striking finding is how strongly the Pakistani diaspora is focused on issues related to social development. Not only do 62 percent consider poverty reduction and helping the needy to be amongst their three most important issues for philanthropic giving, it is also that the next three issues—education and literacy (39 percent), health (27 percent), and human development (12 percent)—are also all related to socio-economic development.

Interesting, the issue of religion comes in at a rather distant fifth with only 11 percent of the respondents including it in their top three most important issues for giving to Pakistani causes in Pakistan.

Causes unrelated to Pakistan

The picture becomes different yet again when one looks at the issues that our respondents consider important for causes unrelated to Pakistan. The most often mentioned issue in this category is religion (51 percent). Based on the discussions we heard during the focus group meetings, it is clear that this refers primarily to giving related to the building, running and maintenance of places of worship in the United States. Following rather close behind is the issue of civil and human rights, which is identified by 39 percent of our respondents as being important to them. Community development (17 percent), poverty and helping the needy (16 percent) and political mobilization (15 percent) take the next three slots in this category but each is well behind the leading two issues in terms of how often they are cited as being important.

The mechanics of giving

We will now turn our attention to a number of factors related to what might be called the mechanics of giving. Does the Pakistani diaspora prefer to give directly to individuals or to organized charities? What channels do they use to make their contributions? Who asks Pakistanis in America for their philanthropic dollars? What effect did the events of September 11, 2001 have on the giving patterns of Pakistanis in America? These are some of the questions that we will explore here in light of our survey findings.

A preference for giving directly to individuals
Looking at the institutional mechanisms that Pakistanis in America prefer to give through, one finds *an overall inclination to give directly to individuals in need and an apparent distrust of formalized institutions* whether they be non-governmental organizations, educational institutions, or religious organizations. Our survey asked respondents to list proportions of their overall giving that went to various types of institutional recipients: kinship networks, other needy individuals, informal local and community groups, friends and family for the purpose of passing on to worthy causes, religious organizations, educational institutions, issue/advocacy groups, and other registered charities (see Figure 24). The results of this question very clearly indicate that there is a strong preference on the part of Pakistanis in America to channel their giving to needy individuals, either directly or through kinship networks (in Pakistan). As we will discuss later, this pattern stems both from a distrust of formalized institutions (including NGOs) and from a strongly held belief that direct giving is more efficient in meeting the needs of the poor and will lead to less wastage and a more effective use of their philanthropic contributions.

According to our survey results, 21 percent of our respondents give half or more ('mostly or predominantly') of their household giving to kinship net-

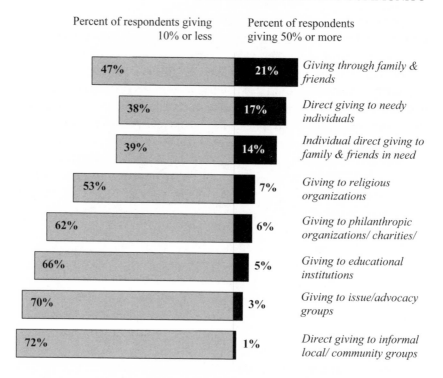

Figure 24: **Who do Pakistanis in America Give to?**

works for that contribution to be passed on to worthy causes and individuals in need. The participants in our focus group discussions made it clear that this was in keeping with the traditional trends in giving in Pakistan and was itself a means of philanthropic accountability.[99] For such givers, a major incentive is that their friends and family can do the 'research' on who is worthy of support, can then provide that support very directly, and can also monitor the use of such contributions. However, in reading these numbers it should also be noted that more than twice as many respondents (47 percent) stated that none or less than 10 percent of their giving is done through this means.

The next two categories on this list are direct giving to extended family and friends in need or to other needy individuals; 17 and 14 percent of respondents, respectively, give half or more of their giving to such needy individuals while about 40 percent of our respondents each give 10 percent or less in these categories. These two categories are better understood together since each is a way of direct giving to needy individuals. Between them, this may be the single most preferred way of giving for those who responded to our survey.

Only 7 percent of our respondents reported giving half or more of their charitable giving to religious organizations, while as many as 53 percent of respondents reported that they give nothing or less than 10 percent to religious organizations. Interestingly, formal philanthropic institutions, charities and NGOs fare equally badly and only 6 percent of our respondents reported channeling half or more of their giving through them and as many as 62 percent say that they give nothing or less than 10 percent through such formal charities. Educational institutions tend to be equally unattractive and advocacy groups and informal community groups fare even worse; 66, 70 and 72 percent, respectively, of our respondents report that they give nothing or less than 10 percent of their giving to these institutions.

More nuance and clarity is added to these results when one juxtaposes them with findings from a different question that directly asked respondents how they distributed their giving between individual and institutional giving (see Figure 25). The striking conclusion here is that *our respondents are much more likely to give directly to individuals when they are giving in Pakistan, but far less likely to do so when they are giving to causes outside of Pakistan.* Indeed, 52 percent of our respondents reported that they gave half or more of their total contribution that was directed to Pakistani causes in Pakistan, directly to individuals in need. By contrast a mere 4 percent and 7 percent say that they give half or more of their giving to Pakistani causes in America and causes unrelated to Pakistan, respectively, as direct contributions to individuals rather than organizations.

Also of note here is that the faith-motivated portion of a household's giving is more likely to be directed to individuals in need than other philanthropic contributions (see Figure 25). Since most (although not all) of our respondents were Muslims, this may be explained by the strong Islamic injunctions about helping individuals in need, and the general view amongst Pakistani Muslims (and certainly a large proportion of our focus group participants) that doing so through direct giving to the needy is preferable to institutional giving to charitable institutions. Although the question was not asked directly in our survey, the numbers do suggest that fairly large proportions of the overall giving to causes in Pakistan goes directly to individuals in need and that faith-motivated portion of giving in the USA tends to go mostly to the building, maintenance and operation of mosques and other places of worship.[100]

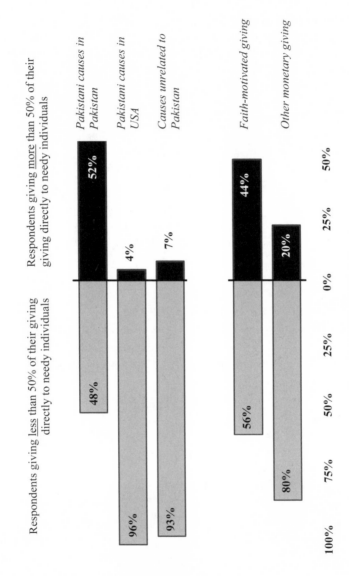

Figure 25: Direct Giving to Needy Individuals

Financial channels

Another question in the survey asked respondents about the financial channels they use in making their contributions (see Figure 26).[101] Within each of the three cause groups, respondents were asked whether they used cash transactions, credit card transactions, or bank transactions in making their monetary contributions.[102] They were asked to check all types that applied to them and, hence, the totals do not add up to 100 percent. The key finding emerging from this question is that bank transactions (bank checks and wire transfers) are the most common channel for financial philanthropic contributions, and is the predominant channel used for contributions to Pakistani causes in America and causes unrelated to Pakistan.

Of respondents who give to Pakistani causes in the USA, 79 percent report using bank transactions for at least some of their contributions; this number is 84 percent for givers to causes unrelated to Pakistan, and 35 percent for givers to Pakistani causes in Pakistan.[103] However, for Pakistani causes in Pakistan, cash contributions remain a popular—and often necessary—channel for philanthropic transfers. Of those who give to Pakistani causes in Pakistan, 87 percent reported that at least some of their contributions were made through cash transactions. By contrast only 43 percent of contributors to Pakistani causes in the US and 37 percent of contributors to causes unrelated to Pakistan reported using any cash transactions.

These results should not be a surprise and should certainly not lead to any unwarranted speculations about intent. Much of the giving in Pakistan tends to be in small amounts and often comes in response to personal appeals—ranging from street beggars to acquaintances in immediate need of relief. Moreover, since documenting philanthropic giving in Pakistan does not offer the same tax incentives as giving in the United States, contributors are less likely to insist on bank or credit card transactions. Finally, and most importantly, this tendency is explained by the fact that bank transfers to Pakistan remain costly and inconvenient and credit cards are still not widely used.

Indeed, the most important implication of this finding is that the difficulties in making bank and credit card transfers to Pakistan is already an important hurdle to giving to causes in Pakistan, and has the potential of becoming a more significant problem for philanthropic organizations in Pakistan since many in the Pakistani diaspora will increasingly prefer using bank and credit card transactions, both because of their convenience and because of post-9/11 concerns.

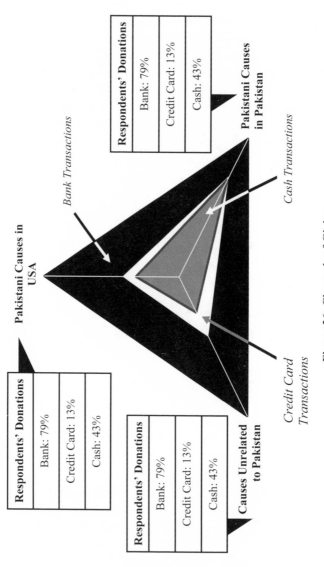

Respondents' Donations

Bank:	79%
Credit Card:	13%
Cash:	43%

Pakistani Causes in USA

Bank Transactions

Respondents' Donations

Bank:	79%
Credit Card:	13%
Cash:	43%

Pakistani Causes in Pakistan

Cash Transactions

Respondents' Donations

Bank:	79%
Credit Card:	13%
Cash:	43%

Causes Unrelated to Pakistan

Credit Card Transactions

Figure 26: Channels of Giving

Areas in the triangle show the relative frequency of each channel mentioned in the responses. The percentages above describe the distribution of giving within each channel. Because respondents could choose more than one channel, the percentages do not add up to 100.

The importance of asking

Another finding that goes to the heart of why charitable organizations in Pakistan may not be doing a good job of reaching the Pakistani diaspora in the United States related to who asks Pakistanis in America for their time, goods or money (see Figure 27 and Figure 28). The results in this case are definitive. *Pakistani causes—whether they are in Pakistan or in the US—simply do not ask the Pakistani diaspora for their contributions as often as causes unrelated to Pakistan.* As many as 81 percent of our respondents reported that they receive three or more requests per month from causes unrelated to Pakistan (equivalent of 36 or more requests per year). By contrast, only 4 percent and 10 percent, respectively, report that they are courted at the same frequency by Pakistani causes in Pakistan or the USA.

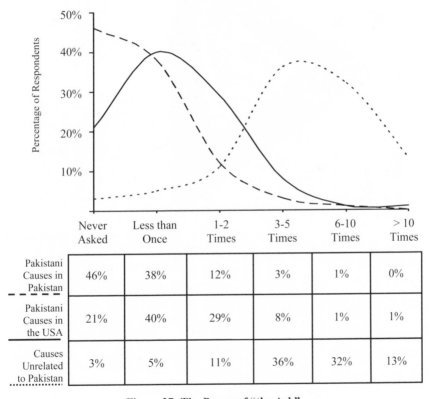

	Never Asked	Less than Once	1-2 Times	3-5 Times	6-10 Times	> 10 Times
Pakistani Causes in Pakistan	46%	38%	12%	3%	1%	0%
Pakistani Causes in the USA	21%	40%	29%	8%	1%	1%
Causes Unrelated to Pakistan	3%	5%	11%	36%	32%	13%

Figure 27: The Power of "the Ask"

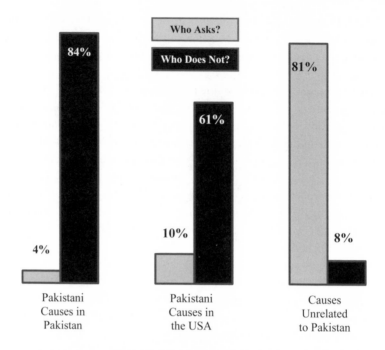

Figure 28: The Power of "the Ask"
Who asks (seen in gray) and who does not (in black)?

However, it is not only that causes unrelated to Pakistan have a high frequency of asking the Pakistani diaspora; it is that the causes related to Pakistan
have a low frequency. As many as 84 percent of our respondents report that on
average they receive less than one – or none – requests to contribute from Pakistani causes in Pakistan.[104] The corresponding number for Pakistani causes in
America is only marginally better, at 61 percent. This is an important finding
worth noting by Pakistani causes and organizations in Pakistan as well as in the
USA because there is clear evidence from national research in the US that
"being asked to give has a strong and significant association with giving behavior" and is amongst the most significant determinants of giving.[105]

The impact of 9/11

A final issue that effects the contemporary mechanics of giving by the Pakistani diaspora in the USA relates to the effect of the 9/11 tragedy and the 'war
on terrorism'. As has been alluded a number of times, the policies put in place

after the 9/11 attacks included a number of steps that called for more vigilance of charitable giving to Muslim organizations. This has understandably triggered much concern within the American-Muslim—including the Pakistani-Muslim—community.

This concern was a central theme of many of our focus group discussions. The fear is centered around the possibility that someone who innocently gives to an organization, believing that it is a legitimate charitable organization, may get into trouble in the future because the organization is later classified as being involved in questionable activities and that this may happen even if the original donor had no knowledge of such activities and had contributed in the belief that the contribution would be used for a worthy cause. Whether warranted or not, the fear is very real and the concern has been that this could dry up the support even for legitimate and worthy organizations that are directly or indirectly associated with Muslim causes.

Although the stated opinion in our focus groups seemed to be divided between those who believed that the events of 9/11 had a very high or rather insignificant impact on the giving patterns of the Pakistani diaspora in America, the result of our survey question on this issue was both surprising and unambiguous (see Figure 29). The response to our survey suggests that *the giving patterns of the majority of Pakistanis in America have remained unchanged since 9/11* and where there has been change, more people have increased their giving since 9/11 rather than decreased it.

The survey questionnaire asked respondents to state whether their household's giving had decreased, increased or stayed the same since September 2001, for each of the three types of causes (Pakistani causes in the USA, Pakistani causes in Pakistan and causes unrelated to Pakistan). In looking at the aggregate of all the responses received across the three cause types, we find that 62 percent of our respondents report that their giving patterns have remained the same, 14 percent report a decrease in their giving, while 24 percent report an increase.[106] In terms of Pakistani causes in Pakistan, the proportion of respondents who reported an increase in their giving was exactly the same as the proportion that reported a decrease (16 percent). The situation was similarly stable in the case of contributions for Pakistani causes in America, where those reporting an increase in giving slightly outnumber those reporting a decrease (20 percent versus 16 percent). Interestingly, however, the number of respondents who report that their contributions to causes unrelated to Pakistan have increased since 9/11 (36 percent) is more than three times the number of respondents who report a decrease in their giving since 9/11 (10 percent).

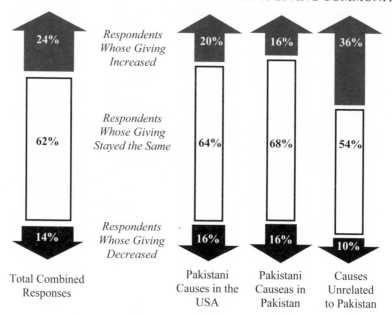

Respondents Whose Giving Increased

Respondents Whose Giving Stayed the Same

Respondents Whose Giving Decreased

Total Combined Responses | Pakistani Causes in the USA | Pakistani Causeas in Pakistan | Causes Unrelated to Pakistan

Figure 29: The 9/11 Effect on Giving by Pakistanis in the USA

Although the survey did not ask any specific questions on this issue, our focus group discussions suggest that this increase is derived largely from the feeling within the Pakistani diaspora that after the events of 9/11 they need to become much more active in community causes within their American neighborhoods than they might have been before.[107] As a result, Pakistanis in America find themselves become more active in community and civic organizations in their neighborhoods. At the same time, one might argue that the events of 9/11 have also heightened the Islamic identity of Pakistani-Muslims and mosques across the country are becoming more vibrant and active venues for social discussions of the role and responsibilities of Muslim-Americans. As such, philanthropic contributions to maintaining and running mosques in America (which would count as causes unrelated to Pakistan) might possibly have also seen an increase. Whether this conjecture is correct or not, it is apparent from our survey results that more Pakistanis have increased their giving since 9/11, and the giving impulse which has seen the greatest increase in this period is for causes unrelated to Pakistan.

CHAPTER #5

Attitudes and preferences

The last two chapters have reported the results of survey questions that asked Pakistani-Americans about their actual giving practices. In this chapter we turn our attention to the philanthropic attitudes and preferences of Pakistanis in America. The issues discussed here are similar, but the focus this time is not on their philanthropic practice, but on their philanthropic beliefs.

The survey questions that we are analyzing in this chapter asked respondents to rate a large number of statements in terms of (a) the importance of various practical factors in influencing their philanthropic decisions, (b) what reasons for giving they find most compelling, (c) the effectiveness of various fundraising methods, (d) their general opinion about philanthropic organizations and NGOs in Pakistan, (e) their sense of the potential for more giving by the Pakistani diaspora in America to philanthropic causes in Pakistan, and (d) their views on what type of measures are most likely to encourage greater philanthropy by the Pakistani diaspora for Pakistani organizations and causes.

It should be noted that the questions and their responses noted in this chapter mostly pertain to institutional (as opposed to direct individual) giving, and a number of them are specific to institutional giving to causes that pertain to, or are in Pakistan.

Why people give

Earlier chapters have looked at the macro-level motivations that propel the philanthropic generosity of Pakistanis in America. In this section we will explore the question of motivation further and in greater depth

The survey questionnaire directly tackled the question of motivation and asked respondents how important each of a set of motivations was in making their philanthropic decisions. They were asked to rate a set of given statements on a five-point scale ranging from 'very high importance' to 'no importance'.

Figure 30 is based on the proportion of respondents who rated the given statements either as being of high to very high importance, or of low to no importance.[108]

The results from this analysis highlight a number of interesting findings, the most important of which is one that was hinted at but not fully discussed through the data presented earlier. *The single most important philanthropic impulse on the generosity of Pakistanis in America is a desire to directly help individuals in need,* including friends and extended family in their kinship networks. Nearly 80 percent of our respondents rated the desire to directly help individuals in need as being of 'high' or 'very high' importance for them and only 4 percent considered this to be of 'low' or 'no' importance. In fact, the second highest ranked category is directly related and only amplifies this result, with nearly 70 percent of our respondents ranking the ability to help their kinship networks (friends and extended family) as being of 'high' or 'very high' importance to them. The only surprise here is that, contrary to what one might have assumed, there is a notable minority (over 10 percent) that considers assistance to kinship networks as being of 'low' or 'no importance.'

In terms of the role of faith as a motivator of giving, it is not a surprise (given what we have already found from other parts of the survey) that over 60 percent of our respondents believe that their religious obligation to give is a major motivation of their philanthropy. What is striking and noteworthy, however, is that *one in five of all respondents believes that the religious duty to give is of 'low' or 'no' importance to their philanthropic decisions.* This should be contextualized with the response to a different statement on this question which referred to causes related to one's religious identity. Interestingly, about as many respondents (a little more than a third each) consider giving to religious causes to be of 'high' or 'very high' importance as those who consider it to be of 'no' or 'low' importance.

Indeed, community motivations seem to be as strong a pull as faith-based motivations. Nearly as many people listed the desire to return something to the community they grew up in as being of 'high' or 'very high' importance to them as those who rated the religious duty to give as an important motivator. More tellingly, the number of respondents who felt that giving back to the community they grew up in is of 'no' or 'low' importance is notably lower than those who rank the religious duty to give as a low motivation. It becomes even more clear that community is a strong motivator of philanthropy by Pakistanis in America as one looks at some of the other results from this question. It is not just that our respondents place value on giving back to the community they grew up in, but more than half (54 percent) also consider giving to the community they now live in as being of 'high' or 'very high' importance. In defining the notion of community more broadly, the same number of respondents (54 percent) consider philanthropy directed at issues important to Pakistan's development to be important to them.

Other possible motivations fail to garner clear enthusiasm from our respondents. Giving to important global issues on the one hand, and giving to religious causes on the other, both show very mixed results with about as many respondents rating these as important motivations as those who did not. What is striking, however, is the very obvious lack of enthusiasm for giving to educational institutions. Nearly half of our respondents felt that returning something to the educational institution they had attended was of 'no' or 'low' importance to them; under 30 percent felt that it was of 'high or 'very high importance'.

This is rather surprising given that one of the most important assets that Pakistani-American professionals (for example, doctors, engineers, etc.) tend to bring with them from Pakistan when they come to the US is their education and training. Arguably, this may also be a function of the fact that (according to many of our focus group participants) most Pakistanis in America are never asked to contribute by the educational institutions they attended in Pakistan. Except for a handful of institutions such as the Lahore University of Management Sciences (LUMS) or the Aga Khan University (AKU), a culture of giving to educational institutions—or even considering these as potential recipients of one's philanthropy—has not really developed amongst the Pakistani diaspora in America. Indeed, more of our focus group participants reported giving back something to the universities they attended in the US than to the institutions they went to in Pakistan.

What makes people give

If motivations are the things that *pull* people towards giving by resonating with the reasons they consider worthy of their philanthropic support, there are also a set of more practical considerations—such as simply how easy or difficult it is to give to a particular cause or organization—that *push* people to convert their intention to give into an actual contribution. We will now turn our attention to these practical motors of philanthropy. What are the types of things that can

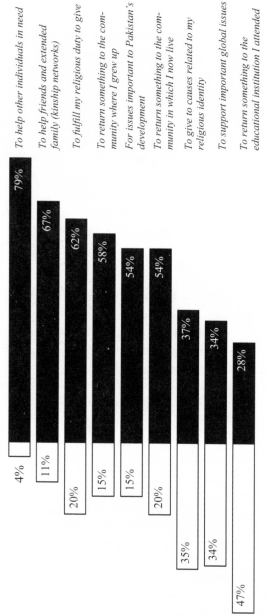

Figure 30: Reasons to Give

The importance of different factors, seen in the issues listed above on the right, in donors' philanthropic decisions.

turn a person's well-meaning desire to be philanthropic into an actual act of philanthropy?

The obvious place to begin exploring this question is to look at our respondents' attitudes to different methods of fundraising. The survey questionnaire presented our respondents with a list of fundraising methods and asked them to rate the effectiveness of each method on a five-point scale ranging from 'very highly effective' to 'not effective'. The critical lesson to be drawn from the analysis of the responses received is clear even from a cursory glance at the accompanying figure (see Figure 31). *Nothing is as effective in raising funds for an organization or cause as personal testimonials and appeals by friends and family in the US or in Pakistan.* Again, we seem to be confirming the adage that 'people do not give to organizations, people give to people.' This result is not surprising, but the intensity with which this view is held is compelling. It is not only that about 65 percent of our respondents consider fundraising appeals by friends and family to be 'highly' or 'very highly' effective, it is also that if we include those who rated these as 'effective' the total number jumps up to over 85 percent.

To an appreciable extent, visits by representatives of the organizations allow people to get a more detailed picture of what the organization is doing and to develop a sense of comfort with the organization that is seeking their support. However, there is lingering skepticism about such visits which were described by one of our focus group participants as "marketing and sales routines." Hence, we see that although 70 percent of respondents do consider these effective to some degree, only 32 percent feel that they are 'highly' or 'very highly' effective. The methods that are probably the most commonly used—cultural events, formal fundraiser events, and celebrity endorsements—seem to solicit only lukewarm approval. In each of these cases, around 20 percent of our respondents do consider these to be 'highly' or 'very highly' effective, but as many as 40 to 50 percent feel they are either 'not effective' or only 'slightly effective'.

Interestingly, *many of the methods that are most popular for fundraising by US organizations—websites, membership dues, mass mailing, media advertising, phone requests and pledges, and email solicitations—receive little enthusiasm from Pakistani-Americans.* Membership dues, mass mailings, media advertising, and phone pledge drives are all immensely popular and powerful fundraising tools for US charitable organizations. Yet, the percentage of our respondents who considered any of these to be 'highly' or 'very highly' effective was in the single digits. In each case, between 60 percent (for membership dues) to 75 percent (for phone pledge drives) of our respondents found these to be either not effective at all or only 'slightly' effective.

Email solicitations received the most negative reaction with over 80 percent of the respondents considering these to be not effective or only 'slightly' effective. This sentiment was also vociferous in the focus groups where a strong case was made many times that email solicitation may not only be ineffective for fundraising, but actually detrimental to an organization's image unless a giving relationship has already been developed through other means between the individual and the organization. Illustrative of this strong view is the fact (not shown in the figure) that as many as 53 percent of the respondents believe that this method is simply 'not effective'. A key factor behind this is the fact that people's emails are already bombarded with too many unsolicited and sometimes unwelcome messages and they consider most mass-mailed emails to be intrusions on their time and private life. This may also be a reason behind the more surprising aversion to phone requests and pledge drives. In this case 45 percent of the respondents found phone pledge drives to be not effective at all. The focus group discussions alerted us to the nuanced view that for many Pakistani-Americans an unsolicited telephone pledge call from another Pakistani is more uncomfortable because the cultural affinity and formality makes it more difficult to say no.

It should be noted, however, that the reaction to websites was not as definitive as to emails. Some 45 percent of our respondents do find these websites to be effective fundraising tools, if only because of the information contained there. Of those who do not, only 25 percent stated categorically that these are 'not effective'. Deciphering this response in the context of responses to other questions discussed later in this chapter, it seems that there is a significant cohort that does find websites a potentially useful device that can assist in fundraising. Our focus group discussions further substantiate the view that although many are still uncomfortable about giving money through a website in general using e-commerce transactions, there is a growing number of people who will look at websites to develop the sense of comfort and trust they need before they contribute through other means. Although the survey results predate the 2005 earthquake in Pakistan, that may well have been a pivotal experience in the community's philanthropic experience in terms of the use of websites for garnering philanthropic information as well as for making philanthropic contributions. As we noted in Chapter #2, a number of institutional and informational websites became the real hub of philanthropic activity amongst Pakistani-Americans in the immediate aftermath of the earthquake.

Respondents' rating of effectiveness:

'Not Effective' or 'Slightly Effective'   'Effective'   'Highly Effective' or 'Very Highly Effective'

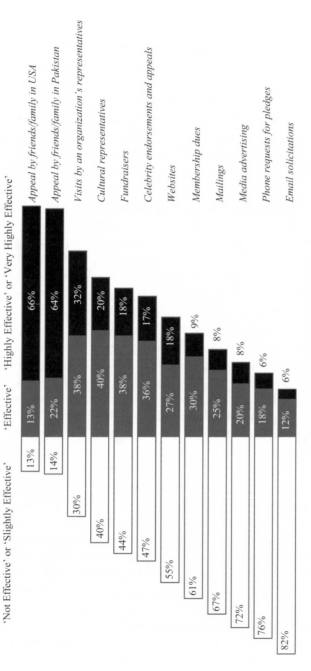

Figure 31: Fundraising Options
The effectiveness of certain fundraising options

Catalysts of institutional giving

The second question we will report on asked Pakistani-Americans to rate a large number of practical factors that might influence their decision to give to institutions on a five-point scale ranging from 'very high importance' to 'no importance'. Figure 32 reports on the percentage of respondents who rated each factor either at the 'low' or 'no' importance level or at the 'high' or 'very high' importance levels.[109] The first, and quite overwhelming, finding from this particular question reinforces what we have also learnt earlier, including in the last section. For an overwhelming proportion (82 percent) of Pakistani-Americans *the single most important factor is the assurance that a large portion of their contribution would go directly to intended beneficiaries.* This not only validates the earlier emphasis on the most direct possible giving to individuals in need but also points towards the lurking distrust (as we will discuss later) of institutionalized philanthropy and the generally held feeling that many organized charities and NGOs are wasteful of resources.[110]

The quality of the people who work for an organization comes in at a rather distant but still impressive second position with nearly 70 percent of our respondents rating this as of 'high' or 'very high' importance to them and only 10 percent feeling that it is of 'low' or 'no' importance. This, again, probably speaks to the well-known adage that people do not give to causes, people give to people. Giving further credence to this view is the fact that over half the respondents (55 percent) considered an organization's reputation to be critical to their giving decisions, and similar proportions consider the recommendation of friends and family in Pakistan (55 percent) and in America (50 percent) to be a critical input for their giving decisions. Given the acute crisis of trust in Pakistani institutions in general, including nongovernmental organizations (NGOs), the importance placed on individuals and on reputations becomes central for the diaspora community. In essence, and not surprisingly, *people tend to listen most to the people they trust the most.*

Results described in the previous chapter had suggested that the events of September 11, 2001 have made the Pakistani diaspora more vigilant but not less giving. This vigilance is also apparent in the responses to this question. For example, over half of our respondents believe that an organization's being officially registered in the United States is of 'high' or 'very high' importance to them.[111] Slightly under half (45 percent) give similar importance to the ease of making financial transfers to that organization. It is surprising, however, that in both cases nearly a quarter of the respondents feel that being registered in the USA or ease of financial transfers is of 'no' or 'low' importance to their philanthropic decisions. These responses, however, might be coming from those respondents who either give mostly to organizations in the US or who largely give to their own kinship networks in Pakistan.

Continuing with surprise results, a number of factors listed in the question did not elicit the type of enthusiasm that might have been expected. For example, organizations working in the region that people 'belong to' get only marginal advantage. Only a third of the respondents give high importance to organizations working in the region or locality that they grew up in or 'belong' to, nearly half felt that this was of 'no' or 'low' importance to them. Similarly, nearly half of the respondents felt that getting tax deductions on their contributions was not critical to whether they gave or not; however, for a significant 30 percent this was of 'high' or very high' importance.

A separate analysis of our data suggests that this factor is much more important to higher income bracket givers, who also tend to give higher amounts and therefore can claim higher tax credits. Strikingly, some 43 percent of our respondents feel that celebrity endorsements are not particularly important. Even more conclusive is the finding that the quality of an organization's marketing material is of little importance to just over half of our respondents. Obviously, people would much rather focus on the quality of the individuals in the organization than on the marketing material. A quite conclusive finding is that most respondents (66 percent) do not consider the size of the organization that is seeking support to be important. This is important in that it implies that even though reputation is a key factor, size is not necessarily a limitation in an organization's success in raising support from the Pakistani diaspora in the USA.

The centrality of institutional trust

An overall theme that emerges from the preceding analysis is the critical importance of trust and comfort in the organization that one is being asked to give to. Factors that can help inspire trust in an organization become critical to the actual giving decisions of Pakistanis in America. As we noted, more than half of our respondents (55 percent) consider an organization's reputation to be critical to their giving decisions. Arguably, being already registered in the US (rated highly by 54 percent), providing regular financial and performance reports (rated highly by 43 percent), and being able to visit and review the operations of the organization (rated highly by nearly 40 percent) all contribute to

Respondents' rating of importance in donation decision:

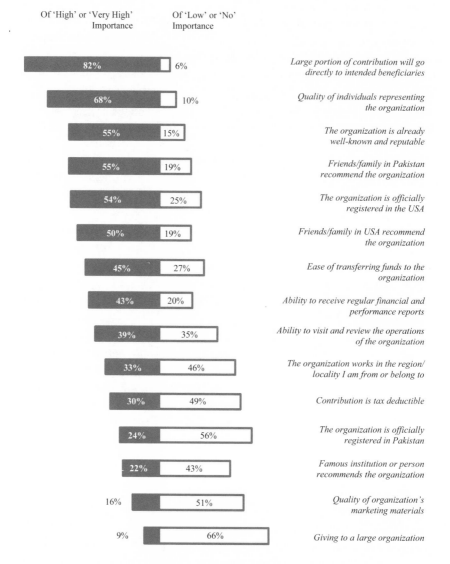

Of 'High' or 'Very High'   Of 'Low' or 'No'
        Importance   Importance

82%	6%	*Large portion of contribution will go directly to intended beneficiaries*
68%	10%	*Quality of individuals representing the organization*
55%	15%	*The organization is already well-known and reputable*
55%	19%	*Friends/family in Pakistan recommend the organization*
54%	25%	*The organization is officially registered in the USA*
50%	19%	*Friends/family in USA recommend the organization*
45%	27%	*Ease of transferring funds to the organization*
43%	20%	*Ability to receive regular financial and performance reports*
39%	35%	*Ability to visit and review the operations of the organization*
33%	46%	*The organization works in the region/ locality I am from or belong to*
30%	49%	*Contribution is tax deductible*
24%	56%	*The organization is officially registered in Pakistan*
22%	43%	*Famous institution or person recommends the organization*
16%	51%	*Quality of organization's marketing materials*
9%	66%	*Giving to a large organization*

Figure 32: Catalysts of Giving
Practical factors in philanthropic decisions

the building of this trust and, therefore, garner important support from our respondents. However, it should be noted that institutional trust does not come easily. As we saw, nearly as many respondents consider the ability to visit and review the operations of an organization as being of little importance, as those who believe it to be critical. Slightly more than half give 'no' or 'low' importance to marketing material from organizations and as many as 43 percent of the respondents choose to give little importance to famous institutions or persons recommending the organization. While these numbers have other significance, they also reflect the views of those many participants in our focus groups who expressed serious concerns about both the ability and sincerity of philanthropic institutions and NGOs in Pakistan.

It is this rather disturbing reputation that NGOs and philanthropic organizations in Pakistan have developed that was the subject of the next question we will report on. In this query, we asked our survey respondents to react to a set of statements about philanthropic organizations and NGOs on a four-point scale ranging from strong disagreement with the given statement to strong agreement. Figure 33 reports of the views of all respondents who expressed an opinion by either disagreeing or strongly disagreeing with the given statement, or agreeing or strongly agreeing.[112] The question was phrased to focus on what the diaspora feels about the sector in general in Pakistan, and not on particular organizations.[113]

The answers received to this question are both surprising and compelling. In essence, *the Pakistani diaspora in America simply does not have much trust in NGOs and philanthropic organizations in Pakistan.* Even though they hold certain organizations in very high regard—the institutional names mentioned most often in our focus groups included the Human Development Foundation of North America (HDFNA), Development in Literacy (DIL), and The Citizen's Foundation (TCF), and the individual names mentioned most often were of Abdul Sattar Edhi and Imran Khan—they are not impressed by what the sector as a whole does or has achieved.

Of those who gave an opinion on this question, over 80 percent 'disagreed' or 'strongly disagreed' with the statement that philanthropic organizations (including NGOs) working in Pakistan use money efficiently and for good use; another 80 percent were equally opposed to the proposition that these organizations are honest and ethical in their use of donated funds; over 70 percent each disagreed with the proposition that they are effective or that they are working on important issues that need attention. This is a serious indictment and suggests that *very large segments of the diaspora Pakistanis per-*

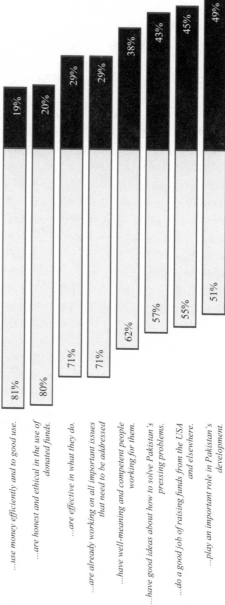

Question: *In general, philanthropic organizations in Pakistan...*

'Disagree' or 'Strongly Disagree'   'Agree' or 'Strongly Agree'

...use money efficiently and to good use.   81%   19%

...are honest and ethical in the use of donated funds.   80%   20%

...are effective in what they do.   71%   29%

...are already working on all important issues that need to be addressed   71%   29%

...have well-meaning and competent people working for them.   62%   38%

...have good ideas about how to solve Pakistan's pressing problems.   57%   43%

...do a good job of raising funds from the USA and elsewhere.   55%   45%

...play an important role in Pakistan's development.   51%   49%

Figure 33: A Crisis of Trust

Individuals' opinions of NGOs and philanthropic organizations in Pakistan *ceive the majority of philanthropic and nongovernmental organizations in Pakistan to be (a) inefficient, (b) ineffective, (c) unethical, and (d) inattentive to the most pressing issues that need attention.* This is not the image that these organizations would like to cultivate and, more importantly, this is not the profile of organizations that are likely to inspire philanthropic giving by Pakistanis in America. It may also be a grossly unfair characterization. Yet, it is a perception that was deep-rooted not only in the survey results but also during the focus group discussions. This perception is clearly an important impediment to institutional giving in Pakistan and needs to be addressed before more significant resources can flow from the Pakistani diaspora to civil society organizations in Pakistan.

The opinions were less stark in terms of whether these organizations have well-meaning and competent people working for them or whether they have good ideas about how to solve Pakistan's pressing problems. However, in both cases around 60 percent of our respondents 'disagreed' or 'strongly disagreed' with these propositions. The fact that significant minorities do believe that the sector has well-meaning and competent people working in it who do have good ideas about Pakistan's development is a silver lining, even if a small one.

On two other statements, the opinion of our respondents was more evenly split – even though in both these cases a slight majority actually chose to 'disagree' or 'strongly disagree' with these sentiments. Nearly as many respondents 'agreed' or strongly agreed' with the view that the nongovernmental sector plays an important role in Pakistan's development as those who 'disagreed' or 'strongly disagreed'. And at least 45 percent 'agreed' or 'strongly agreed' with the view that these organizations do a good job of raising funds in the United States. Both of these, however, are restrained compliments. For example, a number of our focus group participants believe that these organizations end up playing a role in Pakistan's development mostly because other institutions—and particularly the government—do such a bad job of fulfilling their developmental responsibilities.

An image problem for NGOs

It should also be noted that the impression received from the focus group is that the Pakistani diaspora lacks faith not just in the nongovernmental sector in Pakistan, but in all institutions in Pakistan. Between them, the reactions received on these last four statements suggest that there is room for improving the sector's image amongst the Pakistani diaspora, but the sector does have an image building challenge ahead of it.

A few additional points should be kept in mind as we interpret these results. First, it was clear to the respondents that they were being asked to give their views on the Pakistani philanthropic sector as a whole and the collectivity of such organizations rather than about particular organizations. In a number of cases, our respondents made clear (either verbally or by writing notes on the survey forms) that whatever views they were expressing related to such organizations 'in general' and not to particular organizations they knew of. Indeed, it is noteworthy that, based on the focus group discussions, *most people seemed to have a largely negative impression of Pakistani NGOs in general but a largely positive impression of those NGOs that they had themselves come into contact with.* This suggests a serious image problem for the NGO sector in Pakistan that deserves attention and which is eroding faith in the efficacy and sincerity of civil society in Pakistan.[114]

A second point to note is that all eight statements that were tested were worded positively. The fact that most respondents still chose to record very negative impressions is noteworthy. More noteworthy, however, is the fact (not apparent in the accompanying figure) that for each of the eight statements, the number of respondents who *strongly* disagreed with the statement was significantly more than those who *strongly* agreed. In essence, not only do more respondents lack trust in the NGO sector, but those who are critical tend to be very strongly critical while those who are supportive are only mildly supportive. For example, only 3 percent of those who responded, articulated *strong agreement* with the view that NGOs and philanthropic organizations are honest and ethical in their use of donated funds; however, as many as 27 percent *strongly disagreed* with this sentiment. Similarly, only 4 percent said that they *strongly agreed* with the view that in general these organizations used the resources donated to them efficiently and for good use; however, more than 25 percent *strongly disagreed* with this view. It should be disturbing to those in the sector that their distracters hold much stronger opinions about the sector than their supporters.

Finally, by way of comparison it should be stressed that the trend emerging from our survey runs contrary to the general trend around the world.[115] Civil society organizations, and especially charitable organizations, tend to usually have a mostly positive image in society. For example, a similar survey of philanthropic attitudes of the entire US population found that over 70 percent felt that the need for such organizations was more compelling than before,

68 percent believed that most organizations are honest in their use of donated funds, and 82 percent believed that these organizations play an important role in speaking out on important issues.[116] Although our questions are somewhat different, the stark comparison between the generally very positive impression that Americans have of American organizations and the generally very negative impression that Pakistani-Americans have of Pakistani organizations is thought provoking. The finding that the Pakistani diaspora in the United States has such a low opinion of the sector makes one wonder whether Pakistanis in Pakistan feel the same way; after all, the opinion of the Pakistani diaspora is most influenced by the views of their friends, family and the media *in* Pakistan.

Actualizing the giving potential

The final set of questions on our survey related specifically to the attitudes of Pakistanis in America about giving to Pakistani causes, especially in Pakistan itself. The obvious and immediate question that any philanthropic organization in Pakistan might ask itself are (a) whether there is potential for increased giving to Pakistani causes, and (b) to the extent this potential exists, how can it be harnessed. We asked these very questions to our survey respondents, and this section will report on the answers we received.

Giving potential

One of our survey questions asked respondents to think about the future prospects and potential for increased giving to Pakistan-related causes (see Figure 34). The question asked people to answer first in terms of the conditions under which their own future giving might increase (or not) and then to also respond in terms of what they thought about the overall future giving potential of the Pakistani community in the USA as a whole. The most significant finding from this question is both clear and heartening: *an overwhelming majority of our respondents believe that, given the right conditions, their own and the Pakistani community's giving to Pakistan-related causes can increase significantly.*

Overall, as many as 83 percent of our respondents believe that their own giving to Pakistan-related causes can increase significantly and 93 percent feel that if the right conditions were in place the overall Pakistan-related giving by the Pakistani community in America could be significantly higher. It is interesting, however, that while 17 percent of our respondents believe that their giving to Pakistan-related cases "is already as high as it could be and is unlikely to increase unless income increases dramatically", only 7 percent feel that the US-based Pakistani diaspora in general has reached this saturation point in giving.[117]

For those who do believe that the diaspora's giving can increase significantly, *the single most important condition that has to be met before the giving to Pakistani-related causes increases is the creation of greater trust in Pakistani philanthropic organizations and NGOs.*[118] One half of all respondents feel that their own as well as the community's giving to Pakistan related causes could increase significantly but only if they had more trust that their contributions would be put to good use. Logistical difficulties in giving to Pakistan-related causes and the lack of information about such causes were also identified as key hurdles that will need to be overcome before a greater flow of philanthropic giving happens from the Pakistani diaspora in America. Between 20 and 25 percent of those who felt that there is potential for a significantly increased giving to Pakistani causes identified these two factors as the most important likely facilitators of increased giving.

It should be stressed, however, that our respondents set a high bar for the conditions under which their giving to Pakistan-related causes might increase. They are *not* saying that they will automatically give more to such causes in the future. What they are saying is that they would give more to Pakistan-related causes (a) *if* they had more trust that their contributions would be put to good use, (b) *if* it became easier to give to Pakistan-related causes, and (c) *if* they had more and better information about causes in Pakistan. None of these is a small 'if' and it would require some doing to make meet these conditions for increased giving to become possible.

Facilitating more giving

Our next question probed respondents on the relative importance of a set of practical measures that could be used to create these conditions. The question presented the respondents with a list of fifteen possible measures that could be taken to encourage greater philanthropy by the Pakistani diaspora for Pakistani organizations and causes (see Figure 35). It then asked them to rate each on how great a difference each particular measure might make. They were asked to use a five-point scale ranging from 'no difference' to 'great difference'.[119]

A set of six measures—that generally have to do with building greater trust in Pakistani civic organizations and with making giving to Pakistani causes easier—emerge as the top tier of things that the Pakistani diaspora

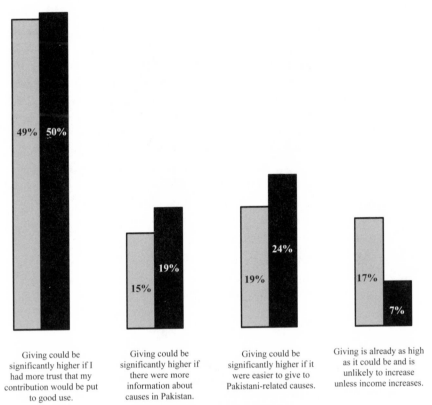

| Giving could be significantly higher if I had more trust that my contribution would be put to good use. | Giving could be significantly higher if there were more information about causes in Pakistan. | Giving could be significantly higher if it were easier to give to Pakistani-related causes. | Giving is already as high as it could be and is unlikely to increase unless income increases. |

Figure 34a: Giving Potential
Potential for an increase in Pakistan-related giving

Respondents' assessment of the future giving potential of the Pakistani diaspora in the USA

Respondents' assessment of their own future giving potential

would like to see getting done. Topmost in people's mind are practical measures that can make giving to Pakistani causes practically easier and clarifying the confusions and misunderstandings that have been created by changes in US regulations related to the 'war on terror'. In particular, according to our respondents, *one of the most important steps that can be taken to encourage greater philanthropy for Pakistan-related causes is to provide greater clarity on US laws and regulations that relate to giving to organizations in Pakistan.* Nearly 70 percent of our respondents feel that such clarity could make a 'significant'

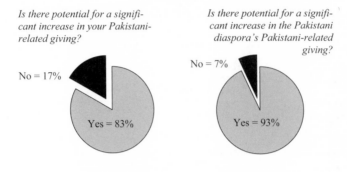

Figure 34b: Giving Potential
Potential for an increase in Pakistan-related giving

or 'great' difference in diaspora philanthropy by Pakistanis in America. Only 14 percent feel that such clarity will make 'no' or only 'slight' difference.

Our focus group discussions suggest that a number of our respondents would like the government of Pakistan to work directly with the US government to define clear and consistent rules about charitable giving to Pakistan, including more general Islamic charities. It was clear that the strong feeling of unease felt by our respondents came not so much from what was in the rules, but from a lack of clarity about what was in the rules. It was repeatedly mentioned that people would feel much more comfortable giving to Pakistani causes if they knew exactly what the rules and regulations were and what they were supposed to do or not to do while making charitable contributions to Pakistan-related causes. In the absence of clear rules, people tend to assume the worst, horror stories get exaggerated, and a general climate of fear and discomfort sets in. For example, at one of our focus groups one participant made a passionate case by asking why "when a corporation breaks a law or does something unethical, the corporation is taken to court and punished, but the shareholders or customers are not; but when [in the post-9/11 world] a charity is found to be diverting the money that was given to it for nefarious purposes, those who had given the money in good faith and with the best intentions are also dragged through the questioning and investigation."

Following close behind, and directly related to this, is the clear call to introduce easier mechanisms for transfer of funds to organizations in Pakistan. As many as 67 percent of our respondents believe that this will make a 'significant' or 'great' difference in how much the Pakistani diaspora gives back to Pakistan-related causes. The focus group discussions suggest that Paki-

Respondents' rating of the impact of potential improvements:

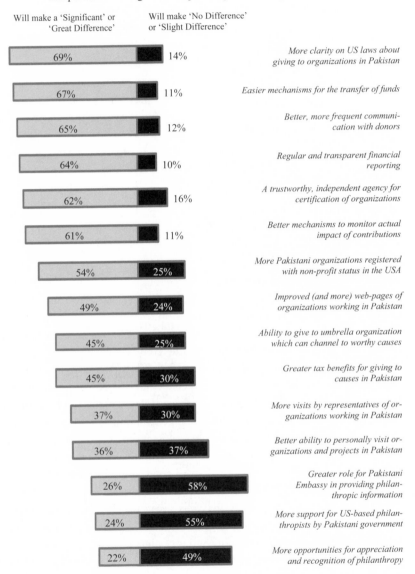

Figure 35: Encouraging Philanthropy
Practical factors in philanthropic decisions

stani-Americans would like to see easier, more accessible and less costly mechanisms for making bank transfers to organizations in Pakistan, and more organizations accepting donations through bank and credit card transactions (especially for smaller amounts). It was repeatedly pointed out that although some bank mechanisms are available, these can become costly if small amounts are being sent regularly. Moreover, many Pakistani organizations do not accept credit card donations and, more importantly, such transactions are not useful when the primary beneficiaries of the philanthropic contribution are needy individuals, as often happens to be the case.

The other four top scoring measures—in each case between 60 and 65 percent of our respondents rated these as measures that can make a 'significant' or 'great' difference—all relate to the creation of greater trust in organizations in Pakistan and in what they are doing. Our respondents felt that the things that can contribute the most to building trust in Pakistani philanthropic organizations and NGOs will include: (a) better and more frequent communication with diaspora donors, (b) regular and transparent financial reporting, (c) a trustworthy and independent agency for the certification of organizations, and (d) better mechanisms to monitor the actual impact of contributions. In essence, our survey respondents are saying that when they make a contribution to an organization in Pakistan they would like to be kept informed of how the contribution is being used and what impact it is having. Because the trust people have in these organizations is fairly low, they are seeking not just information, but *verifiable information from independent sources.*

The importance of regular communication came through clearly from the numbers. However, they are also saying that they particularly want information about how the organization is using its resources and what it is achieving through its actions. A number of our focus group participants pointed out that regular and transparent financial reporting is important not simply because it allows the diaspora donor to keep a tab on the financial health and efficiency of the organization, but even more importantly because an organization's willingness to open its books, to be regularly audited, and to share this information points towards a culture of efficiency and competence.[120] According to one participant, "the very fact that an organization is regularly audited and has a publicly available financial report is as important as what is in that report."

In highlighting the important difference that can be made by having 'a trustworthy, independent certification agency' and also the need for 'better mechanisms to monitor the actual impact of contributions', our respondents are alerting us to the importance of independent quality control. Although these two measures are related, there is a nuanced distinction that needs to be made. In supporting the idea of an independent certification agency, respondents are calling for third-party oversight and outside verification of activities, but they are also insisting that the agency doing the certification has to itself be seen as trustworthy and independent. In this regard, a number of our participants made the point that if such an agency was seen to be lax in its verification and oversight mandate, it could very easily and quickly lose the trust and sense of independence that would be necessary to its success. At the same time, in seeking better mechanisms to monitor the actual impact of contributions, they are sending a signal to organizations as well as their possible certifiers that what is most important to them is not only the financial probity and management efficiency of the organization, but also the charitable impact of their contributions. To put this in the context of other measures discussed here, when they ask for reports of activities, not only do they want to know how their contributions were used, but how that use made a difference in people's lives.

Following at the heel of these top-rated measures is a set of four medium-rated measures that receive more lukewarm responses but where many more people (between 45 and 55 percent) do feel that the measure could make a 'significant' or great' difference than those (between 25 and 30 percent) who think that it can make only 'slight' or 'no' difference. This is an interesting lot because it includes more measures that are frequently discussed as being more important than our survey results seem to imply. An important, but not overwhelming, proportion of our respondents do think that having more Pakistani organizations registered with non-profit status in the US would make a major difference. It is rather striking that as many as 25 percent of our respondents think that this would have 'no' or only a 'slight' effect.

More interestingly, getting greater tax benefits for giving to causes in Pakistan gets a rather tame reaction with as many as 30 percent of the respondents believing that it would make little difference and only 45 percent suggesting that it would make a large impact. This may be explained by the fact that tax benefits make an impact with institutional giving and much of the giving to Pakistan tends to be individual. However, our survey results do suggest (not shown in figure) that higher-income respondents consider tax benefits far more important than lower income respondents. Not surprisingly, of those whose household income is greater than $100,000 per year, as many as 65 percent considered greater tax benefits to be of 'significant' or 'great' importance.

Surprisingly—given earlier results—about half of our respondents do believe that a greater number of improved web pages of Pakistani organizations would make a difference. However, given that people had not rated web pages similarly highly as a fundraising mechanism, one might surmise that the utility people see in more and improved web pages is mainly informational. This was also borne out by our focus group discussions. However, it should be noted that web pages seem to attract the attention of a certain type of Pakistanis in America (younger, more educated, and more technologically connected) but a significant number find them to be a much less impressive measure.

We got a similarly divided response to the idea of creating an umbrella organization (such as the United Way in the USA) which could collect money on behalf of multiple organizations and causes and then channel it to them depending on donor preferences. While 45 percent believe that this could make an important difference, another 25 percent think it will not. Focus group discussions suggest that a major source of the hesitancy is the feeling that creating the requisite trust for this umbrella organization would itself be a problem and that the collection and disbursement of monies is fraught with risks and tensions. Moreover, it was suggested that an umbrella organization might put one more filter between the donors and the ultimate beneficiaries and most Pakistani-Americans want to come closer to their intended beneficiary rather than move away from them.

On two other mechanisms—(a) more visits by representatives of organizations working in Pakistan, and (b) better ability to personally visit organizations and projects in Pakistan—the numbers mimic the results of other similarly worded questions in the survey and demonstrate a rather evenly divided opinion. In each case about as many people think that these measures will make a serious impact as those who think it will not. Building on earlier questions related to these ideas and on the focus group discussion one might postulate that while the existing levels of activity in these areas seem to be generally effective, there is not enough enthusiasm to warrant major investments either in too many more visits by representatives of Pakistani NGOs to the United States, or in massive programs to facilitate visits by diaspora representatives to projects in Pakistan.

Finally, the last three measures on our list are characterized by a very clear lack of enthusiasm. In essence, our survey respondents are telling us that apart from working with the US government to clarify the US regulations about charitable giving abroad, the government of Pakistan has a rather limited role to play in encouraging more philanthropy by Pakistani-Americans. Half or more of our respondents feel that neither the provision of more information by the Pakistan embassy, nor more support or recognition for philanthropists by the Pakistan government will make an appreciable difference to the overall giving by the diaspora to Pakistan-related causes. One should acknowledge that a quarter of our respondents do consider such measures important and they may be worth the effort if they can attract large-scale philanthropy by a few very rich donors. However, putting these results in the context of earlier discussions, it seems that our respondents are sending a rather clear message that the key responsibility and ability to encourage more Pakistan-related philanthropy by Pakistani-Americans lies not with the government of Pakistan but with Pakistani civil society.

CHAPTER #6

Community perceptions

In this chapter we move away from the statistical results of the survey analysis and turn to our own observations based on the 54 focus groups that were conducted around the United States as part of this research. The focus groups were central to this research in many different ways.[121] First, they were the primary source of survey responses. Second, the focus group discussions gave us a robust cross-section of opinion and a much more detailed understanding of the views and attitudes of the Pakistani-American diaspora than the survey alone could have provided. Importantly, this has helped us tremendously in interpreting the survey data and translating its implications not only in light of the survey numbers but also in terms of what we were hearing at the focus groups. Third, and most importantly, unlike the survey forms which provide us with a glimpse of the philanthropic impulses of individual households, the focus groups allowed us the opportunity to look into the nature of particular Pakistani-American *communities*. Because these were group discussions, the discourse revolved not around the individual giving patterns of those present, but around the perceptions of philanthropic attitudes of the particular community that was hosting the focus group and, more broadly, of the Pakistani-American diaspora as a whole.

This chapter will focus on the third of these attributes and present our analysis of what we heard and learnt about the Pakistani-American diaspora as a community, rather than just as an aggregation of individual households. For analytical clarity, we will concentrate primarily on the focus groups in this chapter (just as we have focused primarily on the survey results in earlier chapters). The implications of these two types of data, seen side-by-side, will be pulled together in the following Chapter #7.

The discussion in this chapter is based on a structured analysis of focus group moderators' post-meeting perceptions. This is depicted graphically in the accompanying color-coded matrix, which presents the collated and structured impressions by the moderators about the discussion that had transpired at each focus group meeting (see Figure 36).

Approach to analysis

The moderators' views of what they had heard in the meetings were coded using a methodological framework of 14 key questions and records the research teams' structured impressions of the discussion at each focus group, based on observations, meeting notes, and post-meeting impressions. Each of the 54 focus group meetings conducted for this research was moderated by a member of the research team and each moderator filed a structured written report for these meetings. At the end of the exercise, the moderators of these meetings were asked to record, for each focus group, their responses to a set of structured questions, based on the their observations, meeting notes and post-meeting impressions.

The questions for which the moderators were asked to record their impressions had to satisfy three criteria. First, the questions had to be commonly asked of all groups. Second, they had to have potential for meaningful analysis. And third, they had to have resulted in substantive discussions in the focus groups. These criteria were not hard to satisfy because most of the focus groups had been structured around a common framework, because the structured reporting format for each focus group had allowed different moderators to formulate a common sense of the questions to ask, and importantly because the issues raised by the focus group participants were themselves remarkably consistent. The questions we use for this analysis can roughly be divided into three categories: (a) questions related to the perceptions the group revealed about philanthropy among Pakistanis in general, and about their comparisons with other communities; (b) questions about the structure of the community that the particular focus group represented; and (c) questions regarding the hurdles to and potential for future giving by the Pakistani diaspora in America.

Focus group moderators were independently asked to record their responses on a three-point scale (with two other scale points for outliers or missing data) for a set of 14 questions in total, across the three categories mentioned above. Because the focus groups were conducted on the basis of non-attribution, no identifying tags are included or applied to the analysis. Since none of the groups were designed to be homogenous, the responses are coded to be 'mostly' one way or another. For instance, when recording age, we are asking the moderators to note their impressions on whether the group was 'mostly younger', 'mostly older', or 'mixed'. Similar phrasing applies to the answers of all other questions listed in the legend. As such, when answers to the questions are recorded, they are the moderator's impressions of whether the group discussion 'mostly' leaned one way or the other. The end result is the matrix presented in Figure 36, which codifies the three-point scale, allowing for quick visual checks of the order of magnitude of, and relationships between, the answers recorded. Our analysis is based on studying either the distribution of the focus group responses for a single question, or correlations between multiple questions.

Although analytical, this is not a statistical exercise. We understand the potential danger of (miss-)interpreting the results of such qualitative analysis and have sought to err on the side of caution in reaching any conclusions. We urge the reader to be similarly cautious. Numbers or trends alone without an explanation of their meaning can be worse than no results. It is extremely important, therefore, to understand what our focus group analysis means, and more importantly, what it does not. The primary data for the focus group analysis was the perceptions of the focus group moderators, based on their structured notes and impressions from the meetings, recorded for a set of 14 questions in 3 categories. Quite clearly, these impressions provide one snapshot of one set of experiences. However, let it also be said that subjectivity is not invalidity. We believe this to be an important snapshot (a) because it was taken in a structured fashion with a structured framework for conducting and recording the results of different focus groups, (b) because it was taken across multiple communities which do represent a fair cross-section of the Pakistani diaspora in the USA, and (c) because this analysis allows us a means to capture a very rich set of discussions and perceptions that would be lost if we only concentrated on the survey data.

Presentation of findings

In this chapter we report the obvious and dominant patterns that emerged from these focus group discussions and, in particular, on the phenomena we found either overwhelmingly represented or which we thought our readership will be interested in even if the pattern itself is not surprising. The analysis of qualitative data is intended to make explicit our implicit learning from the focus group interactions. Such learning can sometimes be more insightful than aggregated percentages from survey results.

Did this group perceive
<u>Pakistanis in USA to be:</u>

<u>Did this community appear to have:</u>

<u>Did this group believe that:</u>

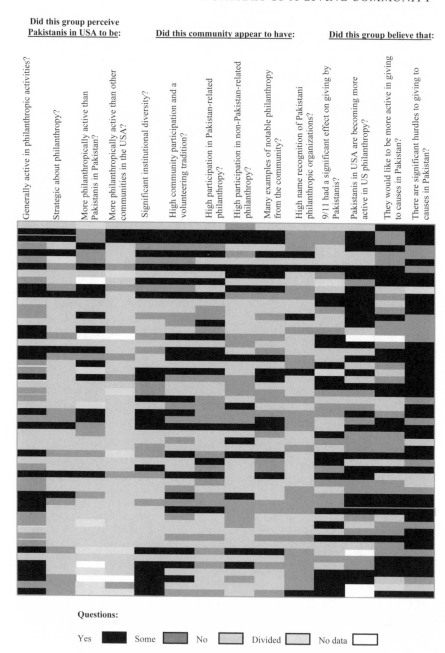

Generally active in philanthropic activities?

Strategic about philanthropy?

More philanthropically active than Pakistanis in Pakistan?

More philanthropically active than other communities in the USA?

Significant institutional diversity?

High community participation and a volunteering tradition?

High participation in Pakistan-related philanthropy?

High participation in non-Pakistan-related philanthropy?

Many examples of notable philanthropy from the community?

High name recognition of Pakistani philanthropic organizations?

9/11 had a significant effect on giving by Pakistanis?

Pakistanis in USA are becoming more active in US philanthropy?

They would like to be more active in giving to causes in Pakistan?

There are significant hurdles to giving to causes in Pakistan?

Questions:

Yes ■   Some ▨   No □   Divided ▨   No data □

Figure 36: Structural Analysis of Focus Group

Simply put, our focus group discussions alerted us to a host of community-level perceptions that were not, and possibly could not be captured in the survey. Although our focus group analysis also strongly reinforces a number of findings from the survey results, we will focus here on those questions and those aspects of the focus group discussions that would not have become possible without our direct experience and interaction with focus groups and analysis of the qualitative data. While not exhaustive, this analysis seeks to capture some key features of the data, particularly about community perceptions and attitudes and about issues that are not equally well covered in the survey data.

The qualitative data from our 54 focus groups provides a different, and arguably more nuanced, picture of the Pakistani-American diaspora than obtained from the survey instrument alone. For instance, our structured analysis of focus group moderators' post-meeting perceptions reveal that *the Pakistani diaspora, as a community, is a dynamic and philanthropically active community but has within it important pockets of philanthropically disengaged subsets, including younger populations; and the community remains quite divided about its self-perception regarding philanthropy and is overwhelmingly unfavorable in comparing its own giving to the giving patterns of other communities* (even though our survey results indicate otherwise).

The following sections will look at some of the more interesting findings from this analysis. These are organized here roughly around the three major questions posed in the analysis: What are the perceptions held by the Pakistani diaspora of its own philanthropic activity in comparison to philanthropy by other peer groups? What are the perceptions held by the Pakistani diaspora about the future of philanthropy by Pakistanis in America? What can we learn from this analysis about the impact of key community attributes on philanthropic giving by that community? In relation to each of these, the findings will be presented in the form of a series of questions that might be asked by those who are interested in better understanding or better mobilizing the philanthropic impulses of the Pakistani diaspora in the United States.

Perceptions about the giving patterns of Pakistani-Americans

The most striking finding from this entire analysis is that the Pakistani diaspora in America has *a very low self-image in terms of how its own philanthropic activities* compared with philanthropy by other peer groups in America. This is striking because, as we had noted earlier, our survey results suggest that Pakistani-Americans are no less generous in their philanthropy than the two most important reference groups: all Americans in America and all Pakistanis in Pakistan. Yet, we found in our focus group analysis that only two groups out of the total 54 that we spoke with seemed to believe that they were more philanthropically active than other communities in America, and an overwhelming majority believed that the Pakistani diaspora is much less philanthropically active. Indeed, in our focus group discussions there was such overwhelming consensus on this issue that in most instances this question was not even discussed at much length. Interestingly, however, it is not that Pakistanis in America do not consider themselves philanthropically active; it is just that they consider other communities to be far more philanthropically active than themselves.

As one might expect, there is significant nuance within this larger finding that needs to be explored. We will do so now by using the lens of a set of questions that might be asked and the potential responses that emerge from our focus group analysis.

QUESTION #1. Did the focus groups perceive Pakistanis in the USA to be generally active in philanthropic activities? And how did they rate giving by Pakistanis in the USA in comparison to giving by to other communities? (See Figure 37)

♦ *Split opinion on the community's own perceptions of the level of its philanthropic activity.* Our focus groups were split roughly evenly between those who considered the Pakistani diaspora as being philanthropically active, and those who disagreed or had no opinion. The locus of opinion in just under half the focus groups (23) was that the Pakistani community in the US is fairly active philanthropically. This split is not simply a statistical artifact, based on the general discussions at the focus group the prevalent sense was that although the community is philanthropically active, it is less active than it should be.

♦ *A clear sense that the community's philanthropy is not strategically directed.* A majority of our focus groups were of the view that philanthropy by Pakistanis in America is not strategically directed. In fact, only 8 groups believed that Pakistanis in the USA do think strategically in targeting their philanthropy for maximum efficacy; but all of them already had favorable opinions of Pakistani diaspora philanthropy. For the majority of the focus groups, and also for the majority of those who discussed this question at the focus

Generally active in
philanthropic activities?

Strategic in thinking about
their philanthropy?

More philanthropically
active than other
communities in USA?

More philanthropically
active than Pakistanis in
Pakistan?

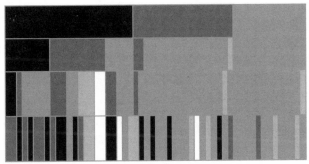

Figure 37: Perceptions About Giving by Pakistanis in America
Note: Gradients represent identical values as those in Figure 36

groups, much of Pakistani diaspora philanthropy is *ad hoc*, untargeted, devoid of strategic focus, and therefore not successful in either cultivating better development in Pakistan or an improved community image in the United States.

♦ *A very strong sense of philanthropic inferiority.* An overwhelming number of focus groups, and focus group participants, felt that the Pakistani diaspora in America is not as philanthropically active as other communities in America (for example, Americans in general, or other diaspora groups within the US). This is remarkable both because a definitive majority of focus groups and focus group participants felt this way, but also because our survey data suggests that Pakistani-Americans are as active and as generous philanthropically as their peer groups. The intensity of this finding can be gauged from the fact that only two of the 54 focus groups felt that Pakistanis compared well in philanthropy with other communities and as many as 38 focus groups (70 percent) recorded definitely unfavorable perceptions.

♦ *'We give but not enough'.* Interestingly, 10 of the 38 groups that compared the Pakistani diaspora unfavorably with other communities thought at the same time that Pakistanis were generally active in giving. This suggests that the sense of philanthropic inferiority mentioned above comes not just from an underestimation of philanthropy by Pakistanis in America, it stems also from an overestimation of the philanthropy by other communities. Importantly, it might also point towards a very high level of philanthropic aspiration within the community.

♦ *A generally high regard for the philanthropic traditions and practice by Pakistanis in Pakistan.* In comparing their own philanthropic practice to that of Pakistanis in Pakistan, a significant number of focus groups (21) felt that, after accounting for earning potential, their compatriots in Pakistan are more philanthropically active than the Pakistani diaspora in the United States. Given that as many as 12 focus groups had divided opinions or no response to this question, the 21 focus groups that considered Pakistanis in Pakistan to be more charitable than themselves constitute exactly half of the focus groups that had a clear response to this question. Indeed, the subject of comparing their own philanthropic behavior with that of Pakistanis in Pakistan was a major and popular issue at most focus groups. Participants did recognize that despite lower earning potentials in Pakistan, the charitable needs as well as avenues for giving were much higher in Pakistan and a culture of giving (even if in very small amounts) is a deep-rooted reality of daily life in Pakistan. Much reference was made of the fact that there are so many needy and deserving individuals and causes in Pakistan. As one focus group participant mentioned, "when I want to give to charity here, I need to research options, find worthy causes, fill out forms, get receipts, and write checks; in Pakistan, all I need to do is to step out into the street and a dozen worthy causes will be standing right there, and even the smallest piece of change in my pocket will make a difference."

QUESTION #2. What are the attributes of the Pakistani- American communities that have high confidence in their own (and the Pakistani diaspora's) philanthropic activities? (See Figure 38)

♦*Older, wealthier and better-educated groups tend to be more philanthropically active.* It is not surprising that groups which included older participants, had higher income levels, and were better educated were more likely to consider the Pakistani diaspora to be generally active in philanthropic activities. These, of course, tend to be the attributes that are directly related to higher levels of giving.

♦*Younger populations seem highly interested but less engaged in Pakistani-American philanthropic activities.* The more important implication of our analysis points towards the possibility that younger populations are less en-

Generally active in philanthropic activities?

Strategic in thinking about their philanthropy?

Figure 38: Perceptions About Communities with High Giving
Note: Gradients represent identical values as those in Figure 36

gaged in diasporic community discussions on philanthropy and tend to have negative perceptions about the level of philanthropic activities that Pakistanis in America are engaged in. Of the 14 focus groups that comprised mostly younger participants, only one believed that the Pakistani diaspora was sufficiently active in philanthropy, while 7 groups were convinced that it is not. The remaining 5 groups had mixed views on the subject. Discussions on this question during the focus groups suggest that this may be because (a) Pakistani community organizations and activities are largely driven by middle-aged Pakistani-Americans; (b) because younger cohorts are often less able to be active in philanthropy themselves, they tend to know less about the various philanthropic activities than older Pakistani-Americans are engaged in, and (c) younger Pakistani-Americans include a large number of 'second generation' youth who were born and/or raised in America and their philanthropic impulses and priorities are significantly different from older cohorts who migrated from Pakistan. This is important because our focus group discussions with younger Pakistani-Americans suggests that there is a very high level of interest on their part to be more active in Pakistani-American activities— especially including philanthropic activities—but that they find a serious dearth of opportunities and activities that respond to their interests and would allow them to participate meaningfully. (It should be noted that this may well have changed with the 2005 earthquake in Pakistan, which mobilized a lot of Pakistani-American youth towards charitable activities).

Perceptions about current and future challenges

It was not a surprise to find that the majority of our focus groups felt that there are strong institutional hurdles in giving to causes in Pakistan. More surprising, however, were the very mixed results regarding the impact of the policy climate in the United States following the tragic events of 9/11. The focus group analysis suggests that the institutional hurdles in Pakistan remain a greater impediment to giving to causes in Pakistan than the post-9/11 policy environment in the United States. Indeed, a key impact of the events following 9/11 seems to have been the emergence of a very strong perception amongst Pakistani-Americans that they need to become much more active in US-based philanthropy, even if that means cutting back on Pakistan-based philanthropy.

Let us explore the implications of these and related findings using the lens of two key questions, one related to the current challenges in giving to causes in Pakistan and the other related to the likely philanthropic priorities of the Pakistani diaspora in the future.

QUESTION #3. Did the focus groups perceive it difficult to give to causes in Pakistan? And to what extent are these difficulties related to the post-9/11 policy environment in America? (See Figure 39)

◆ *It is not easy to give to causes in Pakistan; particularly because of institutional hurdles in Pakistan.* There was an overwhelming sense during the focus groups that philanthropic giving to causes in Pakistan is not easy. Only 4 groups out of 54 indicated that there were no significant hurdles in giving to Pakistan, and as many as 35 groups believed that significant hurdles existed. During the discussions some participants even argued that these hurdles were serious enough to dissuade Pakistani-Americans who might otherwise be interested in contributing to causes in Pakistan. Importantly, many of the hurdles mentioned in the focus groups related to the institutional conditions *within* Pakistan. Amongst the ones mentioned most often are (a) the lack of affordable, transparent and efficient means of transferring philanthropic funds to Pakistan, (b) lack of information about, and trust in, charitable and nongovernmental organizations in Pakistan, and   (c) lack of ability to monitor and verify that the philanthropic contributions are being put to intended use.

◆ *The 9/11 effect is real, but is not overwhelming.* Our survey results had showed that about as many respondents reported decreased contributions post September 11, 2001 as those who reported increased contributions. Similarly, our focus group analysis suggests that about as many groups felt that the events of 9/11 had serious and significant effects on giving by Pakistanis as those who believed the opposite. An interesting implication of this finding is that even amongst those groups which believe that there are significant hurdles to giving in Pakistan, the opinion is divided nearly equally on whether 9/11 has had a significant effect on Pakistani giving or not. From the focus group discussions

Figure 39: Perceptions About Hurdles to Giving
Note: Gradients represent identical values as those in Figure 36

it was quite clear that the events of 9/11 and the various policies initiated in the USA since then have had a significant impact on how Pakistani-Americans think about philanthropy. However, people's actual giving does not seem to have been changed. The sentiment that was repeated many times during the focus groups was that people had become much more careful and vigilant about who they give to and how they give, but the actual giving itself had not changed.

♦ *All across the board:* It is also worth noting that the institutional hurdles in giving to causes in Pakistan as well as the impacts of the post-9/11 policies in America are felt across the board and no meaningful demographic patterns are evident. Variables such as age groups, income, education and gender seem to have no measurable impact on whether a group is more likely to feel the pinch of institutional hurdles in giving to causes in Pakistan or whether it is more likely to feel the impact of post-9/11 policies. When these hurdles hurt, they seem to hurt across the board. At one level, this seems surprising, since lower income groups would *a priori* seem more vulnerable to the post 9/11 policies. However, in our discussions we did not find this to be the case and lower income groups had adapted to the post-9/11 realities as quickly as higher income cohorts.

QUESTION #4. Are Pakistanis in America likely to give more to causes in the United States and/or to causes in Pakistan in the future? (See Figure 40)

♦ *Pakistanis in America are likely to become increasingly active in US-based philanthropy.* Nearly half of all our focus groups (26) perceive a strong trend towards Pakistani Americans becoming increasingly more active in US philanthropy over the next few years. Only a fifth of the focus groups (11) believed that this is not likely to happen, while the remaining groups either had mixed views or no view on this issue. This perception was voiced quite strongly in many of the focus groups and a number of participants made a pas-

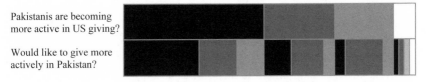

Pakistanis are becoming more active in US giving?

Would like to give more actively in Pakistan?

Figure 40: Perceptions About Prospects for Future Giving
Note: Gradients represent identical values as those in Figure 36

sionate case that not only is this trend taking place, but also that it *should* take place. Although groups which had mostly older, higher-income and more educated participants were particularly articulate in making this case, the focus group analysis suggests that the general perception of this emerging trend is fairly consistent across demographic categories.

♦ *But the Pakistani diaspora in the US is not necessarily going to become less active in Pakistan-based philanthropy.* Even though the perception that Pakistanis in America need to become (and are becoming) more active in US-based philanthropy is strong as well as consistent, this does not mean that the Pakistani diaspora's interest in Pakistan-based philanthropy is likely to recede. As many as 22 of our focus groups (about 40 percent) felt that they would like to get more active in giving to causes in Pakistan, another 21 groups had mixed views, and only 9 focus groups expressed the opposite opinion. This suggests that there is a fairly robust contingent within our focus groups which perceives that giving to causes in Pakistan is and will remain important and the new interest in US-based philanthropy will be fueled with new and additional sources rather than by directing resources now going towards Pakistan-based philanthropy. For the most part, this perception also cuts across the board and no major demographic trends seem apparent. However, it is striking that no lower-income or lower-education focus groups indicated that they would like to give more to causes in Pakistan. This may be because these groups already tend to give large proportions of their philanthropic contributions to causes in Pakistan. Interestingly, only one of the four focus groups that were composed mostly of women suggested that they would like to increase their involvement in giving to causes in Pakistan.

Impact of community attributes on giving

Our mapping of focus groups reveals a landscape of communities with varying levels of institutional diversity, community participation and philanthropic activity. There are hubs of amazingly active communities spread between relatively quite communities. There are large centers with multiple communities that nearly never coincide despite living in the same metropolitan area, and there are intricately well-knit medium-sized communities that have developed deep relations not only amongst themselves but also with their neighboring communities. In this final section we look at what attributes define the most active of these communities.

QUESTION #5. Can we identify some attributes that are likely to be found in communities that are more active givers? (See Figure 41)

♦ *Active communities tend to be mature in age, but neither income nor education is particularly important.* Our focus group data suggests that high community participation does correlate with age. Older groups tended to be better organized and more active. This is not a surprise since older groups can have greater economic and time stability in their life and often bring with them networks of relationships and experience that can be very useful. Moreover, as we had noted earlier, younger groups can often feel isolated and disengaged from the mainstream of Pakistani-American activities, and this can itself further marginalize their role. Interestingly, however, there seems to be no significant correlation between income or education and levels of community participation. Both high- and low-income focus groups were equally likely to demonstrate high levels of participation and the same was true for high- and low-education groups. Extrapolating from a number of focus group discussions, one could argue that the defining feature for high community participation is

Significant institutional
diversity?

High community participation
and a volunteering tradition?

High participation in Pakistan-
related philanthropy?

High participation in non-
Pakistan-related philanthropy?

Many examples of notable
philanthropy from the
community?

High name recognition of
Pakistani philanthropic
organizations?

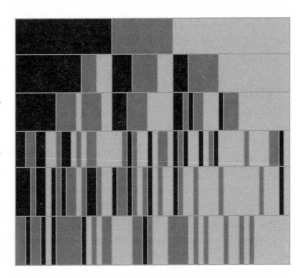

Figure 41: Perceptions About Active and Giving Communities
Note: Gradients represent identical values as those in Figure 36

the network of relationships and trust within the community rather than any particular demographic attribute.

♦ *Institutional diversity matters.* To the extent one could define a critical variable, it would be the level of institutional diversity within the community, as measured by a variety of different Pakistani institutions serving different needs (for example, identity needs, religious needs, intellectual needs, political needs, etc.). The presence of institutional diversity correlates fairly well with a number of positive variables, including high community participation, active Pakistan-related philanthropy, active non-Pakistan related philanthropy, and the presence of examples of notable community philanthropy. The vast majority of the focus groups with high community participation and a volunteering tradition were in institutionally diverse communities. However, there were pockets of high activity in low institutional diversity communities, reflecting perhaps the presence of an individual or a small group which formed the center of community life.

♦ *Different communities develop different philanthropic persona.* A total of 13 focus groups were identified by the moderators as being significantly active in non-Pakistan related philanthropy. 15 focus groups were identified as being similarly active in Pakistan-related philanthropy. Interestingly, however, 5 groups were significantly active *both* in Pakistan-related and non-Pakistan related philanthropy. This suggests that different communities develop different philanthropic persona and tend to focus on particular types of philanthropic initiatives. However, given some of our earlier findings, particularly the trend towards greater involvement in US-based philanthropy, it is likely that this distinction and specialization might begin to blur.

♦ *Very low recognition of Pakistani philanthropic organizations.* One rather sad but strikingly consistent finding is that across the board there was very low name recognition for even the largest Pakistani philanthropic or non-governmental organizations. This was true even for the most active and informed focus groups and points towards the failure of Pakistani charitable organizations to make serious inroads into the Pakistani diaspora in America. The names of Imran Khan and Abdus Sattar Edhi were well known to most focus groups, but it was clear that they were known as celebrities rather than institutional entities. For example, while the name of Imran Khan was very well known as was his philanthropic success, relatively few participants actually knew the name of the trust or the hospital (Shaukat Khanum) that he operates. Only three organizations seemed to have national recognition and were regularly recognized in focus groups around the country – these were the Human Development Foundation, Development in Literacy (DIL), and The Citizens's Foundation (TCF). Tellingly, all three of them have very strong roots in the Pakistani diaspora in the US itself.

QUESTION #6. How do the views of active communities relate to larger trends within the Pakistani diaspora in the United States? (See Figure 42)

♦ *Communities that are institutionally vibrant and diverse are also philanthropically active.* Not surprisingly, our analysis finds that groups that demonstrated a high degree of institutional diversity and had high levels of community participation in general, also tended to be themselves more active in philanthropy and had a high assessment of philanthropic activity by the Pakistani diaspora. Institutional diversity, in particular seemed to be a leading indicator of a community's philanthropic vibrancy. Of the 23 groups with positive perceptions of Pakistani-American philanthropy, only 4 were in communities with low institutional diversity. More remarkably, none of the groups with low opinions of philanthropic activity were in communities with significant institutional diversity.

♦ *High community participation does not necessarily mean an ability to*

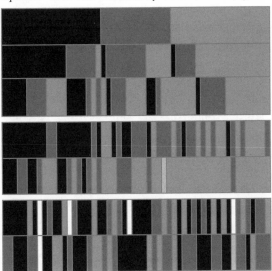

High community participation tradition?

Active in Pakistan-related philanthropy?

Active in non-Pakistan-related philanthropy?

Generally active in philanthropic activities?

Strategic in thinking about their philanthropy?

Pakistanis are becoming more active in US giving?

Would like to give more actively in Pakistan?

Figure 42: Perceptions About Making Communities Active
Note: Gradients represent identical values as those in Figure 36

give more to causes in Pakistan. Almost 4 out of 20 groups with high community participation and a volunteering tradition recorded they would not like to be active in giving more to causes in Pakistan. In fact, only about half (9) responded yes, while the others were mixed or ambivalent. Similarly, institutionally diverse communities were not significantly more likely to say they would like to be more active in giving to causes in Pakistan. This may be partly explained by the fact that the most active communities are more likely to have already deployed their philanthropic resources and have the least ability to add further resources to the mix. It may also stem from the fact that the most active communities are likely to have thought most hard about how they want to channel their philanthropy and are, therefore, least likely or able to respond to new claimants to their philanthropy.

♦ *Untapped communities would like to be more active in giving to causes in Pakistan.* Related to the above, there may be an opportunity to cultivate new communities that are not currently very active but have the potential to become more philanthropically active. In practical terms, this means that sometimes it is far better to seek new and 'ripe' communities to target for philanthropic campaigns rather than mature and saturated communities that are already as active as they can be. For example, in our focus group analysis we found that amongst the groups that reported low levels of community participation and volunteering tradition there were as many as seven groups that also said they would like to be more active in giving to causes in Pakistan.

♦ *Lack of a community participation tradition should not be confused with a lack of desire to contribute.* In looking at the communities that are marked as having little tradition of community participation and volunteering, it is striking to note that these same communities can sometimes also express a high desire to contribute more to causes in Pakistan as well as a recognition that the Pakistani diaspora in general is fairly active, plus a realization that more and more Pakistanis are going to become active in US-based philanthropy in the near future. All of this suggests that even if these communities are not currently well organized, they have a high potential for better community mobilization. Our focus group analysis cannot predict how many such communities exist, but between this analysis and the discussions we heard at the focus groups themselves, it is fairly obvious that there are many Pakistani-American communities across the United States that are fairly eager to become more involved in philanthropic activities but have not yet been able to organize themselves to do so.

CHAPTER #7

What did we learn and what should we do?

The many findings of our research are spread all over the previous chapters of this book. It is not particularly useful to re-summarize and restate them here. We will use this final chapter, instead, to draw out key trends and larger lessons that emerge from looking at these findings as a whole. We want to focus here on dominant and emergent themes that are of greatest conceptual and practical value to some key audiences: to Pakistani-Americans; to those in Pakistan who wish to encourage diaspora philanthropy from the USA for Pakistan's equitable development, particularly the Pakistan Center for Philanthropy (PCP); Pakistan-related philanthropic organizations that wish to engage the Pakistani diaspora; and the scholarly and policy communities interested in understanding the dynamics of diaspora philanthropy.

To do so, we will ask ourselves three questions, and seek to answer each in light of the findings of this study. *First*, what are the most important general lessons and trends that we discovered about philanthropy by Pakistani-Americans? *Second*, what can be done, to attract and channel more and better-directed philanthropic contributions from Pakistani-Americans, especially for more equitable development in Pakistan? And, *third*, what are some of the questions that this study has not been able to look at but which are worth looking at in the future?

The next sections will look at each of these questions. In trying to identify the key trends and the most strategic interventions, we will build upon all elements of this study including the lessons learnt from analyzing the 461 survey responses that we received to our research questionnaire, the general findings of the community perceptions analysis of the 54 focus groups that were conducted across the USA, and also the specific discussions within these focus groups which often included discussions about 'what can be done'.

Lessons learnt

There is a growing interest in diaspora philanthropy, and Asian diasporas in the United States have received particular attention. This is the first systematic enquiry about philanthropy by Pakistanis in America and amongst the few studies on any diaspora that estimates actual giving patterns based on a broad-based survey instrument. What we learn from this study is, therefore, of interest not only to the Pakistani-American diaspora and those who study it but also to those who are interested in diaspora philanthropy in general. Our research points us towards a set of seven key lessons about philanthropy by Pakistanis in America.

#1. Pakistani-Americans are a generous,
giving and active community

We estimate that the overall giving by Pakistani-American includes about $250 million in cash and in-kind contributions and nearly 43.5 million hours of volunteered time, or the equivalent of 25,000 full-time jobs. If a monetary value is placed on the time volunteered, this comes to approximately $1 Billion per year in total giving (cash, in-kind and volunteered time) by Pakistanis in America. For a community of around half a million people, this is a very impressive set of numbers.[122]

Although this is a relatively affluent community, we find that charitable instincts are spread across all income classes. We estimate that, on average, the Pakistani-American household contributes 3.5 percent of its income to philanthropic giving, which compares very favorably with the giving habits of the average American household and with the average Pakistani household in Pakistan. Given these findings, it is both striking and surprising that the community suffers from a strong sense of 'philanthropic inferiority' with many Pakistani-Americans believing that they are not very philanthropically active and with most feeling that the community's giving is not strategically directed.

Importantly, the Pakistani-American diaspora is not only a giving community, it is a very active giving community. For a community of this size it is remarkably prolific in building and supporting institutions for a very wide variety of causes. The community invests 43.5 million hours—or the equivalent of 25,000 full time jobs—of volunteered time and supports a rich and diverse tapestry of organizations that provide the diaspora with sustenance in a variety of areas that range from the arts and culture, to sports and recreation, to community support, to institutions of faith, to professional fraternities, to research and intellectual enquiry, and much more. Indeed, the community support structures that Pakistani-Americans have constructed through these myriad community organizations may be their biggest philanthropic achievement, which not only provides members of the Pakistani-American community with a sense of cultural connectedness to Pakistan but also gives the community (and Pakistan-related issues) a greater prominence in American society.

#2. There is a strong preference for giving directly to individuals in need

By a very clear margin, the single largest chunk of overall giving by Pakistanis in America goes directly to individuals in immediate need, rather than to institutions and organized charities. There is a very strongly held belief amongst Pakistani-Americans that giving directly to the needy and the deserving is superior to institutional giving. This belief comes from (a) cultural and social habits that people have grown up with, (b) a rather deep sense of distrust in the honesty, efficiency or effectiveness of organized charities and NGOs, (c) a sense that direct giving encourages greater accountability, and (d) a feeling that more of the contribution will reach and benefit the deserving.

Kinship networks of friends and extended family (as opposed to organized charities) play a critical role in this direct giving to needy individuals. Kinship networks are important both for identifying and relaying resources to the deserving individuals in need, and also as recipients of such charity. Importantly, however, although much of the charitable giving going to Pakistan goes directly to needy individuals, the vast majority of the contributions made in the US do not. This may simply be a case of the availability of, and accessibility to, deserving and needy individuals which is obviously so much greater in Pakistan.

Similarly, giving motivated by injunctions of faith tends to go much more to needy individuals than issue-motivated giving. Importantly, the preference for direct giving to individuals in need is also matched by (and possibly influenced by) a striking lack of trust in nonprofit and philanthropic institutions in Pakistan. Although the Pakistani diaspora in America is quite willing to direct its giving to philanthropic and nonprofit organizations in terms of what is given to causes outside of Pakistan (whether Pakistan-related or not), it is quite hesitant to do so in Pakistan. Large proportions of Pakistani-Americans have a very low opinion about the honesty, efficiency or efficacy of NGOs in Pakistan and would much rather give through (and to) their kinship networks than through such institutions.

#3. People are motivated by faith, but mostly give to social issues

The desire to help individuals in need, including the needy within one's extended kinship networks, is by far the most important reason why Pakistani-Americans give. In fact, this is cited as an even more important reason to give than the motivation of faith.

Social issues—especially the issue of poverty and helping the needy but also including education, health, civil and human rights, and community development—are amongst the most cited issues that people contribute to and wish to contribute to. Like other communities in the USA, Pakistani-Americans have a strong sense of a moral duty to be charitable that is motivated by their faith. However, the responses we received suggest that they channel far *less* of their contributions to religious organizations than Americans in general. Instead, more of their faith-motivated giving is channeled directly to poor and deserving individuals in dire need.

Our results suggest that a sense of faith-based moral duty to be charitable and to give to the poor is a major motivator of philanthropy by Pakistanis in America, but according to the responses we received faith-based organizations are *not* a major direct recipient of their giving. To the extent they give to faith-based organizations, the vast bulk of this giving is to places of worship in the US that are as much centers of community and social congregation as of religious congregation.

The distinction that people make between faith as a motivation for giving and faith-based organizations as a recipient of their giving is a critical one and is probably valid not only for Pakistani-Americans but for many other categories in the study of philanthropy. Our survey and focus group data suggests that even when people's giving habits are motivated by a strong sense of moral and spiritual obligation to give to those in need, the giving itself is often directed to secular social causes. Given that Pakistan is a developing country it is not surprising that much of this giving directed towards Pakistan gets channeled towards social development issues, especially including poverty and helping the poor, education, health and human development.

#4. The philanthropy of Pakistani-Americans
is not limited to Pakistan

Although the giving of the Pakistani diaspora is firmly rooted in its 'Pakistani' identity, this is not the only identity that pulls at its philanthropic generosity. We estimate that about 40 percent of the monetary and in-kind giving by the Pakistani diaspora goes to Pakistani causes in Pakistan, another 20 percent to Pakistani causes in the US, and the remaining 40 percent to causes unrelated to Pakistan. In terms of time volunteered, slightly more than half (54 percent) goes to causes unrelated to Pakistan, about 40 percent goes to Pakistani causes in America, and the remaining 6 percent goes to causes in Pakistan.

Although religion constitutes a major portion of the giving that is not related to Pakistan, there are very clear indications in our findings that the real growth area in terms of the giving by Pakistani-Americans is in giving to causes in the United States that are related to their 'American' identity. The trends imply that the giving patterns of Pakistani-Americans tend to resemble the giving of their American neighbors more than it resembles the giving of their erstwhile compatriots back in Pakistan.

Two important trends should be highlighted here. First, the longer someone has lived in the US, the more likely they are to give a larger proportion of their philanthropy to causes unrelated to Pakistan. However, they tend to do so by diverting additional philanthropic resources to non-Pakistan-related causes and without necessarily reducing their giving to causes in Pakistan. Second, largely as a result of post-9/11 effects, the Pakistani diaspora in America is becoming increasingly active in USA-based philanthropy including in mainstream US charitable organizations.

#5. 9/11 made the Pakistani diaspora
more vigilant, but not less-giving

There is grave and justifiable concern within the diaspora that the tragic events of September 11, 2001 have had a serious and debilitating impact on the Pakistani-American community. There is a strong unease about the potential impacts of the post-9/11 government policies and how these might impact the giving by all immigrant communities and especially Muslim communities in America. However, the unease comes not as much from what the policies are but from the uncertainty and lack of clarity about what the new policies are.

Despite this very strong sense of unease, there is no evidence—either in the survey results or in focus group discussions—that Pakistani-Americans have actually stopped giving or decreased their giving. Instead, the clear and unambiguous finding is that people have become extremely careful and vigilant in terms of who they give to, how they give and what they give for, but they have not actually become less giving.

Indeed, our survey suggests that while the bulk of our respondents (62 percent) say that their giving has remained unchanged since 9/11, far more respondents report that their giving has increased (24 percent) than those who say their giving has actually decreased since 9/11 (14 percent). Most significantly, as many as 34 percent of our survey respondents say that their giving to causes unrelated to Pakistan has increased since 9/11 and our focus group discussions suggest that this increase has come mostly in giving to causes that relate to being better and more active citizens within their American neighborhoods and communities.

#6. Significant potential for more giving, including more giving to Pakistan

All indications suggest that there is significant potential for more giving by Pakistanis. Overwhelming numbers of our respondents feel that, given the right conditions, their own Pakistan-related giving could increase significantly (83 percent); an even more overwhelming majority (93 percent) feels that there is great growth potential for the overall giving by the Pakistani-American diaspora.

Our research also points towards a strong desire in the community to increase its giving to non-Pakistan-related issues, including involvement to mainstream US philanthropic causes. There is clearly a desire within the Pakistani diaspora in America to become ever more involved both in philanthropy related to Pakistan and in civic life in the US.

Our focus group discussions suggest that there are also a significant number of locations and Pakistani communities within the United States that have the willingness to give more to Pakistan-related causes but which are grossly under-serviced in that they are only infrequently approached by institutional philanthropic initiatives which tend to concentrate their activities in a few large metropolitan areas. There is a palpable eagerness on the part of the community to remain in touch with its Pakistani roots while also growing new roots in the USA.

There was a great willingness to talk about the subject of philanthropy directed towards Pakistan and many expressions of the diaspora's desire to give more to Pakistani causes. However, it was also clear that for this potential to be realized a number of serious hurdles will first have to be cleared. That notwithstanding, we estimate that there is significant potential for more overall giving by Pakistanis in America, including more giving to Pakistan-related causes in Pakistan.

#7. There are serious hurdles that make it difficult to give more to Pakistan

Although this community is ready to give significantly more than it does now, there are high barriers to accessing this additional giving. This is particularly true if one seeks to direct new or existing philanthropy to institutional giving in Pakistan. There are three major hurdles that need to be addressed before significant resources might be directed towards charitable institutions and NGOs in Pakistan.

The first hurdle is the *chronic lack of trust in the civic sector in Pakistan.* Over 80 percent of our survey respondents believe that such organizations are inefficient as well as dishonest, over 70 percent feel that they are also ineffective and inattentive to the most pressing problems in Pakistan. Although people have high opinions of the organizations and individuals that they have themselves worked with, they have a deep suspicion of the sector as a whole and do not believe that institutional philanthropies are good custodians of their giving. The intensity of this suspicion is not only embarrassing for the sector, it is also an unfair assessment. Importantly, however, it is the single most critical, and possibly debilitating, challenge for the future of organized philanthropy in Pakistan.

The second important hurdle relates to the *practical difficulties in giving to causes in Pakistan* including unclear US regulations about charitable giving abroad (especially after 9/11) and a lack of convenient mechanisms to transfer funds to Pakistan. There is also a dearth of reliable mechanisms to monitor the performance of organizations and a lack of opportunities to interact directly with organizations and their workers.

The third barrier is that there is *very little information available to Pakistani-Americans about philanthropic organizations in Pakistan.* This becomes particularly important because it feeds on, and exacerbates, both the barriers mentioned earlier. For example, people do tend to trust the organizations that they know; however, they know of very few philanthropic organizations and NGOs in Pakistan. Very few organizations are recognized by name, and even then there is only a rudimentary familiarity with what these organizations do and have achieved. Pakistan-related causes—especially those in Pakistan, but also those operating in the US—just don't ask for contributions as often as other causes. Over 80 percent of our respondents say that, on average, they are asked to give to causes unrelated to Pakistan six or more time per month; only 4 percent of our respondents say that they are asked at the same frequency to give to a Pakistani cause in Pakistan.

In essence, most Pakistani-Americans tend to have little trust in institutions in Pakistan, including in NGOs and philanthropic organizations; those who are willing to give, face serious logistical difficulties in giving to causes in Pakistan, including difficulties related to transferring money; and finally, the Pakistani diaspora in America has fairly scant, often inaccurate, and generally negative information about the NGO and philanthropic sector in Pakistan which keeps them from giving more. These barriers have to be addressed before the potential for giving can be realized.

Recommendations

Those who seek to mobilize more philanthropic resources from Pakistanis in America for equitable development in Pakistan should take particular note of the last two lessons highlighted above. On the one hand, there is a significant potential for increased giving by the Pakistani diaspora in America. On the other, there are also some very serious barriers that keep Pakistani-Americans from giving more to causes in Pakistan. In particular, we have identified three sets of challenges that are particularly pressing and deserving of attention. First, there is a chronic crisis of trust in the civic sector. Second, giving to Pakistan has been, and is becoming, ever more difficult in terms of legal uncertainties and logistical hassles. Third, there is a lack of information about, and familiarity, with Pakistani philanthropic organizations and NGOs amongst the Pakistani diaspora in the United States.

These issues are both important and urgent and they deserve immediate attention from the Pakistani philanthropic sector as a whole and particularly from the Pakistan Center for Philanthropy, which was created specifically for encouraging philanthropy in Pakistan. The barriers identified in this study are important because the latent potential for increased giving cannot be realized unless these barriers are somehow removed. However, there is also an urgency because if left in place, these barriers could have the effect of diverting philanthropic resources away from Pakistan and towards other more attractive and logistically convenient philanthropic options. We believe that three types of measures are required.

♦ Measures that build greater confidence in the civic, and especially the philanthropic, sector.

♦ Measures that facilitate an easier giving process for Pakistani-Americans who wish to give to causes in Pakistan.

♦ Measures of outreach that better familiarize Pakistani-Americans with the work of specific philanthropic organizations in Pakistan.

The rest of this section will outline specific recommendations that emerge from this study about the type of initiatives in each of these three areas that are likely to make a difference. These suggestions flow directly from the findings and analysis of our survey results and, for the most part, emerge from and were discussed at our focus group meetings. To make this discussion relevant, practical, and useful, this section focused on what can be done by the key actors including the Pakistani-Americans themselves, organizations in Pakistan, and others. Table 11 organizes these various suggestions by which actor is best suited to operationally which recommendation.

Building confidence in Pakistan's civic sector

As already elaborated, the lack of trust in the civic sector is the single most important challenge that needs to be addressed before institutional giving to Pakistan can be significantly enhanced. Our survey results and, especially, our focus group discussions point us towards a number of practical measures that could help address the trust deficit.

There is significant, but guarded, support for the idea of *creating a trust-worthy, independent agency for certification* of philanthropic organizations and NGOs. The PCP already has an initiative in this direction and is very well placed to take on this role. A large majority of our survey respondents and focus group participants would welcome independent certification of philanthropic organizations. They argue that this could go a significant distance in allaying their suspicions and creating residual trust for the certified organizations. However, they are guarded in their enthusiasm because the trust invested in any certification program is a factor of the trust reposed in the certifying agency. They warn that given the climate of general distrust, the bar is now set very high for the certifying agency. Questionable performance by any certified

Table 11: Harnessing Greater Diaspora Philanthropy for Pakistan

What are some of the most important things that key constituencies of change can do to encourage greater diaspora philanthropy by Pakistanis in America?

	What can be done by PCP?	What can be done by individual organizations?	What can be done by other actors?
Building confidence in Pakistan's civic sector	• Initiate independent certification of NGOs. • Develop guidelines for standard financial and management reporting of NGO performance. • Develop guidelines for better impact reporting of NGO performance.	• Ensure regular and transparent financial audits and reporting. • Develop mechanisms to calculate and report development impact at the level of organization as well as individual contributors. • Seek outside certification; e.g., financial audits, management reviews, impact monitoring, registration in Pakistan as well as the US, etc.	• Role for media in Pakistan to better report the positive activities and impact of civic sector initiatives.
Facilitating easier mechanisms for giving to causes in Pakistan	• Conduct survey of emerging US laws and regulations on diaspora giving. • Facilitate 'pooled funding drives' by sets of smaller NGOs and philanthropic organizations. • Support educational institutions in harnessing diaspora funding through 'pooled funding drives' as well as capacity development.	• Ask, and ask frequently. • Offer reliable and transparent international money transfer; e.g., ability to accept credit card payments. • Offer convenient and innovative options for contribution; e.g., ability to give in small monthly installments, web-based giving, etc. • Register for US tax-free status to offer peace of mind, tax incentive, and ease of giving.	• Role for State Bank of Pakistan to facilitate easier and cheaper international transfers to nonprofits in Pakistan. • Role for government of Pakistan to work with US government to bring clarity and regulatory uniformity on how philanthropic remittances to Pakistan will be dealt with in the US.
Improving outreach on impacts and achievement of civic sector in Pakistan	• Establish a web-based clearinghouse of information on philanthropies and NGOs in Pakistan that showcases best practice and performance. • Facilitate visits to the United States by team delegations of NGO and philanthropic sector leaders, especially from smaller organizations.	• Create channels of better and more frequent communication to existing and potential donors, including websites, annual reports, financial audits, and impact assessments. • Target visits by representatives around key diaspora events in the USA for outreach activities. • Seek diaspora involvement through non-monetary giving, especially through knowledge-giving and volunteering.	• Role for diaspora institutions, including diaspora media, in better acquainting itself with the activities and achievements of NGOs and philanthropic organizations in Pakistan.

organization will erode the trust not only in that organization but also in the certifier.

There is a strong desire on the part of the Pakistani diaspora in America to see financial and management reports from the organizations they give to. This desire comes partly from the fact that they have become accustomed to seeing such reports from US organizations and is highlighted because of their low level of trust in civic institutions in Pakistan. However, it was also pointed out that those organizations that do offer some sort of financial reports, tend to offer reports that are of variable quality and variable detail (for example, a number of our focus group participants were concerned that executive compensation within Pakistani nonprofits or the percentage of total expenditure that goes to salaries is not reported). An important role for PCP would, therefore, be to *develop guidelines for standard financial and management reporting* of NGO performance so that diaspora donors could better compare the performance of different organizations working in Pakistan.

It was also clear, however, that the diaspora donor is sophisticated enough to realize that an NGOs performance should be gauged not just by its financial and management probity but even more so by the actual impact its work has on society. Much time was spent during the focus groups discussing the difficulties of measuring such impact and also the importance of trying to do so in some systematic fashion. It was often argued that a key contribution by an institution such as the PCP might be to *develop guidelines for standard impact reporting* of NGO performance so that diaspora donors could better compare the performance of different organizations working in Pakistan.

It is the responsibility of NGOs and philanthropic organizations in Pakistan *to develop a culture of regular audits and transparent reporting of financial and management performance.* This issue came up in many of our focus groups and it was repeatedly pointed out that the very fact that an organization would open itself to regular and transparent audits was a signal that would inspire trust; in some respects, knowing that at organization is open to audits was deemed even more important than reviewing the details of the audit reports themselves. Many of our focus group participants stressed that any representative of Pakistani organizations coming to the United States for fundraising should make sure that they are willing to discuss and disclose their financial and management performance to potential diaspora donors.

Similarly, and even more importantly, it is clear that *organizations working in Pakistan need to better measure and better communicate the impacts of their work.* As one focus group participant said, "I am much less interested in hearing about how you will do what you want to do, and much more interested in finding out what difference that will make.... And even more interested in finding out what difference you have already made." This is both a reporting challenge and a communication challenge. As people make their giving decisions they want to make sure that each dollar they give to an institution in Pakistan will somehow have a bigger impact than the same dollar being given to a needy individual. Given the propensity for giving to individuals rather than institutions, our respondents were most keen on information that would convince them that the value addition of institutional giving was enough to offset the personal satisfaction they gain from direct individual giving.

Importantly, our study suggests that one way for organizations to overcome the deficit of trust is to *acquire as many types of outside verification of their impact and influence as they can.* For example, any forms of independent certification, financial audits, management reviews, monitoring reports, media reports, mention in academic studies, etc., all go a long way in building the confidence that people have in a particular organization. Indeed, our focus groups suggest that many Pakistanis in America value organizations that are registered in the US not simply for the tax benefit such registration provides but also because it suggests that the organization meets some minimal standards of legitimacy and performance and is not simply a fly-by-night outfit. In essence, this echoes one of the overarching lessons from this study: reputation matters. Anything that an organization can do to build its reputation as an above board and effective outfit will enhance its chances of gaining support from diaspora donors.

Finally, there is a clear need to address the trust deficit at its source. Pakistani-Americans tend to be suspicious of the organized philanthropic sector in Pakistan largely because their friends and family in Pakistan are suspicious of such organizations. It is very clear from a number of our findings that the people who influence the giving decisions of Pakistani-Americans the most are their friends and family back in Pakistan. This would suggest that *the key to changing the views of Pakistani-Americans is to first change the views of Pakistanis in Pakistan.* Stated differently, the best way to attract more diaspora funds to organized charities in Pakistan is to first attract more contributions from Pakistanis in Pakistan to such charities. In this regard, the diaspora Pakistani may be a more cautious follower and the lead might well have to come first from Pakistanis in Pakistan.

Facilitating easier mechanisms for giving to causes in Pakistan
Although the single most important reason (for half of our survey respondents) for not giving more to Pakistani organizations is a chronic lack of trust, the second most important reason (20-25 percent of our respondents) was that it is not easy to give to Pakistani organizations. This suggests that there is a significant cohort of Pakistani-Americans who are ready to give more, if only it was made easier to give. Here are some suggestions we heard that could make that giving potentially less difficult.

Our focus group participants recognized that the role of an organization such as the PCP is rather limited in terms of making giving to Pakistani organizations easier; particularly in the post-9/11 world where many of the hurdles come from unclear, uncertain and unfriendly US government policies for international financial transactions. However, many of our participants felt that it would be a significant contribution if someone could *prepare a user-friendly inventory of exactly what the new US laws and regulations say about international philanthropic transactions.* Pakistani-Americans have already become far more vigilant in their international giving but are very interested in finding clear, concise, and credible information on exactly what they can and cannot do, who they should and should not give to, and what the limits of donor liability are.

A practical area where umbrella agencies in Pakistan or in the United States could make a difference is to *facilitate 'pooled funding drives' for sets of smaller NGOs and philanthropic organizations* which may not have the ability to harness the philanthropic generosity of the Pakistani diaspora. Many Pakistani-Americans are willing (even eager) to give to small NGOs and community organizations whose work is rooted in ground realities at local levels. However, they find that giving to such organizations is particularly difficult because they do not have the ability to either approach Pakistani-Americans or receive support from them (sometimes simply because they do not have dedicated accounts in which to receive individual donations).

Given that a large proportion of successful Pakistani-Americans owe their success to their education and large numbers within this group were educated in Pakistan, it was felt that there might be considerable untapped potential for alumni giving to educational institutions in Pakistan. However, the hurdles here are those of capacity. Outside actors can help by building the capacity of these organizations to (a) run 'pooled funding drives' in the USA and (b) to organize offices of alumni relations within their institutions to keep a tab on, and to regularly seek the support of, their former students. It was also felt that since education is one of the highest priorities for giving by Pakistani-Americans, educational institutions in Pakistan should target not only their former students but also the larger Pakistani diaspora in America.

Notwithstanding all of the other points already made, it is quite clear that Pakistani NGOs and philanthropic organizations (Pakistan-based as well as US-based) should *ask for contributions from Pakistani-Americans, and ask more often.* There is immense learning available from US-based philanthropy and fundraising research on how important it is to ask, and how to ask.[123] Pakistan-related organizations seeking support from the Pakistani diaspora will do well to learn from this research. It is, of course, important that one should never be offensive in the way one asks for support, nor should be offended if support is refused. However, the art of gentle, repeated, and persuasive asking for support is something that Pakistan-related organizations need to cultivate.

Another set of practical recommendations for NGOs and philanthropic organizations in Pakistan is to *offer reliable and transparent options for international money transfer.* This would include, importantly, the ability to accept credit card payments and various types of bank transactions. Our survey results suggest that only minimal amounts of philanthropic transfers to Pakistan are made through credit cards, largely because most NGOs and organizations in Pakistan do not have the ability to receive support through credit card transfers. This has become more important in the post 9/11 climate because it maintains a monetary trail. However, it is also important for the ease and convenience that it provides to donors in the United States. Indeed, credit card transactions are also a preferred mode of transaction for the recipients because the money is transferred reliably, immediately and at minimal cost.

Related to the above, many of our focus group participants suggest that it would be advisable for individual NGOs and philanthropic organizations **to offer convenient and innovative options for contributions.** For example, a number of our participants pointed out that while many organizations in America encourage donors to give in small regular installments, most Pakistani organizations simply do not have the ability to receive contributions in small regular installments. This makes giving more difficult for donors and serves as an important disincentive to give. Illogical as it might sound to some, the fact of the matter is that many people who are able to have $10 deducted from their credit card every month for a year, find it much more difficult to write a single check for $120 once a year.

Another key recommendation is to suggest to individual organizations to *seek registered nonprofit status in the US*. To many donors—particularly high net-worth donors—the tax incentive can be a major draw. In addition, as we have discussed, being officially registered in the United States can also give donors relative peace of mind in terms of possible legal and regulatory concerns, and can make giving easier simply because the transaction becomes domestic to the USA rather than international.

Our focus group participants also see a role for the *government of Pakistan*, in general, in working directly with the US government to promote clarity and regulatory uniformity in how philanthropic remittances to Pakistan will be dealt with at the US end. There is a general sense within the diaspora communities that charitable remittances to Pakistan may be in for uneven and unfair scrutiny, and they would like clarity on (a) how they need to be vigilant, and (b) what the limits of their liability in charitable giving is.

Improving outreach on impacts and achievements of the civic sector in Pakistan

The bad news coming from this study is that Pakistani-Americans lack information about the size, scale, scope, achievements and impacts of the civic sector in Pakistan, including NGOs and philanthropic organizations. The good news is that, in general, Pakistani-Americans are quite eager to learn more about what and how the civic sector in Pakistan is doing. This suggests that there is both the need and the opportunity for serious outreach to the Pakistani diaspora in America on what the civic sector in Pakistan has achieved till now and the impacts it can have in the future.

A large number of our focus group participants suggest that they would find a *web-based clearinghouse of information on philanthropies, charities and NGOs in Pakistan* to be a very useful resource. Such a web-based clearinghouse of information could serve to showcase the best practices and performance of civic organizations. The type of information that people would find of interest in such a clearinghouse would include financial and management audit information, impact reports, certification information, inventories of projects, independent monitoring reports, media reports, links to websites of organizations and other resources, etc.

Pakistani-Americans are eager to meet representatives from the Pakistan civic sector themselves. This inspires a sense of pride in them as well as greater confidence in the organizations that these personnel represent. Although the representatives of a few of the biggest organizations do regularly visit the United States, they tend to move only in restricted circles and meet select groups of Pakistani-Americans. Moreover, many other civic sector leaders do not visit the US at all. The PCP and other organizations that seek to encourage diaspora philanthropy could facilitate visits to the USA by team delegations of NGO and philanthropic sector leaders. Such visits, similar in some respects to trade delegations, should focus particularly on representatives not only from larger organizations but also from smaller and more novel civic sector organizations. In addition, such visits should focus not only on the 'usual suspects' of stops in terms of the cities and organizations that they interact with, but should also target under-served Pakistani-American communities which have a high willingness and potential to give to causes in Pakistan, but are seldom visited.

Pakistani NGOs and philanthropic organizations should seek to *establish channels of better and more frequent communication with existing and potential diaspora donors*. Because they are distant from Pakistan, diaspora donors wish to hear more and more often about the causes they are giving to. At one level, that sense of connection is itself a major motivator of their giving. It could also include communication through websites, annual reports, financial audits, impact assessments, newsletters, etc.

Organizations in Pakistan which do send representatives to the United States for outreach and fundraising activities should invest time and effort in better understanding the 'rhythms' of the diaspora institutional life of Pakistani-Americans and should structure their visits around these 'rhythms'. Practically, this means targeting visits by representatives around key diaspora events in the US for outreach activities. Visits should be targeted as reputation-building events as much as fundraising events. Our study suggests that a funding base can be built only *after* a good reputational base has been built; investing in a reputational base is, therefore, a good idea.

It is understandable that much of the focus of seeking philanthropic support from the Pakistani-American diaspora revolves around monetary fundraising. However, it is a mistake to focus solely on monetary giving. Our study suggests that Pakistani-Americans are active volunteers who have a strong urge to also give their time and skills to the causes that they are passionate about. Pakistan-related organizations—in America as well as in Pakistan—should actively seek diaspora involvement through non-monetary giving, especially though knowledge-giving and volunteering. This is important because the

Pakistani diaspora is a highly skilled knowledge community and its knowledge-contribution to Pakistan can be as significant as its monetary giving.

There is a palpable eagerness amongst Pakistani-Americans to give much more of their time to causes in Pakistan. However, many of them find it difficult to match up with organizations that are willing and able to use their skills. This is unfortunate because the skills they bring—medical, engineering, management, information technology, scholarship, teaching, etc.—are valuable and much needed in Pakistan. Creating avenues for non-monetary giving in and to Pakistan by Pakistani-Americans is also important because we know that *people who give their time to an organization are also highly likely to give their money to the same organization.*

Finally, the responsibility for better outreach about the roles, relevance and achievements of the Pakistani civic sector rests largely with the Pakistani civic sector itself. However, there is also a *crucial role to be played by the institutions of the Pakistani diaspora in America.* In particular, the growing Pakistani diaspora media in the US, as well as community and professional organizations of Pakistani-Americans, should also seek to better acquaint themselves with what the civic sector in Pakistan is doing and what it has achieved. This is already happening to some extent, particularly through more civic sector leaders being invited by the Pakistani diaspora organizations to come to USA and speak at their events and conferences, and is a process which should be encouraged and accelerated.

Next Steps

This book is a preliminary attempt to systematically analyze a complex and understudied topic. This book stems from the belief that there is a need to move beyond anecdotal stories and more empirical analysis of the how Pakistanis in America cope with the task of juggling multiple identities, particularly through their philanthropic practices.

However, this research is presented with all humility, due vigilance and transparent caution. We strongly believe that the results we have highlighted are, in fact, robust and reflective of the reality of the charitable impulses and philanthropic practices of Pakistani-Americans. However, we also recognize that quantitative research on these topics is not only difficult, it can also give a sense of false precision. We have, therefore, tried to err on the side of caution in terms of what results we highlight as well as how we present them. Our expectation, and hope, is that future researchers will be able to use this first attempt to refine better methodologies, mine better information, and arrive at even more nuanced insights.

This research has also alerted us to important questions and issues that deserve more attention than we have been able to afford them. Let us end with identifying at least three avenues of further research that we hope others will pursue and which can make a huge difference in our understanding the lives and struggles of Pakistanis in America.

Fist, there is clearly a need for better baseline estimates of the size, scale, scope and texture of this and other diaspora communities. The Pakistani-American community is now large enough, organized enough, and interested enough in such research to invest in this itself. One hopes that the pioneering population estimates calculated by the Pakistan Embassy in Washington, DC, will be updated, that its methodology will be made more transparent and subject to expert review, and that it will be converted into a periodic and regular exercise. The highest priority within this area of research is to get better baseline estimates of the economic activity and income distribution of the diaspora. Without the availability of better baseline estimates, any other research on the subject will necessarily remain tentative and hesitant in its conclusions. It is also important to begin getting a temporal picture of the giving habits of this and other communities. What we have presented here is a snapshot in time. Our hope is that others may be able to follow this up at other moments in time so that one can get a sense of how and why these giving habits change over time.

Second, there is a need for more comparative research on diaspora giving by various diaspora communities. A lot of excellent research is coming forth on diaspora philanthropy in general and on the philanthropic profiles of various diaspora communities, especially in the United States. What has not happened as much, as yet, is robust analysis that compares the philanthropic profiles of various diaspora communities. For example, it would be most interesting to compare the philanthropic activities of Pakistanis in America with those of Indians in America or of Filipinos in America; or, to compare philanthropy by Pakistanis in America to philanthropy by Pakistanis in the United Kingdom, or to Pakistanis in the Middle East, and so on. Such research is especially necessary if we are to arrive at broader conceptual lessons about diaspora philanthropy in general. It could also lead to a better understanding of why diasporas from different countries evolve differently in the same host country, or why diasporas from the same country evolve very differently in different host countries. Such insights could be valuable in a globalizing world and could also have significant public policy implications in host as well as home countries.

Third, even though this book is based on broad, nation-wide research of general and generalizable trends, it is quite clear that we also need more in-depth, location-specific research on the nuances of the philanthropic practices of particular Pakistani-American. For example, how is the philanthropic life of Pakistani-Americans in Pasadena, California different or similar to that of Pakistani-Americans in Peoria, Illinois? How do the various Pakistani-American communities in New York City manage their philanthropic activities? What are the differences, similarities, linkages, amongst and between these communities? Such questions can best be answered by in-depth case studies that can ask the type of more nuanced questions and arrive at complex explanations that broad, nation-wide research cannot. Ultimately, more location-specific studies will help us in better explaining the results of the nation-wide research, just as better nation-wide research is required to properly contextualize the location-specific variant.

References

Abraham, Sameer Y. and Nabeel Abraham (editors). 1983. *Arabs in the New World: Studies on Arab-American Communities*. Detroit: Wayne State University Center for Urban Studies.

African Foundation for Development. 2000. *Globalization and Development: A Diaspora Dimension*. London: AFFORD.

Ahmed, Gutbi Mahdi. 1991. 'Muslim Organizations in the United States.' In *The Muslims of America* edited by Yvonne Yazbeck Haddad. New York: Oxford University Press.

Akbar, Raana (undated).'KEMCAANA History' at: http://www.kemcaana.org/Aboutsociety.htm.

American Association of Fundraising Counsel (AAFRC). 2004. *Giving US 2004: Annual Report on Philanthropy,* Washington, DC: AAFRC.

Bagai, Leona B. 1967. *The East Indians and Pakistanis in America*. Minneapolis, MN: Lerner Publications.

Bagby, Ihsan, Paul M. Perl and Bryan T. Froehle. 2001. *The Mosque in America: A National Portrait*. Washington, DC: Council on American-Islamic Relations (CAIR).

Barnes, Jessica S. and Claudette E. Bennett. 2002. *The Asian Population: 2000*. Washington, DC: US Census Bureau.

Ba-Yunus, Ilyas and Moin Siddiqui. 1998. *A Report on the Muslim Population in the United States*. Richmond Hill, NY: Center for American Muslim Research and Information.

Bonbright, David and Asad Azfar. 1999. *Enhancing Indigenous Philanthropy for Social Investment: A Report of the Initiative on Indigenous Philanthropy*. Karachi: The Aga Khan Foundation-Pakistan.

Brittingham, Angela and G. Patricia de la Cruz. 2002. *Ancestry: 2000*. Washington, DC: US Census Bureau.

Burki, Shahid Javed. 2005a. 'Another Kind of Influence.' *Dawn* (daily), Karachi, Pakistan, March 22, 2005 (available at www.dawn.com).

Burki, Shahid Javed. 2005b. 'Expatriates' Economic Role.' *Dawn* (daily), Karachi, Pakistan, March 29, 2005 (available at www.dawn.com).

Burki, Shahid Javed. 2005c. 'Anatomy of Remittances.' *Dawn* (daily), Karachi, Pakistan, April 5, 2005 (available at www.dawn.com).

Burki, Shahid Javed. 2005d. 'Expatriates' Investments.' *Dawn* (daily), Karachi, Pakistan, April 12, 2005 (available at www.dawn.com).

Burki, Shahid Javed. 2005e. 'Utilizing Expatriate Money.' *Dawn* (daily), Karachi, Pakistan, April 19, 2005 (available at www.dawn.com).

Chan, Sucheng. 1991. *Asian Americans: An Interpretive History.* Boston: Twayne Publishers.

Coward, Harold, John R. Hinnells and Raymond Brady Williams (editors). 2000. *The South Asian Religious Diaspora in Britain, Canada, and the United States.* Albany: State University of New York Press.

Durrani, Tehmina. 1996. *Abdul Sattar Edhi: An Autobiography.* Islamabad: National Bureau of Publications.

Embassy of Pakistan. 2004. *Pakistani American Demographics: 2003 Annual Report.* Washington, DC: Embassy of Pakistan.

Friedman, Lisa. 2004. 'Muslims shy away from philanthropy.' *Los Angeles Daily News.* October 30, 2004.

Geithner, Peter F., Paula D. Johnson, and Lincoln C. Chen (editors). 2004. *Diaspora Philanthropy and Equitable Development in China and India.* Cambridge, MA: Harvard University.

Ghayur, Arif M. 1981. 'The Muslim Population in the United States.' *Annals of American Academy of Political Science,* 454: 150-163.

Greembaum, Thomas L. 1997. *The Handbook for Focus Group Research* (second edition). New York: Sage Publications.

Haddad, Yvonne Yazbeck (editor). 1991. *The Muslims of America.* New York: Oxford University Press.

Huda, Qamal-ul. 2006. *The Diversity of Muslims in the United States.* Special Report 159 of the United States Institute of Peace (USIP). Washington, DC: USIP.

Johnson, Paula. 2001. *Global Social Investing: A Preliminary Overview.* Boston, MA: Philanthropic Initiative.

Khalidi, Omar. 2000. 'Approaches to Mosque Design in North America.' In *Muslims on the Americanization Path*, edited by Yvinne Yasbeck Haddad and John L. Esposito, pages 317-332. New York: Oxford University Press.

Koenig, Angela T. 2004. *Pakistanis in America.* Chanhassen, MN: The Child's World.

Krueger, Richard A. 1997. *Analyzing and reporting Focus Group Results.* New York: Sage Publications.

Kumar, Gopa. 2003. *Indian Diaspora and Giving Patterns of Indian Americans in the U.S.* New Delhi: Charities Aid Foundation India.

Leonard, Karen Isaksen. 1997. *The South Asian Americans*. Westport, CT: Greenwood Press.

Lethlean, Esther. 2001. *Diaspora: The New Philanthropy?* New York: Center for Philanthropy, City University of New York.

Levitt, Peggy . 2001. *The Transnational Villagers*. Berkeley: University of California Press.

Lovell, Emily Kalled. 1983. 'Islam in the United States: Past and Present.' In *The Muslim Community in North America*, edited by Earle H. Waugh, Baha Abu-Laban and Regula B. Qureshi. Edmonton: University of Alberta Press.

Mamdani, Mahmood. 2004. *Good Muslim, Bad Muslim: America, the Cold War and the Roots of Terror*. New York: Pantheon Books.

McChesney, Robert D. 2004. 'Charity and Philanthropy in Islam.' In *Philanthropy in America: A Comprehensive Historical Encyclopedia*, edited by Dwight F. Burlingame, Washington, DC: ABC-CLIO.

Merz, Barbara J. 2005. *New Patterns for Mexico: Observations on Remittances, Philanthropic Giving, and Equitable Development*. Cambridge, MA: Harvard University.

Miles, Matthew B. and Michael Huberman. 1994. *Qualitative Data Analysis: An Expanded Sourcebook* (second edition). New York: Sage Publications.

Naff, Alixa. 1983. 'Arabs in America: A Historical Overview.' In *Arabs in the New World: Studies on Arab-American Communities*, edited by Sameer Y. Abraham and Nabeel Abraham. Detroit: Wayne State University Center for Urban Studies.

Najam, Adil. 1996. 'Understanding the Third Sector: Revisiting the Prince, the Merchant and the Citizen.' *Nonprofit Management and Leadership, 7(2)*: 203-19.

Najam, Adil. 1994. 'The Brain Drain Sabotage.' In *Pakistan: Our Identity*, pages 4-18. Islamabad: GOY Publications.

Najam, Adil. 1996. 'NGO Accountability: A Conceptual Framework.' *Development Policy Review, (14)1*: 339-53.

Najam, Adil. 2000. 'The Four C's of Third Sector-Government Relations: Cooperation, Confrontation, Complementarity, and Co-optation.' *Nonprofit Management and Leadership, 10(4)*: 375-396.

Nimer, Mohamed. 2002. *The North American Muslim Resource Guide: Muslim Community Life in the United States and Canada*. New York: Routledge.

Pribbenow, Paul. 2005. 'Public Character: Philanthropic Fundraising and the

Claims of Accountability,' in *New Directions for Philanthropic Fundraising*, 47: 13-27, 2005.

Ratha, Dilip. 2003. 'Workers' Remittances: An Important and Stable Source of External Development Finance.' In *Global Development Finance*. Washington, DC: World Bank.

Reis, Thomas K. and Stephanie J. Clohesy. 2001. 'Unleashing New Resources and Entrepreneurship for the Common Good: A Philanthropic Renaissance,' in *New Directions for Philanthropic Fundraising*, 32: 109-144.

Saxon-Harrold, Susan K.E., Susan J. Wiener, Michael T. McCormick and Michelle A. Weber. 2000. *America's Religious Congregations: Measuring Their Contribution to Society*. Washington DC: Independent Sector.

Schmidt, Garbi. 2004. *Islam in Urban America: Sunni Muslims in Chicago*. Philadelphia: Temple University Press.

Sidel, Mark. 2004. 'Diaspora Philanthropy to India: A Perspective from the United States.' In *Philanthropy and Equitable Development in China and India* edited by Peter F. Geithner, Paula D. Johnson and Lincoln C. Chen, pages 215-258. Cambridge, MA: Harvard University.

Sowell, Thomas. 1996. *Migrations and Cultures: A World View*, New York: Basic Books.

Stone, Carol L. 1991. 'Estimate of Muslims Living in America.' In *The Muslims of America* edited by Yvonne Yazbeck Haddad, New York: Oxford University Press.

The Philanthropic Initiative. 2003. *Global Giving: Making a World of Difference*. Boston, MA: Philanthropic Initiative.

Toppe, Christopher M., Arthur D. Krisch and Jocabel Michel. 2002. *Giving and Volunteering in the United States, 2001: Findings from a National Survey*. Washington DC: Independent Sector.

Toppe, Christopher M., Arthur D. Krisch, Jocabel Michel, Susan J. Wiener and Nadine T. Jalandoni. 2002. *Faith and Philanthropy: The Connection Between Charitable Behavior and Giving to Religion*. Washington, DC: Independent Sector.

Waugh, Earle H., Baha Abu-Laban and Regula B. Qureshi (editors). 1983. *The Muslim Community in North America*. Edmonton: University of Alberta Press,.

Williams, Raymond Brady. 1988. *Religions of Immigrants from India and Pakistan: New Threads in the American Tapestry*. New York: Cambridge University Press.

Wolfe, Michael (editor). 2002. *Taking Back Islam: American Muslims Reclaim Their Faith*. New York: Rodale Inc.

Yin, Xiao-huang and Zhiyong Lan. 2004. 'Why Do They Give? Chinese American Transnational Philanthropy Since the 1970s.' In *Philanthropy and Equitable Development in China and India* edited by Peter F. Geithner, Paula D. Johnson and Lincoln C. Chen, pages 79-128. Cambridge, MA: Harvard University.

Notes

1. This book uses the terms 'Pakistani diaspora in the United States', 'Pakistanis in America', and 'Pakistani-Americans' inter-changeably to refer to people of Pakistani descent now living in the USA, irrespective of their immigration status. We use these multiple terms to break the monotony for the reader but also because our focus is on all of those for whom Pakistan makes up a part of their identity, and not on whether they have or have not acquired US citizenship or permanent residence.

2. Peter F. Geithner, Paula D. Johnson and Lincoln C. Chen (editors). *Diaspora Philanthropy and Equitable Development in China and India*, Cambridge, MA: Harvard University, 2004; Gopa Kumar (editor) *Indian Diaspora and Giving patterns of Indian Americans in the U.S.*, New Delhi: Charities Aid Foundation India, 2003; The Philanthropic Initiative, *Global Giving: Making a World of Difference*, Boston, MA: Philanthropic Initiative, 2003; Paula Johnson, *Global Social Investing: A Preliminary Overview*, Boston, MA: Philanthropic Initiative, 2001; Peggy Levitt, *The Transnational Villagers*, Berkeley: University of California Press, 2001; Esther Lethlean, *Diaspora: The New philanthropy?*, New York: Center for Philanthropy, City University of New York, 2001.

3. 'Overview', pages xiii-xxii in Geithner, Johnson and Chen. *Diaspora Philanthropy and Equitable Development in China and India*.

4. 'Preface' by Barry D. Gaberman (p. vii), in Geithner, Johnson and Chen. *Diaspora Philanthropy and Equitable Development in China and India*.

5. Shahid Javed Burki has, most recently, laid out his arguments for the importance of economic and social investments by Pakistani expatriates in a series of essays in the daily *Dawn* (Karachi; available at www.dawn.com). These include: 'Another kind of influence' (March 22, 2005), 'Expatriates' economic role' (March 29, 2005), 'Anatomy of remittances' (April 5, 2005), 'Expatriates' investment' (April 12, 2005) and 'Utilizing expatriate money' (April 19, 2005).

6. This trend, of course, is not limited to Pakistan. The World Bank, in particular, has been identifying a similar trend in the social and economic value of expatriate remittances as a potential motor of development. See Dilip Ratha, 'Workers' Remittances: An Important and Stable Source of External Development Finance,' in *Global Development Finance*, World Bank, 2003; African Foundation for Development, *Globalization and Development: A Diaspora Dimension,* London: AFFORD, 2000.

7. Mohamed Nimer reflects on a fairly similar phenomenon within American Muslims, of whom Paksitani-Americans make up the single largest national immigrant contingent (see Mohamed Nimer, *The North American Muslim Resource Guide: Muslim Community Life in the United States and Canada*, New York: Routledge, 2002). Xiao-

huang Yin and Zhiyong Lan identifies similar trends within the Chinese-American diaspora and Mark Sidel does likewise for the Indian diaspora in the USA (see 'Why Do They Give? Chinese American Transnational Philanthropy Since the 1970s' by Xiaohuang Yin and Zhiyong Lan (pages 79-128) and 'Diaspora Philanthropy to India: A Perspective from the United States' by Mark Sidel (pages 215-258), both 'in Geithner, Johnson and Chen. *Diaspora Philanthropy and Equitable Development in China and India*). More generally, the literature on diaspora communities suggests that the desire to maintain a link, including a philanthropic link, to the country of origin is common to most diaspora communities and that the forces of globalization only enhances the opportunities to maintain such links (see Levitt, *The Transnational Villagers*; Thomas Sowell, *Migrations and Cultures: A World View*, New York: Basic Books, 1996).

8.For more on the legendary philanthropist Abdul Sattar Edhi, see Tehmina Durrani, *Abdul Sattar Edhi: An Autobiography*, Islamabad: National Bureau of Publications, 1996.

9.For more on these and on PCP and its activities, see www.pcp.org.pk. Also see, David Bonbright and Asad Azfar, *Enhancing Indigenous Philanthropy for Social Investment: A Report of the Initiative on Indigenous Philanthropy*, Karachi: The Aga Khan Foundation-Pakistan, 1999.

10. For example, the fundraising initiatives of the Shaukat Khanum Memorial Trust (SKMT), the Layton Rehmatullah Benevolent Trust (LRBT), the Human Development Foundation (HDFNA), The Citizen's Foundation (TCF), Development in Literacy (DIL), the SOS Children's Village, etc. have become regular features in the social calendars of many Pakistani-American communities.

11. Bonbright and Azfar, *Enhancing Indigenous Philanthropy for Social Investment;* Also see www.pcp.org.pk.

12. See http://www.usccr.giv/pubs/sac/il0503/ch7.htm.

13. 'Muslims shy away from philanthropy' by Lisa Friedman, *Los Angeles Daily News*, October 30, 2004. Accessed at http://www.montereyherald.com/mld/montereyherald/news/state/10056199.htm.

14. 'Under Suspicion' a report by Jeffrey Kaye, *NewsHour with Jim Lehrer*, September 12, 2004. Transcript accessed at http://www.pbs.org/newshour/bb/religion/july-dec02/muslims_9-12.html.

15. The majority of focus group discussions were led by Dr. Adil Najam or Dr. Salal Humair. A large number of focus groups were led by Dr. Bilal Zuberi. A few each were led by Dr. Musadik Malik, Sabahat Ashraf, Momina Suleman. A number of other team members also actively participated in various focus groups.

16. The number of survey forms completed is significantly different from the number of focus group participants for a variety of reasons: (i) in many cases multiple members of the same household (usually couples) participated in the same focus group; however, only one forms per household was collected.; (ii) some participants of the focus groups chose not to complete the survey forms; (iii) some of the completed survey forms had insufficient information for analysis and were discarded; (iv) a significant

minority of survey forms were received from participants who did not attend any focus groups.

17. The team that participated in the development of the survey forms included Dr. Adil Najam, Durriya Farooqui, Dr. Salal Humair, Dr. Bilal Zuberi, and Hasan Usmani. Useful feedback was received from multiple reviewers on the various drafts of the survey questionnaire.

18. This includes focus groups held in Maryland and Virginia, which are counted as part of the District of Columbia (DC) metropolitan region.

19. See Thomas L. Greembaum, *The Handbook for Focus Group Research* (second edition), New York: Sage Publications, 1997; Matthew B. Miles and Michael Huberman, *Qualitative Data Analysis: An Expanded Sourcebook* (second edition), New York: Sage Publications, 1994; Richard A. Krueger, *Analyzing and reporting Focus Group Results*, New York: Sage Publications, 1997.

20. See, for example, Sidel in *Diaspora Philanthropy and Equitable Development in China and India;* Kumar, *Indian Diaspora and Giving Patterns of Indian Americans in the U.S.*

21. See, for example, Nimer, *The North American Muslim Resource Guide*; Carol L. Stone, 'Estimate of Muslims Living in America', in *The Muslims of America* by Yvonne Yazbeck Haddad, New York: Oxford University Press, 1991; Karen Isaksen Leonard, *The South Asian Americans*, Westport, CT: Greenwood Press, 1997; Raymond Brady Williams, *Religions of Immigrants from India and Pakistan: New Threads in the American Tapestry*, New York: Cambridge University Press, 1988; Sidel in *Diaspora Philanthropy and Equitable Development in China and India*; Qamar-ul Huda, *The Diversity of Muslims in the United States*, Special Report 159, Washington, DC: United States Institute of Peace (USIP), 2006.

22. Leonard, *The South Asian Americans*; Kumar, *Indian Diaspora and Giving Patterns of Indian Americans in the U.S.*

23. Leona B. Bagai, *The East Indians and Pakistanis in America*, Minneapolis, MN: Lerner Publications, 1967.

24. Kumar, *Indian Diaspora and Giving Patterns of Indian Americans in the U.S.*

25. For more on the early Punjabi agriculturalists in California, see, Leonard, *The South Asian Americans* (pages 39-65).

26. Kumar, *Indian Diaspora and Giving Patterns of Indian Americans in the U.S.*, (pages 23-5).

27. First figure from Bagai, *The East Indians and Pakistanis in America* (page 29); second figure from Kumar, *Indian Diaspora and Giving Patterns of Indian Americans in the U.S.*

28. Bagai, *The East Indians and Pakistanis in America*; Leonard, *The South Asian Americans* (pages 39-65); Kumar, *Indian Diaspora and Giving Patterns of Indian Americans in the U.S.*

29. See Nimer, *The North American Muslim Resource Guide*; Gutbi Mahdi Ahmed, 'Muslim Organizations in the United States,' in *The Muslims of America*; Williams,

Religions of Immigrants from India and Pakistan; Alixa Naff, 'Arabs in America: A Historical Overview,' in *Arabs in the New World: Studies on Arab-American Communities*, edited by Sameer Y. Abraham and Nabeel Abraham, Detroit: Wayne State University Center for Urban Studies, 1983; Emily Kalled Lovell, 'Islam in the United States: Past and Present,' in *The Muslim Community in North America*, edited by Earle H. Waugh, Baha Abu-Laban and Regula B. Qureshi, Edmonton: University of Alberta Press, 1983.

30. Bagai, *The East Indians and Pakistanis in America*; Ahmed, in *The Muslims of America*.

31. According to Garbi Schmidt (*Islam in Urban America: Sunni Muslims in Chicago*, Philadelphia: Temple University Press, 2004, p. 21) the annual allowance for Pakistanis was capped at 100 per year.

32. All three examples are detailed in Bagai, *The East Indians and Pakistanis in America*.

33. A children's' book (Bagai, *The East Indians and Pakistanis in America*) written for school libraries and published in 1967, very much conveyed the sense that these were 'model' immigrants. The title and the lumping together of 'East Indians' and 'Pakistanis' is also interesting; by the year 2004 a similar book (Angela T. Koenig, Chanhassen, *Pakistanis in America*, MN: The Child's World, 2004) was no longer lumping these two communities together.

34. Schmidt, *Islam in Urban America: Sunni Muslims in Chicago*.

35. Sucheng Chan, *Asian Americans: An Interpretive History*, Boston: Twayne Publishers, 1991; Kumar, *Indian Diaspora and Giving Patterns of Indian Americans in the U.S.*

36. Leonard, *The South Asian Americans*.

37. Kumar, *Indian Diaspora and Giving Patterns of Indian Americans in the U.S.*

38. Adil Najam, 'The Brain Drain Sabotage,' in *Pakistan: Our Identity*, pages 4-18, Islamabad: GOY, 1994.

39. Leonard, *The South Asian Americans* (page 71).

40. The year 1991 saw huge once-off jump in the number of immigrants admitted from a host of countries. This includes a 50 percent jump in Indian immigrants (from 30,667 in 1990 to 45,064 in 1991), a 110 percent jump in Pakistani immigrants (from 9,729 to 20,355) and a 150 percent jump in Bangladeshi immigrants (from 4,252 to 10,676). Although the law changed in 1986, it would have taken a few years for the applications of those seeking immigrant status change to work its way through the legal system.

41. Leonard, *The South Asian Americans* by Karen Isaksen Leonard (page 71).

42. Nimer, *The North American Muslim Resource Guide*.

43. Embassy of Pakistan, *Pakistani American Demographics: 2003 Annual Report*. Washington, DC: Embassy of Pakistan.

44. These higher population estimates are usually extrapolated from assumptions based on very high estimates of total Muslim population in America (in the 5-7 million

range) and of a high proportion of Pakistanis (20-25 percent) within that population. However, as the recent analysis (see, Nimer, *The North American Muslim Resource Guide*) suggest, both of these assumptions are likely to be severely exaggerated.

45. A recent and detailed analysis of total Muslim population in the USA is to be found in Nimer, *The North American Muslim Resource Guide*. Nimer estimates the total Muslim population in the United States to be between 2,560,000 and 4,390,000, or an average of 3.5 million (page 27); moreover, his calculations suggest that 15 percent of Muslim immigrants coming into the US are from Pakistan (pages 24-25). Both lower and higher (but less convincing) estimates and projections of the Muslim population can be found in, for example, Stone, in *The Muslims of America*; Arif M. Ghayur, 'The Muslim Population in the United States,' *Annals of American Academy of Political Science*, 454: 150-163, 1981; Ilyas Ba-Yunus and Moin Siddiqui, *A Report on the Muslim Population in the United States*, Richmond Hill, NY: Center for American Muslim Research and Information, 1998.

46. Embassy of Pakistan, *Pakistani American Demographics* (page 9).

47. For a discussion of census results on these two questions, see Jessica S. Barnes and Claudette E. Bennett, *The Asian Population: 2000,* Washington, DC: US Census Bureau, 2002; Angela Brittingham and G. Patricia de la Cruz, *Ancestry: 2000,* Washington, DC: US Census Bureau, 2002.

48. For example, Nimer, *The North American Muslim Resource Guide* (page 29).

49. What this means, for example, is that our confidence in the Embassy's estimate about there being around 480,000 Pakistanis living in America in 2002 is higher than our confidence that, in fact, there are only 37(and not 36 or 38) Pakistanis living in Wyoming. It should also be pointed out that the Embassy's estimates are based on 2001-02 data and regional distributions can change over short period.

50. Embassy of Pakistan, *Pakistani American Demographics*.

51. The list of Metropolitan areas mentioned here is not exhaustive. The purpose is to highlight some of the cities, outside of the 'big five,' that have significant number of Pakistani-Americans. This does not suggest that these cities are in some way more important than other cities not mentioned here.

52. See, the 2002 Annual Demographic Survey (March Supplement) conducted by the US Bureau of Labor Statistics and the US Bureau of the Census (http://www.bls.census.gov/cps/ads/adsmain.htm).

53. Leonard, *The South Asian Americans*; Sidel in *Diaspora Philanthropy and Equitable Development in China and India*; Kumar, *Indian Diaspora and Giving Patterns of Indian Americans in the U.S.*; Koenig, *Pakistanis in America*.

54. This is quite different, for example, from the Indian case where the most active civic associations tend to be regionally or ethnically focused. The difference is probably explained by the India's much larger size and internal diversity as well as by its larger diaspora. See, Sidel in *Diaspora Philanthropy and Equitable Development in China and India*.

55. See http://www.embassyofpakistan.org/community.php.

56. In some cases, depending on the size and leanings of the Pakistani students there, Pakistan-related activities become part of larger South Asian Student Associations or Muslim Student Associations.

57. See http://www.pakistanlink.com/Community/2004April04/ 30/02.html.

58. Raana Akbar, 'KEMCAANA History,' at: http://www.kemcaana.org/ Aboutsociety.htm, undated.

59. Raana Akbar, 'KEMCAANA History.

60. See http://www.openglobal.org/news1.htm.

61. Williams, *Religions of Immigrants from India and Pakistan* (page 279)

62. Schmidt, *Islam in Urban America: Sunni Muslims in Chicago*; Williams, *Religions of Immigrants from India and Pakistan*; Nimer, *The North American Muslim Resource Guide*.

63. Christopher M. Toppe, Arthur D. Krisch, Jocabel Michel, Susan J. Wiener and Nadine T. Jalandoni, *Faith and Philanthropy: The Connection Between Charitable Behavior and Giving to Religion*, Washington, DC: Independent Sector, 2002.

64. Williams, *Religions of Immigrants from India and Pakistan*.

65. *Zakat* is a mandatory activity for every Muslim (one of the five mandatory personal obligations) to give a proportion of their wealth (usually around 2.5 percent) every year to prescribed categories of the needy. It is sometimes described as an 'alms tax' precisely because the prescribed categories relate principally to helping the poor and the needy within the giver's community. *Sadaqah* refers to voluntary charity by Muslims and is strongly encouraged in religious doctrine but is not mandatory. For many practicing Muslims *sadaqah* is an integral part of being a good Muslim, even if it is not a duty like *zakat*. *Waqf* (endowment or trust) is a particular type of endowed *sadaqah*, which is also encouraged as a means for charitable giving. Importantly, Islam establishes a clear priority for helping the poor, the destitute, and the needy and clearly seeks good citizenship and an economically just society through its doctrine of charity. For more on these concepts and related discussion, see, Robert D. McChesney, 'Charity and Philanthropy in Islam,' in *Philanthropy in America: A Comprehensive Historical Encyclopedia*, edited by Dwight F. Burlingame, Washington, DC: ABC-CLIO, 2004.

66. The debate on whether *zakat* can be used for building mosques or not is particularly relevant to Muslim communities in America and those raising funds for establishing mosques. Such projects nearly always result in intense community involvement because these tend to be sizeable fundraising and construction projects and also because of their spiritual importance. For example, the *Islamic Center of Boston*, in Wayland, Massachusetts (which has a mixed congregation with Muslims from various countries, but with a large Pakistani component) recently completed a $3 million expansion process and went through a passionate but inspiringly transparent and open community discussion, using its website as a means of transparent decision-making (www.icbwayland.org/buildingexpansion).

67. See, Ihsan Bagby, Paul M. Perl and Bryan T. Froehle, *The Mosque in America: A National Portrait*, Washington, DC: Council on American-Islamic Relations, 2001. A listing of mosques in the United States is available in Nimer, *The North American Muslim Resource Guide*.

68. For more see, Bagby et al., *The Mosque in America*. Also see Omar Khalidi, 'Approaches to Mosque Design in North America,' pages 317-332, in *Muslims on the Americanization Path*, edited by Yvinne Yasbeck Haddad and John L. Esposito, New York: Oxford University Press, 2000.

69. For a detailed discussion on the denominational profile of Muslims from South Asia (especially Nizari Ismaili Muslims) and profiles of religious organizations in the Houston and Chicago areas, see, Williams, *Religions of Immigrants from India and Pakistan*.

70. See Durrani, *Abdul Sattar Edhi*.

71. For example, in our sample only 1.97 percent of respondents reported household incomes of less than $20,000 per year. By comparison, the 2000 US Census reports that 22.58 percent of all US respondents and 17.34 percent of Asian respondents were in this income category. Similarly, in our sample, nearly 13 percent of respondents reported incomes of $200,000 per year or more. According to US Census numbers, only 2.36 percent of all US households and 4.03 percent of all Asian households fall within this income category. (*See* http://www.bls.census.gov/cps/ads/adsmain.htm).

72. Question 6 of the US Census 2000 Form asks respondents to identify the race and the choices including six 'Asian' categories (Asian Indian, Chinese, Filipino, Japanese, Korean, and Vietnamese). In addition, the 2000 Census Form allowed respondents to write in their own category under 'other Asian' and 'Pakistani' was the second largest response in this write-in category with 204,309 respondents choosing it (this makes Pakistanis the eighth largest Asian community in America according to the 2000 US Census after the six that are directly named in the Census form and Cambodians). However, it is assumed that the number reported for Pakistanis under this question is an under-representation because at least some respondents of Pakistani descent are likely to choose the official catchall category of 'Asian Indian' that is spelled out in the 2000 US Census while others are likely to leave this question unanswered because it is not mandatory.

73. According to the 2002 Annual Demographic Survey (March Supplement) conducted by the US Bureau of Labor Statistics and the US Bureau of the Census (http://www.bls.census.gov/cps/ads/adsmain.htm) the mean household income for all US households in 2002 was $57,852. This figure was $60,166 for white households, $62,115 for white households not including Hispanics; $40,011 for black households, $44,887 for Hispanic households, and $70,047 for Asian households.

74. Leonard, *The South Asian Americans*; Sidel in *Diaspora Philanthropy and Equitable Development in China and India*.

75. For more census details on Asians in the USA see Barnes and Bennett, *The Asian Population.*

76. Christopher M. Toppe, Arthur D. Krisch and Jocabel Michel, *Giving and Volunteering in the United States, 2001: Findings from a National Survey,* Washington DC: Independent Sector, 2002.

77. *Zakat* is a mandatory requirement for every Muslim (one of the five mandatory personal obligations) to give a proportion of their wealth (usually around 2.5 percent) every year to prescribed categories of the needy. *Sadaqah* refers to voluntary charity by Muslims and is strongly encouraged in religious doctrine but is not mandatory. See earlier footnote for a more detailed description.

78. For example, a survey of philanthropic giving in the United States (conducted much more elaborately and with far better quality baseline data than our own) notes with caution that the primary value of such survey findings "is to discern identifiable giving and volunteering patterns among the population and relate them to different variables." It goes on to suggest that aggregate numbers should not be derived from such surveys and that when they are, they tend to be less than the actual number, primarily because relatively few very large gifts can change the total significantly and these are likely to be undercounted in most survey instruments. (See Toppe, et al., *Giving and Volunteering in the United States, 2001,* page 15).

79. The survey instrument (see Annex) asked responding households to indicate their annual giving in cash, in kind and in time. Giving in cash and in kind were reported in US dollars by the respondents while the giving in time was reported in hours and was then converted into equivalent value in US dollars based on the standard method used by the US Department of Labor.

80. Toppe, et al., *Giving and Volunteering in the United States, 2001.*

81. For the year 2003, each hour of volunteered time is valued at $17.19. This number is based on the average hourly wage for nonagricultural workers in the USA and is derived from US Department of Labor statistics. *Independent Sector,* a nonprofit consortium focusing on philanthropy and volunteering research, provides the appropriate value of an hour of volunteered time in the US on its website (www.IndependentSector.org). We also follow *Independent Sector's* methodology by using a 1,700 hours work-year to convert total hours volunteered into equivalent full-time employees.

82. The aggregate calculations were rounded off *after* aggregation.

83. For more detailed discussions of how places of worship assume far greater social, cultural and community relevance for immigrant and diaspora communities, see Levitt, *The Transnational Villagers*; Sowell, *Migrations and Cultures*; Williams, *Religions of Immigrants from India and Pakistan*; and Harold Coward, John R. Hinnells and Raymond Brady Williams (editors), *The South Asian Religious Diaspora in Britain, Canada, and the United States,* Albany: State University of New York Press, 2000.

84. This discussion is related only to the patterns emerging from an analysis of the actual amounts that our respondents reported as faith-motivated monetary giving. Re-

sults from a separate set of *perceptional* questions about the same issue will be discussed later in Chapter 5.

85. No question was asked about the motivations behind in-kind contributions. However, it seems fair to assume that the motivation behind in-kind giving is not different from that behind monetary giving.

86. Not surprisingly, faith-motivated giving was slightly greater than half (54%) of the total monetary giving in Pakistan while it was slightly less than half of the total in cases of monetary giving to causes unrelated to Pakistan (48%) or to Pakistani causes in America (47%). But, in general, the half-and-half rule seems to be validated by this distribution.

87. Toppe et al., *Giving and Volunteering in the United States, 2001,* page 57.

88. In response to another question in the US survey by *Independent Sector,* just over half of Americans who give (52.4% of contributing respondents) considered the fulfillment of their religious obligations as a main reason for giving. By comparison, a similarly phrased question in our survey found that about 60% of our respondents rated religious duty to be charitable as being of 'high' or 'very high' importance.

89. Toppe et al., *Faith and Philanthropy*; Also, Susan Saxon-Harrold, Susan J. Wiener, Michael T. McCormick and Michelle A. Weber, *America's Religious Congregations: Measuring Their Contribution to Society,* Washington DC: Independent Sector, 2000.

90. Toppe et al., *Giving and Volunteering in the United States, 2001,* page 33.

91. Levitt, *The Transnational Villagers*; Sowell, *Migrations and Cultures: A World View.*

92. Bonbright and Azfar, *Enhancing Indigenous Philanthropy for Social Investment.*

93. American Association of Fundraising Counsel (AAFRC), *Giving US 2004: Annual Report on Philanthropy,* Washington, DC: AAFRC, 2004; see www.aafrc.org.

94. Toppe et al., *Giving and Volunteering in the United States, 2001.*

95. Toppe et al., *Giving and Volunteering in the United States, 2001,* page 138.

96. In general, the tendency for about half the total monetary giving to be faith-motivated with the remaining half motivated by other issues and identities applies nearly uniformly across the various demographic variables identified here. Since the general 'half-and-half principle' has already been discussed earlier, this section will not repeat that discussion.

97. The numbers mentioned in the accompanying table refer to the percentage of respondents who consider this issue to be important to them; it does *not* reflect the actual amount of giving that may be devoted to this issue.

98. For more on this theme see, Mahmood Mamdani, *Good Muslim, Bad Muslim: America, the Cold War and the Roots of Terror,* New York: Pantheon Books, 2004; Michael Wolfe (editor), *Taking Back Islam: American Muslims Reclaim Their Faith,* New York: Rodale Inc., 2002; Huda, *The Diversity of Muslims in the United States.*

99. See Adil Najam 'NGO Accountability: A Conceptual Framework.' *Development Policy Review,* (14)1: 339-53, 1996.

100. For more on the importance of the mosque to the community life of Muslim-Americans, see Bagby, et al., *The Mosque in America.*

101. This particular question elicited less responses than any other question in the survey and some respondents raised concerns about its purpose. The legitimate concern of some respondents was that in the post-9/11 climate, the responses to this question could very easily be misunderstood or misused.

102. Respondents were asked to check the appropriate form of transaction if any of their contributions in the previous year (irrespective of amount) was made using the particular channel (cash, bank or credit card transaction). Hence, someone who might have contributed $5 in cash to a street beggar in Pakistan and also $100 in bank check to an organized charity in Pakistan would select both 'cash transactions' and 'bank transactions'.

103. It should be noted that the numbers mentioned here and in the accompanying figure refer to the percentage of respondents who used these channels as one of the means to transfer contributions. They do *not* refer to the proportion of actual money transferred through this particular channel.

104. The number of average 'asks per month' may seem like a discrete variable, but is not. The somewhat oddly named category of 'less than one' asks per month refers to incidences where the asks are actually between 1 and 11 asks per year, and would therefore average to less than one ask per month; similarly, someone saying that they are asked 1-2 times per month are actually implying that they get between 12 and 24 requests to give per year.

105. Toppe et al., *Giving and Volunteering in the United States, 2001,* page 44.

106. It should be noted that the numbers mentioned here and in the accompanying figure refer to the percentage of respondents who reported an increase, decrease, or stability in their contributions. They do *not* refer to the proportion of contribution change in dollar terms.

107. Huda, *The Diversity of Muslims in the United States.*

108. The percentage of respondents who considered each statement to be of 'medium importance' is not shown in the figure and can be easily calculated by adding the two numbers that are shown for each statement and subtracting the sum from 100.

109. The percentage of respondents who considered each statement to be of 'medium importance' is not shown in the figure and can be easily calculated by adding the two numbers that are shown for each statement and subtracting the sum from 100.

110. See Najam 'NGO Accountability: A Conceptual Framework.'

111. Interestingly, being registered in Pakistan does not inspire similar confidence and more than half of our respondents (56 percent) feel that it is of 'no' or 'low' importance to their philanthropic decisions.

112. The fifth option in this question was stating that one had no opinion. The accompanying figure reports on all responses that gave an opinion along the four-point

scale. The numbers in the accompanying figure, therefore, add up to 100 for every statement.

113. Although the question used the phrase 'philanthropic organizations', our respondents made it clear (in how they filled the forms and in focus group discussions) that they understood this to include the larger NGO sector and also that their views related not only to how private philanthropic donations are used but also institutional support from government and international assistance agencies.

114. See Adil Najam, 'Understanding the Third Sector: Revisiting the Prince, the Merchant and the Citizen.' *Nonprofit Management and Leadership,* 7(2): 203-19, 1996; Adil Najam, 'The Four C's of Third Sector-Government Relations: Cooperation, Confrontation, Complementarity, and Co-optation,' *Nonprofit Management and Leadership,* 10(4): 375-396, 2000.

115. See Najam, 'Understanding the Third Sector: Revisiting the Prince, the Merchant and the Citizen.'

116. Toppe et al., *Giving and Volunteering in the United States, 2001,* page 111.

117. It should be noted that those who filled out our survey forms and attended our focus groups are likely to be amongst the more philanthropically active. However, this may also be explained by the generally low self-image that the community has of its own giving patterns (see Chapter #6).

118. The survey question gave respondents four choices (as stated in the accompanying figure) to choose from and asked them to choose only the one statement they considered *most important.*

119. The respondents were given five choices to choose from: 'no', 'slight', 'some', 'significant' and 'great' difference. The figure shows the percentage of respondents who chose 'no' or 'slight' difference on the one hand or chose 'significant' or 'great' difference on the other. The percentage of respondents who responded with 'some difference' is not shown in the figure but can be easily calculated by adding the two numbers that are shown for each statement and subtracting the sum from 100.

120. It is rather interesting that in an earlier but differently worded question—about the catalysts of giving—our respondents had highlighted the importance of regular financial reports but less passionately than in this question. The difference may well be explained by the fact that in this case the notion of 'transparent' reporting has been incorporated; if so, the emphasis we are hearing is on independent and transparent reporting, rather than just reporting.

121. Chapter #6 is based on a first draft written by Dr. Salal Humair. The analysis presented here was also done principally by Dr. Humair.

122. These numbers should be understood within the limitations of survey-based analysis and the constraints of working without good baseline data that would be needed for more structured scientific sampling.

123. See, for example, Paul Pribbenow, 'Public Character: Philanthropic Fundraising and the Claims of Accountability,' in *New Directions for Philanthropic Fundraising,* 47: 13-27, 2005; Thomas K. Reis and Stephanie J. Clohesy, 'Unleashing New Re-

sources and Entrepreneurship for the Common Good: A Philanthropic Renaissance,' in *New Directions for Philanthropic Fundraising*, 32: 109-144, 2001.

INDEX

ANNEX

Survey Form

Opinion Survey on Philanthropy by
Pakistanis in America

This survey is part of an independent research project being conducted for the Pakistan Centre for Philanthropy (PCP) and being funded by the Aga Khan Foundation. The Pakistan Centre for Philanthropy is an independent, non-funding, support organization. It aims to increase the volume and effectiveness of indigenous philanthropy in Pakistan.

The goal of this research project is to highlight the current dimensions and future potential of philanthropy by Pakistanis in the United States of America. The research seeks to identify and analyze patterns, motivations, effectiveness and hurdles to philanthropy by Pakistanis in America. It will also highlight selected case studies of successful individual and institutional philanthropic initiatives. The research team is composed of researchers and scholars of Pakistani origin and is led by Prof. Adil Najam (adil.najam@tufts.edu) of the Fletcher School of Law and Diplomacy, Tufts University.

(For more detailed information on the PCP and this project, visit www.pcp.org.pk).

The survey should take between 20-30 minutes to fill.

Only one person per household should fill the survey. Survey respondents should be knowledgeable about and willing to respond to questions about their household's philanthropic activities.

For this survey, philanthropy includes activities of voluntary giving and serving, primarily for the benefit of others beyond one's own family. Individual giving to needy members of the extended family may be included but do not include support of immediate relatives/dependents that you consider 'obligatory' (e.g., parents).

Section B of the survey asks questions about three types of philanthropic contributions:

    Volunteering (e.g. giving time and services to organizations and events related to philanthropic causes.)

    Goods/In-kind (e.g. donation of books, materials, clothes, computers, etc.)

    Money (this also includes money given as religious charity, such as *zakat*, etc.)

Section B of the survey asks about three different kinds of causes to which people give:

    Pakistani Causes based in the U.S. (organizations, initiatives and events located in the U.S.)

    Pakistani Causes based in Pakistan (organizations, initiatives and events located in Pakistan)

    Causes unrelated to Pakistan (located in the US or other parts of the world but not directly related to Pakistan)

Questions in Section B relate to household philanthropy (except those related to volunteering).

Questions in Section C relate to your personal opinions and preferences.

Section A: Demographic Information
(for analysis; not for identification)

Current residence in USA, State?

Nearby metropolitan center?

Age?

    20-30; 30-40; 40-50; 50-60; 60-70; over 70

    All respondents must be at least 20 years old

Gender?

Marital status?

Education?
Less than high school; High school; Bachelor's degree; Master's degree; Ph.D.; Other (please specify)

Primary occupation *(choose only one)*?
Academics (Teaching & Research); Accounting/Finance; Administrative support; Agricultural; Armed Forces/Police/Fire; Doctor/Dentist/ Veterinarian; Educator (K-12); Engineering/Scientific; Factory/Warehouse Work; Finance/Banking/Insurance; Government Service; Homemaker; Information Technology; Law/Legal Services; Management/Business Consulting; Managerial/Executive; Media/Journalism/PR/Advertising; Non-profit/social services; Nurse/Pharmacist/Allied Health; Professional Services; Real Estate/Construction; Restaurant/Hotel Services; Retail Store/Gas Station; Sales and Marketing; Student; Taxi/Limo/Transport Services; Other (please specify)

Employment status *(choose only one)*?
Employed full-time (incl. self-employed); Employed part-time (incl. self-employed); Student; Home-maker; Retired; Unemployed; Other (Please specify)

Origin *(choose only one in each category)*?
You: Raised in Pakistan, Pakistani Origin; Not Raised in Pakistan, Pakistani origin; Not of Pakistani origin
Your spouse (if married): Raised in Pakistan, Pakistani Origin; Not Raised in Pakistan, Pakistani origin; Not of Pakistani origin

Have been living in USA for *(years)*?
5 years or less; 5-10 years; 10-15 years; 15-20 years; 20-30 years; Over 25 years

Residence status in USA?

U.S. Citizen; U.S. Permanent Resident; Student; Status in USA; Working Non Resident; Other (please specify)

How do you stay connected to Pakistan *(choose no more than three)*?

Newspapers/Magazines; Television; Radio; Internet; Community events & gatherings; Pakistan Embassy; Contact with friends & family in Pakistan (including visits, emails, phone, etc.); Do not stay connected; Other (please specify)

What is the level of your participation in Pakistani community organizations and events?

No participation; Infrequent participation; Moderate participation; Frequent participation; Very active participation

Annual household income?

Less than $10,000; $10,000 to $20,000; $20,000 to $30,000; $30,000 to $40,000; $40,000 to $50,000; $50,000 to $60,000; $60,000 to $70,000; $70,000 to $80,000; $80,000 to $90,000; $90,000 to $100,000; $100,000 to $110,000; $110,000 to $120,000; $120,000 to $130,000; $130,000 to $140,000; $140,000 to $150,000; $150,000 to $160,000; $160,000 to $170,000; $170,000 to $180,000; $180,000 to $190,000; $190,000 to $200,000; More than $200,000

Number of individuals in household?

Usually you, your spouse, and dependents

Sources of household income?

You only; Your spouse only; You and your spouse jointly; Other (please specify)

Who makes primary decisions about philanthropic contributions?

You only; Your spouse only; You and your spouse jointly; Other (please specify)

Are you knowledgeable about and willing to respond to questions about your households philanthropic activities?

Yes; No *(If you answered YES, please proceed with survey. If you answered NO, please stop here. Thank You.)*

Section B: Philanthropic Giving

1. Does your household in any way 'give' (money, time or in-kind) to the following category of causes? *(Answer 'Yes' or 'No' for each category; if you answered 'No' to all three categories, please skip to Question 17).*
Pakistani Causes based in the US
Pakistani Causes based in Pakistan
Causes unrelated to Pakistan

2. What is the range of the money contributions your household makes (per year) for each of the three categories? *(For each of the following, choose amongst these categories: Not at all; Less than $100 per year; $100-500 per year; $500-1000 per year; $1000-2000 per year; $2000-3000 per year; $3000+ per year).*
Giving money: Obligatory religious (e.g., *zakat*)
Pakistani Causes based in the US
Pakistani Causes based in Pakistan
Causes unrelated to Pakistan
Giving money: Other philanthropic giving
Pakistani Causes based in the US
Pakistani Causes based in Pakistan
Causes unrelated to Pakistan

3. What is the approximate value of the goods and in-kind donations your household makes (per year) for each of the three categories of causes? *(For each of the following, choose amongst these categories: Not at all; Less than $100 per year; $100-500 per year; $500-1000 per year; $1000-2000 per year; $2000-3000 per year; $3000+ per year).*
Goods/In-kind
Pakistani Causes based in the US
Pakistani Causes based in Pakistan
Causes unrelated to Pakistan

4. Approximately how much time (per month) do you and others in your household volunteer for each of the three categories of causes? *(For each*

*of the following, choose amongst these categories: Not at all; Less than 5
hours/month; 5-10 hours/month; 10-20 hours/month; 20-30 hours/month; 30-
40 hours/month; 40+ hours/month).*

Volunteering: Your time
    Pakistani Causes based in the US
    Pakistani Causes based in Pakistan
    Causes unrelated to Pakistan

Volunteering: Time of others in household
    Pakistani Causes based in the US
    Pakistani Causes based in Pakistan
    Causes unrelated to Pakistan

**5. What you give for. Please list the THREE MOST IMPORTANT issues
that you usually contribute to for each of the three causes listed here.**
*(Please choose from the following options, or suggest your own: Arts, culture
and sports; Children and youth; Civil and Human Rights; Community Development; Disabilities and handicaps; Education (Higher); Education (Literacy
and basic); Environment; Health; Housing/shelter; Human Development;
Politics; Poverty (incl. helping needy individuals); Religious; Science and
Technology; Women).*
    Pakistani Causes based in the US
    Pakistani Causes based in Pakistan
    Causes unrelated to Pakistan

**6. What financial channels do you use to contribute money to the following
causes?** *(Check ALL that apply: Cash transactions; Credit card transactions;
Bank transactions; Other).*
    Pakistani Causes based in the US
    Pakistani Causes based in Pakistan
    Causes unrelated to Pakistan

**7. Approximately what portion of your households giving in each category
of causes, and by each type was to NEEDY INDIVIDUALS (rather than to
organizations)?** *(For each of the following, choose amongst these categories:
None; Some-Less than 10%; Significant-10-25%; Large portion-25-50%;
Mostly-50-75%; Predominantly-75% or more).*
By type of giving (directly to individuals)
    Volunteering: Your time

Volunteering: Others in household
Goods/In-kind
Money: Obligatory religious
Money: Other philanthropic
By cause (directly to individuals)
Pakistani Causes based in the US
Pakistani Causes based in Pakistan
Causes unrelated to Pakistan

8. What proportion of your households giving in each category is 'repeat giving' to the same individual or organization (giving for the **third** time or more to the same individual or organization)? *(For each of the following, choose amongst these: None; Some; Significantly; Large Portion; Mostly; Predominantly).*
Pakistani Causes based in the US
Pakistani Causes based in Pakistan
Causes unrelated to Pakistan

9. WHO YOU GIVE TO. How much of your households recent overall giving has gone to each of the following types of recipients ? *(For each of the following, choose amongst these: None; Some-Less than 10%; Significant-10-25%; Large portion-25-50%; Mostly-50-75%; Predominantly-75% or more).*
Individual direct giving to extended family and friends in need
Direct giving to other needy individuals
Direct giving to informal local/community groups
Giving though family and friends – who pass on to worthy causes
Giving to religious organizations
Giving to educational institutions
Giving to issue/advocacy groups
Giving to other registered philanthropic institutions/charities

10. Since September 2001, how has your household's giving pattern changed in each of the following categories? Please answer for each relevant category. *(Choose from: Decreased; Stayed the Same; Increased).*
Pakistani Causes based in the US
Pakistani Causes based in Pakistan
Causes unrelated to Pakistan

11. Approximately how many times PER MONTH are you approached by organizations in each category asking for your contribution of time, goods or money? Please answer for each relevant category. *(For each of the following, choose amongst these: Never; Less than once per month; 1-2 times per month; 3-5 times per month; 6-10 times per month; More than 10 times per month).*

Pakistani Causes based in the US

Pakistani Causes based in Pakistan

Causes unrelated to Pakistan

Section C: Philanthropic Preferences

12. How important is each of the following practical factors in influencing your philanthropic decisions (in giving to institutions and organizations)? Please leave blank if you have no opinion. *(For each of the following, choose amongst these: No importance; Low importance; Medium importance; High importance; Very high importance).*

My contribution is tax deductible

Ease of transferring funds to organization

Large portion of my contribution will directly go to intended beneficiaries

Ability to visit and review the operations of the organization

Ability to receive regular financial & performance reports

The organization is already well-known and reputable

The organization works in region/locality I am grew up in or 'belong to'

The organization is large in size

Quality of organization's marketing materials

Quality of individuals representing organization

Famous institution or person recommend the organization

Friends/family in USA recommend the organization

Friends/family in Pakistan recommend the organization

The organization is officially registered in Pakistan

The organization is officially registered in USA

13. How effective are the following fundraising methods in your giving (to institutions and organizations)? Please leave blank if you have no opinion. *(For each of the following, choose amongst these: Not effective; Slightly effective; Effective; Highly effective; Very highly effective).*

Fundraising meetings
Cultural events
Membership dues
Mailings
Phone requests for pledges
Media (Newspaper/TV) advertising
Websites
Email solicitations
Visits by organization's representatives
Celebrity endorsements and appeal
Appeal by friends/family in USA
Appeal by friends/family in Pakistan

Are there other means of fundraising that have been very effective in your experience:

14. MOTIVATION. How important is each of the following in making decisions about how you give? Please leave blank if you have no opinion. *(For each of the following, choose amongst these categories: No importance; Low importance; Medium importance; High importance; Very high importance).*

To help friends and extended family
Ease of transferring funds to organization
To help other individuals in need
To return something to the community I grew up in
To return something to the community I now live in
To return something to the educational institution I attended
To give to causes related to my religious identity
To fulfill my religious duty to give
To give for issues important to Pakistan's development
To support important global issues

15. What is your general opinion about philanthropic organizations in Pakistan? *(For each of the following, choose amongst these: Strongly disagree; Disagree; Agree; Strongly agree; No opinion).*

IN GENERAL, philanthropic organizations working in Pakistan ....
… are honest and ethical in the use of donated funds
… use money donated to them efficiently and to good use

... have well-meaning and competent people working for them

... are effective in what they do

... play an important role in Pakistan's development

... have good ideas about how to solve Pakistan's pressing problems

... are already working on all the important issues that need attention

... do a good job of raising funds from USA and elsewhere

16a. Please choose the ONE statement that best captures your sense of the future prospects on your own and the general Pakistani community's giving to Pakistan related philanthropic organizations.
My giving to Pakistan-related philanthropic causes...

Is already as high as it could be and is unlikely to increase unless income increases dramatically.

Could be significantly higher if it was easier to give to Pakistan-related causes.

Could be significantly higher if there was more information about causes in Pakistan.

Could be significantly higher if I had more trust that my contributions would be put to good use.

16b. Please choose the ONE statement that best captures your sense of the future prospects on your own and the general Pakistani community's giving to Pakistan related philanthropic organizations.
The overall giving by the Pakistani community in USA to Pakistan-related philanthropic causes...

Is already as high as it could be and is unlikely to increase unless income increases dramatically.

Could be significantly higher if it was easier to give to Pakistan-related causes.

Could be significantly higher if there was more information about causes in Pakistan.

Could be significantly higher if I had more trust that my contributions would be put to good use.

17. In your opinion, how large a difference will each of the following measures make in encouraging greater philanthropy by the Pakistani Diaspora for Pakistani organizations and causes? Please leave blank if you have no opinion. *(For each of the following, choose amongst these categories: No*

difference; Slight difference; Some difference; Significant difference; Great difference).

More Pakistani organizations had registered non-profit status in USA

More clarity and information on US laws about giving to organizations in Pakistan

Easier mechanisms for transferring funds to organizations in Pakistan

Greater tax benefits for giving to causes in Pakistan were available

More opportunities for appreciation and recognition of philanthropy were available

More support for US-based philanthropists by Pakistan Embassy and government

Better mechanisms to monitor actual impact of contribution

Ability to give to an umbrella organization which can channel money to various worthy causes in Pakistan

Regular & transparent financial reporting

Better and more frequent communication from organizations to donors

Improved (and more) web-pages of organizations working in Pakistan

More visits by representatives of organizations working in Pakistan to USA

Greater ease and ability to personally visit organizations and projects in Pakistan

Greater role for Pakistan Embassy in providing philanthropic information

A trustworthy, independent agency could certify various organizations

Can you suggest any other measure that would make a particularly great difference?

DATE DUE